Faith
and Philosophy

BL51 .R47
religion-philosophy

by

JAMES RICHMOND

M.A., B.D., Ph.D.

J. B. LIPPINCOTT COMPANY
Philadelphia and New York

EDITOR'S PREFACE

To judge by the unending flow of religious literature from the various publishing houses there is an increasingly large demand on the part of ordinary intelligent people to know more about what Christianity has to say. This series is designed to help meet this need and to cater for just this kind of people.

It assumes that there is a growing body of readers, both inside and outside the Church, who are prepared to give serious attention to the nature and claims of the Christian faith, and who expect to be given by theologians authoritative and up-to-date answers to the kind of questions thinking people want to ask.

More and more it becomes clear that we are unlikely to get any answers that will satisfy the deepest needs of the human spirit from any other quarter. Present-day science and philosophy give us little help on the ultimate questions of human destiny. Social, political and educational panaceas leave most of us unpersuaded. If we are not to end our quest for the truth about ourselves and the world we live in in cynicism and disillusionment where else can we turn but to religion?

Too often in the past two thousand years the worst advertisement for Christianity has been its supporters and advocates. Yet alone of all the great world religions it has shown that a faith which was Oriental in origin could be transplanted into the Western world and from there strike root again in the East. The present identification of Christianity in the minds of Asians and Africans with European culture and Western capitalism or imperialism is a passing phase. To say that no other religion has the same potentialities as a world-wide faith for everyman is neither to denigrate the God-given truth in Buddhism, Islam and the rest, nor to say that at this stage Christianity as generally practised and understood in the West presents much more than a caricature of its purpose.

Perhaps the best corrective to hasty judgment is to measure these two thousand years against the untold millions of years of man's development. Organized Christianity is still in its infancy, as is the mind of man as he seeks to grapple with truths that could only come to him by revelation. The half has not yet been told and the full implications for human thought and action of the coming of God in Christ have as yet been only dimly grasped by most of us.

It is as a contribution to a deeper understanding of the mystery that surrounds us that this series is offered. The early volumes deal, as is only right, with fundamental issues — the historical impact of Christianity upon mankind based upon its Jewish origins and establishing itself in the wider world; the essence of the Christian faith and the character of Christian behaviour. Later volumes in the series will deal with various aspects of Christian thought and practice in relation to human life in all its variety and with its perennial problems.

The intention is to build up over the years a library which under the general title of "Knowing Christianity" will provide for thinking laymen a solid but non-technical presentation of what the Christian religion is and what it has to say in this atomic age.

The writers invited to contribute to this series are not only experts in their own fields but are all men who are deeply concerned that the gulf should be bridged between the specialized studies of the theologian and the untheologically minded average reader who nevertheless wants to know what theology has to say. I am sure that I speak in the name of all my colleagues in this venture when I express the hope that this series will do much to bridge the gap.

WILLIAM NEIL

The University,
Nottingham

AUTHOR'S PREFACE

It has often been said that no one should write a book without having some idea of the public for which he is writing. Certainly this book has been written with two fairly definite classes in mind. First, theological students in universities and colleges who require an introduction to some of the main tendencies, problems and movements in philosophical theology during the past couple of centuries. Unless the author is mistaken, British students are not so well served in this way as their American counterparts. Accordingly, the books referred to in the notes are, in the main, easily accessible ones, and, where possible, fairly recent ones. It ought to be unnecessary, but, unfortunately, it is not, to remind theological students that the notes are designed to help them follow up problems and historical periods on their own by working on the books and articles cited in them. Second, intelligent and enquiring laymen who wish to keep abreast of what philosophical theologians are saying, and to be informed of what the significant growing-points in the philosophy of religion are. With both classes in mind, technical philosophical and theological terminology has been kept to the absolute minimum. Where it has seemed unavoidable, it has been defined. It can therefore, I think, be claimed that there is nothing in these pages that both classes cannot understand if they really want to.

Since the manuscript of this book was written, a certain number of books have been published, mention of which might reasonably have been expected. But to do so would have involved re-writing large portions of the book, and also its enlargement, and for this there was, unfortunately, no time. But two of these deserve to be mentioned here. First, Richard R. Niebuhr's *Schleiermacher on Christ and Religion* (London, 1965), is an exceedingly full and important treatment of some of the themes discussed in the second chapter. Second, all who are interested in the theme of the third chapter should read and ponder well H. P. Owen's *The*

Moral Argument for Christian Theism (London, 1965).

The omissions, of course, are glaring. Why have I omitted, for example, lengthy treatments of the thought of Hegel, Kierkegaard, Reinhold Niebuhr, and Paul Tillich? Why are there no discussions of philosophical theologians in the Eastern and Roman Catholic traditions? Why are there not lengthy chapters on American scholars? The answer is simple: there was simply no space. To have included these omissions would have required several bulky volumes. Rather than write nothing at all, it has seemed to the author not without value to select several *types* of theological tendency in the past couple of centuries, and concentrate upon them. The inevitable exclusion of other theologians and traditions does not at all mean that the author regards them as unimportant or irrelevant. Rather, the opposite is the truth.

My thanks are due in several directions. I am greatly indebted to the general editor of this series, my colleague Dr. William Neil, Reader in Biblical Studies in this university, for much kindly help and encouragement. The writing of these pages has encroached upon the leisure-time of my wife as much as upon my own; I am very grateful to her for her patience and help. Finally, I am in the debt of an anonymous, but very real group of Nottingham Theology undergraduates; their discussion with me in seminars of almost all of the themes discussed in these pages has helped me more than I can say.

JAMES RICHMOND

Department of Theology,
The University,
Nottingham

CONTENTS

TO

MY FATHER AND MOTHER

INTRODUCTION

The main concern of this book is the *philosophy of religion* (or *philosophical theology*), and we must begin by attempting some sort of definition. The philosophy of religion is a border-discipline, composed of the area of overlap between two subjects, such as economic history, social psychiatry, chemical engineering, or the sociology of education. It tries to marry two important areas of discussion and enquiry, a marriage not uncommonly characterized by tension and discord. It is with various attempts to bring about such a marriage that we are going to be concerned. But first, what is philosophy? It is incredibly hard to offer a definition, since philosophers themselves notoriously disagree about the scope and content of their subject-matter, and also because it is hard to appreciate what philosophy is without having done some. But perhaps we may put forward two tentative working-definitions, which may help to communicate what philosophy is about. First, a short definition: "Philosophy is reflexion on experience in order to apprehend its ultimate meaning."[1] Second, a longer definition: philosophy is a rational examination of reality as a whole, aiming at a systematic set of universal maxims, principles or beliefs. Even a superficial discussion of these definitions involves us in actually doing philosophy.

Philosophy is an enquiry into "reality as a whole". This has important implications. It does not select or isolate a "slice" of reality, such as the chemical, biological or astronomical spheres, and proceed to examine their structure. Philosophy tries to look at that reality which includes but transcends such spheres. That is, philosophy is not a *science*, like chemistry or biology. Within these fields, tests or experiments are possible which indicate whether certain hypotheses are true or false, tenable or untenable. But within philosophy, such tests are out of the question. Rather, the philosopher appeals to the plausibility, the intellectual satisfaction inherent in his theories and convictions themselves.

[1] George Galloway, *The Philosophy of Religion*, Edinburgh, 1914, p. 1.

We can make the same point in a slightly different way, by pointing to the words we used above, that philosophy aims at "*universal* maxims, principles or beliefs". Philosophy asks *universal* rather than *particular* questions. It does not ask: Is this *particular* biochemical, economic or bacteriological theory true?, but rather: What is *universally* meant by terms like "true" or "truth"? It does not ask: Does this *particular* man possess moral freedom?, but rather: Does the *universal* class of men *universally* possess freedom of choice? And philosophy does not ask and answer questions haphazardly. The questions with which it deals tend to fall into certain fairly definite groups. Thus when philosophy asks: What is goodness? What is rightness? How do we make moral judgments?, it is classified as *ethics* or *moral philosophy*. When it asks: What is argument? What is a fallacy? In what ways ought conclusions to be derived from premises? What do we mean by saying that one set of beliefs is *entailed* by another set?, it is classified as *logic*. When it asks: How is the mind related to the body? Is human behaviour determined or free? How are space and time related to each other? Is there some single substance underlying all particular entities in space and time?, it is classified as *metaphysics*.

When it asks: How do we know? Does man possess certain notions or ideas innately? Does all our knowledge derive from impressions received through our senses in our day-to-day experience?, it is classified as theory of knowledge or *epistemology*. It is obvious that contact between philosophy and theology is inevitable, because theology too is concerned with "reality as a whole", with universally true maxims or beliefs, with an enquiry concerning good and evil, right and wrong (ethics), with the ultimate nature of things (metaphysics), with the nature of human knowledge (epistemology). According to the answers supplied to its questions, philosophers have of course tended to form schools of thought, philosophical movements; these standpoints have almost always been denoted as *-isms*. In the chapters that follow we shall examine some of these and their implications for religious belief, such as empiricism, positivism, naturalism, existentialism, and so on.

It is of course easy to disagree with that type of definition of philosophy that we put forward above. Many contemporary philosophers, for example, would look askance at a definition like Galloway's, with its stress on the quest for the "ultimate meaning" of the world or our experience. They would consider such a quest futile, and the language of "ultimate meanings" meaningless. But, we must note, to take up such an attitude is itself to do philosophy. It is not enough to express scepticism about the knowability or existence of ultimate meanings in an emotional way. Nor can such scepticism merely be asserted arbitrarily. It is a philosophical standpoint and we are justified in asking for the arguments, grounds and reasons upon which it is held. Disagreement about the nature of philosophy is itself a philosophical matter, and of course varying attitudes to philosophy, considering it to be the highest conceivable human activity or a futile waste of time, are themselves philosophical ones, requiring their holders to produce grounds and reasons for their support of the attitudes.[1]

Philosophical analysis and evaluation have of course been increasingly brought to bear upon certain important areas of human thought and experience in an attempt to clarify them. Thus we have the emergence, for example, of the philosophy of art, of mathematics, of history, of science, of education, and so on, all of them now established intellectual disciplines. But while in general artists, mathematicians and educational theorists have welcomed philosophical clarification and the dialogue with philosophers, it has by no means been as simple as that in the case of the philosophy of religion. The fact is that many theologians and religious believers have looked with intense suspicion and often downright hostility at philosophy, and have deplored in the strongest terms any attempt to mingle or synthesize the two. Nor is this ancient attitude by any means dead today. Hence the philosopher of religion, before he begins his task, must try to frame answers to the question: What has philosophy to do with religion? The *locus classicus* of such a question is of course to be found

[1] For the varying attitudes of philosophers themselves to the nature of their subject, see the source-book, *What is Philosophy?*, edited by Henry W. Johnstone, Jr., Sources in Philosophy Series, New York, 1965, in which eleven philosophers put forward their conceptions of what philosophy is.

in the writings of the great African Church Father Tertullian (c. 160–c. 220): "What is there in common between Athens and Jerusalem? What between the Academy and the Church? What between heretics and Christians? . . . Away with all projects for a 'Stoic', a 'Platonic' or a 'dialectic' Christianity! After Christ Jesus we desire no subtle theories, no acute enquiries after the gospel. . . ."[1]

Tertullian's question is of no mere antiquarian interest, and, as we shall see in our fourth chapter, it expresses the attitude to philosophical reflection upon religion of an important twentieth-century school of theological thought. But at this stage we must try to indicate some lines along which the question may reasonably be answered. What, then, has philosophy to do with religion? Why should theologians try to think philosophically, why should they note philosophical theories and trends, and why should they read philosophical books? The kind of answer we should like to put forward is that *all* theologians are implicitly also philosophers, and that all attempts to isolate theology from philosophical considerations are futile ones.

The question, Why should we be philosophers?, is, in a sense, a silly one. All of us, whether we know it or not, whether we admit it or not, have some "philosophy" of life. The question is: Has it been clearly formulated, scrutinized, criticized? Is it a good one, a reasonable one, or not? We all live, act and think on the basis of a set of assumptions, beliefs and answers to questions. Do we trust reason, or not? Are we free to choose courses of action, or not? Is there a God, or not? Does it matter? Are certain values preferable to others, or not? Does it matter? Are there things we can know and others that we cannot? Is this present life all there is, or is there another? How can we find out? Does it matter? What difference would it make, anyhow? What is man, ourselves and our neighbours? An intelligent animal, a skin filled with chemicals and water, a complicated machine, a child of God with an immortal soul? Is there a difference in *degree* or in *kind* between man and animals? Can we know? Does it matter? Is it right to hang murderers? Is it wrong?

[1] *De Praescriptione haereticorum* (c. 200), vii, quoted in *Documents of the Christian Church*, edited by H. Bettenson, London, 1943, p. 8.

Are murderers merely deficient machines who cannot help behaving as they do? Does it matter?

Everyone who comes to grips with everyday questions like these, and tries to answer them consistently, is a philosopher, whether conscious of it or not. And as religious believers live in the same world as everyone else, they cannot avoid them, nor the rational evaluation of the answers they give to them. The impression that "philosophers" are somehow to be found only *outside* the Church, and "theologians" only *inside* the Church, and that these separate groups must somehow try to get into contact with each other, is a thoroughly misleading one. Rather, the truth is that the philosophico-theological dialogue is something that goes on *within each of us*, whether we are convinced believers trying to reconcile the insights of our faith with the insights of our reason, or sceptics struggling to make sense of the mass of evidence to which religion directs our attention. Religious believers too are modern men. Unless they have sealed themselves in an intellectual vacuum, they too drink in the ideas of the contemporary world. They too have to find answers to philosophical questions. Otherwise the result might well be grave damage to their faith, or to their intellectual integrity, or to both—in short, a kind of intellectual schizophrenia destructive of human personality.

One of the concrete historical ways in which theology has become involved in philosophical considerations is in the attempt to formulate a *natural theology*. Sometimes (especially in the Thomist or Cartesian traditions), this has taken the form of *proving* or *demonstrating* by rational means alone certain essential truths of religion, such as God's existence, some of his attributes, and the immortality of the soul. At other times (especially in the Augustinian-Anselmian tradition), this has taken the form of "faith seeking understanding" (*fides quaerens intellectum*). That is, by accepting the data of faith, and by looking in the directions in which they point, the attempt is made to show that an examination of reality and our experience of it demonstrates that it is perfectly rational to indulge in religious attitudes, exercises and practices. Other more modern types of natural theology will be explored in the chapters that follow. There are two reasons at least why theologians ought not to evade the historic forms of natural theology, one ecclesiastical and the other philosophical.

The ecclesiastical reason, and this applies particularly to the demonstrative type of natural theology, is that in the highly ecumenical atmosphere of the second half of the twentieth century, it would be dangerous to overlook that one of the factors separating the Western Roman Church from the main Western non-Roman Communions is a thoroughly philosophical one. The Roman Catholic Church holds that God's existence can be known with certainty *by reason alone* from an examination of the created universe, and more especially by the fact that the principle of causality requires us to believe in God as the originator of all that is. She believes, conversely, that it is heretical to deny this.[1] Clearly, therefore, the possibility and nature of natural theology is a factor which dare not be overlooked or ignored in the contemporary ecumenical dialogue. The philosophical reason is this: the not uncommon theological rejection of natural theology is itself a philosophical matter. If it is not to be merely an arbitrary, irrational prejudice, it must involve an examination of the arguments of which a given natural theology is composed, and a demonstration of their invalidity or irrelevance. But, of course, the attempt to do this, and the attempt to put forward an alternative kind of theology, involves the theologian in becoming a competent philosophical theologian.

Again, philosophical issues are theologically inescapable because in our world philosophers *do* discuss theological questions. In the context of their philosophical work, philosophers take up issues like the existence of God, the knowability of God, the nature of God. In what sense, they sometimes ask, does God *exist*? Is God a *thing*? Is God the name of a cosmic process? Is God really the ultimate *quality* of the universe? Is God the descriptive title we give to our

[1] The official, authoritative documents of the Roman Church referring to this are to be found in H. Denzinger, *Enchiridion Symbolorum*, edited by Karl Rahner, S. J., 31st edition, Freyburg-im-Breisgau 1960, paras. 1391, 1785, 1806, 2145. Cf. Ludwig Ott, *Fundamentals of Catholic Dogma*, edited by J. Bastible, Cork, 1960, Book One, Part I, Section 1, "The Existence of God", pp. 13–17.

response to certain aspects of or occurrences in the universe? Does it make sense to talk of the *supernatural*? Are theologians obliged to use this word? How could we check up if such a sphere existed or not? Does a word like "goodness" make sense when applied to persons? Are persons free to choose this goodness? Does "goodness", when applied to God when believers say that "God is good", mean the same thing as when applied to actions and persons? Does it mean that we *judge* God to be good, *confer*, so to speak, goodness upon God, because we already know what goodness is? If so, is goodness somehow superior to, more ultimate than God Himself? If so, how can God be described as ultimate or absolute? Or, rather, does it mean that a thing is good merely because God wills it? How exactly *is* goodness related to God? What does all this add up to? It means "that there is no one problem which can be labelled 'the theistic question'. Proof, intro-spection, laws of nature, free-will, falsifiability—almost all the topics of philosophy arise in a theistic context. The conceptual problems of the theistic philosopher are thus for the most part the ordinary conceptual problems of philosophy raised from a particular point of view."[1] But these philo-sophical questions, and the answers given to them, have vitally important consequences for theology. Theologians have no monopoly in them. They cannot forbid trespassers. It follows that unless theologians want to live in a vacuum, dialogue between them and philosophers on such issues is inevitable.

A parallel reason is to be found in the fact that all theolo-gians, whether conscious of it or not, *do* discuss philosophical questions. In discussing the Bible and the Creeds they discuss themes and concepts like these — God, free-will, good, evil, miracle, time, history, nature, and the like. Such themes and concepts are obviously of central importance for the philosopher also. It would appear again that dialogue on such issues is inevitable. At this point, it is not uncommon for the theologian to insist that *what he means* by God, good, evil, miracle, nature and the rest, is not at all what the philosopher means by them. Clearly the philosopher is to be pardoned if he finds this objection a puzzling, even a meaningless one!

[1] The article "Theism", *The Concise Encyclopaedia of Western Philosophy and Philosophers*, edited by J. O. Urmson, London, 1960, pp. 377–9.

If the theological and the philosophical meanings of these common key-terms diverge *absolutely*, the long-standing use of the same terms by both groups for different things becomes absolutely unintelligible. Surely, the philosopher may ask, there is an extremely ancient and idiotic misuse of language going on somewhere? The theologian must then soften his objection by saying: "No, what I mean by God, good, evil, miracle, nature and history, is *not exactly* what you philosophers mean by them. There are *dissimilarities* as well as *similarities* between the two sets of meanings." The theologian has, in saying this, conceded that his job is a thoroughly philosophical one. For the attempt to analyse similarities and dissimilarities in the use of terms in one context as compared with their use in another, for example, in the theological elucidation of biblical analogical terms such as "Father", "forgives", "creates", "saves", "redeems", "wills", "justifies", "loves", and so on, is one which overlaps with, has much in common with, linguistic or semantic philosophy. Once again, philosophical considerations cannot be excluded from theology.

Theology has of course also become thoroughly involved in philosophy in defending itself against accusations that its doctrines are untrue, irrelevant, outworn or meaningless. In coming to grips with such accusations, theologians have re-formulated, re-shaped and re-stated theological materials in order to undermine and overcome the accusation in question. Hence the emergence of *apologetics*, or *apologetic* theology.[1] But, of course, in order to do this, theologians have been obliged to understand thoroughly those hostile criticisms in the light of which they have re-interpreted their materials. In short, they have had to become philosophers. In the following chapters, we shall see again and again the Christian faith being shaped in the light of contemporary philosophical criticisms.

[1] For classical examples of this kind of theology, see Joseph Butler, *The Analogy of Religion* (first published in 1736), Everyman's Library, London, 1906; William Paley, *Evidences of Christianity* (first published in 1794), 7th edition, Cambridge, 1880; Robert Flint, *Anti-Theistic Theories*, 4th edition, Edinburgh, 1889; A. B. Bruce, *Apologetics; or Christianity Defensively Stated*, Edinburgh, 1892.

Philosophical theology has been rooted in another consideration—the dominical commission to the Church in the Bible
to communicate the gospel to all men. In the light of this, we
must say that there is a solemn obligation upon theologians
to think and write philosophically. Now obviously, there is a
sense in which theology, in common with other academic
disciplines like archaeology or mathematics, is worth
studying for its own sake, for the scholarly training and
satisfaction derivable from it. No one should wish to detract
from the worth of those areas which theology has in common
with philology, ancient history, archaeology and textual
criticism. Nevertheless, it must be insisted that the limitation
of theology to these areas is both wrong and very dangerous.
Just as the Christian *message* is not the possession of a religious
group, clique or club, so Christian *theology* cannot be an
esoteric discipline practised by a few specialized "initiates",
who speak in jargon understandable only among themselves.
It is unthinkable that the highly dangerous situation should
ever be reached where theology has been reduced to the
status of a sub-compartment of philology, ancient history,
archaeology, literary criticism or antiquarianism. A theology
may be absolutely correct and simultaneously boring and
irrelevant!

The Christian message belongs (literally and not merely
metaphorically) to all men, and these of course are living,
thinking, criticizing, hoping, speculating and enquiring men.
It is quite wrong to assume high-handedly and arbitrarily that
their awareness is devoid of the issues with which the Bible
and theology are concerned—issues like God, man, good, evil,
death, freedom, guilt, values, happiness, blessedness and
ecstasy. Indeed, if they knew absolutely nothing about what
these terms refer to, and if they were quite unconcerned
about them, it is very hard to see how they could even begin
to understand one word of the Bible.[1] Also, within traditional
Christian doctrine we find the notion of man's creation in the
"image of God" (*imago dei*); that is, that man's possession
of conscience, awareness of beauty, appreciation of order
and rational mind, however spoiled by sin, bears witness to

[1] In this connection, see Rudolf Bultmann, "The Problem of Hermen-
eutics", *Essays: Philosophical and Theological*, London, 1955, pp. 234–61.

the God by whom and for whom he was created.[1] If so, it is only rational to expect that man's thinking, judging, aspiring, hoping and fearing concretely point towards man's origin and destiny, and to do theology accordingly.

If so, there are certain inescapable implications. The first is that philosophical theologians, in interpreting their materials, have done so with one eye on the theological data and the other on those whom they have tried to persuade, convince, communicate with. Any other method has been to them unthinkable. They have tried to find contact-points between biblical and credal materials on the one hand and men's thinking, enquiring and questioning on the other, in order to show that they are relevant, that they have something to do with and to say to human lives and situations in a concrete way. Hence we have the emergence of what Paul Tillich calls "situation-theologies", formulated in the light of definite human situations. Hence also, we have the emergence of theologies formulated in the light of contemporary philosophical trends, such as Neo-Platonism, Neo-Aristotelianism, Romanticism, Idealism and, more recently, Existentialism.

The second implication is really a consequence of the first; it is that theologians in every generation cannot evade the difficult problem of how, to use classical terminology, *nature* is related to *grace*, of how what man knows by *reason* is related to what he knows by *faith*. So far as philosophical theologians are concerned, eternal vigilance is required against any attempt to relax the tension between the two by the irresponsible denigration of nature and reason for the alleged benefit of faith and grace. They are convinced that the problem requires different treatment, and to different forms of this we shall turn in the chapters that follow.

Perhaps one of the most stubborn types of objection to philosophical theology is rooted in the notion that theology is, when all is said and done, essentially a *biblical* discipline, revolving around the learned interpretation of the biblical texts. Now it is not the business of the philosophical theologian, nor of any theologian, to indulge in depreciating the worth

[1] See John Burnaby, *The Belief of Christendom*, London, 1959, pp. 43-9.

of the scholarly attempt to understand the original meaning of the biblical writings in their historical settings, by means of philological, historical and textual tools. Obviously, the health of theology depends vitally upon this. Nevertheless, the philosophical theologian will understandably protest against any attempt to limit theology to biblical exegesis, to so-called "biblical theology". Philosophical theologians too are concerned with the biblical text, although from rather different points of view, and they will rightly insist that philosophical criticism has indispensable contributions to make towards biblical science. Perhaps it is the case that philosophical criticism's greatest contribution to biblical theology lies in focussing attention upon fundamental theological method, upon theological prolegomena; in brief, in insisting upon the importance of *theological methodology*.

They are aware, for example, that theology cannot be done merely by grouping or classifying texts under headings, which, arranged in a certain order and taken together, are regarded as *The Theology of the Old Testament* or *The Theology of the New Testament*. They are aware that such groupings and classifications are literally mathematically infinite, pointing towards an infinite number of "biblical theologies". Hence their insistence upon a study of theological *method*—that is, of the complex presuppositions which usually underlie the patterns in which biblical materials are grouped and should be grouped. The ignoring of the methodology of theology may have quite disastrous consequences. Even a slight knowledge of the history of theology is sufficient to impress upon one the extent to which theology has often been done in various periods according to presuppositions which were unconscious, unexamined and unscrutinized. The examination of and discrimination between these is, partly at least, a philosophical matter.

The philosophical theologian is sometimes puzzled by the claim that there is somehow an authoritative theology of the Old Testament or of the New. He is so, partly at least, by the fact that X's *Theology of the New Testament* (highly regarded in some quarters but not in others!) may diverge in varying degrees from Y's or Z's. At this point his contribution is the analysis of the various assumptions, predispositions, presuppositions and preconceptions which underlie and shape different *types* of biblical theology, predispositions which may be psychological, national, confessional and historical. Any attempt to ignore the existence and operation of such pre-dispositions leads to irresolvable theological confusion. And in so far as philosophical theology has strong affinities with, and is (especially in the United States, Germany and Scotland) included within, *systematic theology*, another contribution it has to offer is the plea that a theology should be self-consistent; that is, that theological problems should not be treated in isolation from each other; that, for example, its talk about God should be consistent with its talk about man, that its talk about sin should not contradict its talk about salvation, and so on. But, in general, it may be said that from the point of view of the biblical disciplines, the function of philosophical theology is to act as a corrective against an exclusive indulgence in biblical exegesis in abstraction from methodological considerations, from fundamental human concerns and from the pressing apologetic needs of the day.[1]

It has probably emerged by now that there can be a relationship of tension between the philosophy of religion and other theological disciplines, and also between the philosophy of religion and secular, non-religious philosophy. Writing of the recent past in the history of theology in America, John E. Smith has this to say: "In addition to the claim that theology (or more frequently, Christianity) is *sui generis* and hence not to be treated philosophically, there are those who regard the philosophy of religion as no more than a name for 'unorthodox theology' and for them the discipline becomes a masquerade. Objections of this sort prove that apparently innocent names may take on pejorative meanings so that it becomes possible to express a critical judgment upon a system of religious thought by saying that it represents no more than

[1] Speaking of pressing contemporary theological problems, the late J. N. Sanders expressed this opinion: "The fashionable biblical theology is no real solution. It does indeed represent an earnest attempt to understand the New Testament in its own terms, but it is unable to communicate its understanding satisfactorily to men who think in terms radically different. It is self-contained and self-consistent, but out of touch with experience", *Soundings*, edited by A. R. Vidler, Cambridge, 1962, p. 130.

'a philosophy of religion'."[1] Smith further tells us that some of Paul Tillich's critics "would prefer to see him classified as a 'philosopher of religion' with the implication that his thought omits or radically transforms some favorite doctrine in the theology of the critic".[2] Howard Root, after reminding us that Ninian Smart has called natural theology "the sick man of Europe", tells us that "there are theologians who would be glad to let the sick man die. Natural theology, outside Catholic traditions, has generally been regarded as the poor relation, if not the black sheep of the family. Theologians have never been convinced that he had a proper job of work to do. If he did do any work the result usually embarrassed the rest of the family. On the other side, philosophers have seldom been happy to acknowledge the philosophical theologian as one of their family."[3]

The reasons for the tension are not hard to seek. The philosopher of religion has quite understandably appeared as somewhat uncommitted to "either side" in the philosophico-theological dialogue! If he claims to take his stand on the Christian faith, he nevertheless enters into a sympathetic understanding of the doubts of the sceptic to such an extent that he inevitably appears to some of his theological colleagues to share them. Consequently, the questions he asks within the theological camp appear as very awkward indeed, and he is not infrequently, if very unjustly, accused of "sniping from within". Nonetheless, he insists that intellectual integrity demands that these questions be asked and answered. The position and task of the philosopher of religion has been neatly summarized by John E. Smith: "On the one hand religion and theology must not be kept in a separate compartment safe from all criticism at the hands of philosophy and, on the other, philosophy must not attempt to shield itself from dealing with those difficult questions about the nature of things and the status of man in reality that have ever been the concern of religious faith.

[1] John E. Smith, the "Philosophy of Religion" section of *Religion* (The Princeton Studies in Humanistic Scholarship in America), edited by Paul Ramsay, Englewood Cliffs, N. J., 1965, p. 358.

[2] *Ibid.*, n. 1.

[3] *Soundings*, p. 3.

23

Stated in other language, religion separated from the critical prod of philosophy is constantly in danger of falling into obscurantism and complacency; philosophy untouched by the goad of religion and its concern for the most urgent questions of human life is constantly in danger of formalizing itself and of occupying its time with strictly preliminary questions of method and meaning while neglecting the larger and more difficult questions."[1]

Applying this understanding to this book, we must make this point: throughout we try to look at theological systems, some of them massive, rich, intricate and impressive, from the point of view of philosophers. We try to show the principal difficulties apparently involved in them, the apparent weaknesses of their structure. We have tried to put to them the kind of questions philosophers would ask, enquiring how far adequate answers to these can be found. To do so is of course to invite protests from the committed defenders of such systems, protests which claim that these systems, in being subjected to such criticism, have been either over-simplified, or distorted, or both. If this has happened it is very regrettable. Nevertheless, it has seemed worth while to imagine sympathetically how theological systems appear to the "outsiders" and the "uncommitted". And, perhaps, nothing but good can come of seeing those ways in which theological systems lend themselves to "over-simplification" and "distortion".

Our final point is one of some importance. The method of treating our material that we have chosen is unashamedly *historical*. Theologians and theological problems have been treated in relation to their position on a time-scale, within a historical setting. This has been done in the conviction that it is futile to treat philosophical and theological issues in abstraction from the history of ideas. The "de-historicization" of modern man and much modern scholarship is one of the most sinister and tragic features of the contemporary scene. But there are hopeful signs that it may soon be recognized that the attempt to unravel a complex present inevitably throws one back into the recent past; the investigation of this throws one back into a slightly more remote past, and so on.

[1] From his introduction to the source-book, *Philosophy of Religion*, New York, 1965, p. 25.

The conviction expressed in the present volume is that the unravelling of our complicated theological present throws us back at least to the closing decades of the eighteenth century, and also, perhaps, to the beginnings of the sixteenth century.

Still, it must be conceded that over-emphasis on the historical approach has its dangers. It is vital that theologians, theological problems, and theological methods be studied "in depth" as well as "in length". It is not too much to claim that were we able to find the perfect combination of the two approaches, we would have found the perfect method by which to do philosophical theology. The chapters that follow, it is hoped, may contribute a little to the attempt helpfully to combine these two.

Chapter One

THE SIGNIFICANCE OF HUME AND KANT

THE contemporary philosopher with an interest in theological issues has clearly had his attitudes shaped by the works of the Scottish philosopher David Hume (1711–76), and the German philosopher Immanuel Kant (1724–1804). It is hardly possible to understand much of the modern philosophical discussion of religion without some knowledge of the standpoints of these two thinkers. The contemporary philosopher rightly includes these two amongst the founders of modern Western philosophical thought. He is aware that the contemporary crisis or predicament in the dialogue between theology and philosophy has its roots, partly at least, in their work, and can only be understood in the light of it. This crisis has come about in this way. For almost seventeen centuries it was scarcely doubted that the framework of Hebrew-Christian theism could be securely erected by means of certain rational arguments and demonstrations.[1] The apostle Paul, for example, had been convinced that "the invisible things of him (i.e. God) from the creation of the world are clearly seen, being understood by the things that are made, even his eternal power and Godhead".[2] Christian philosophical theologians such as St. Augustine of Hippo (354–430), St. Anselm of Canterbury (1033–1109), St. Thomas Aquinas (1225–74) and René Descartes (1596–1650) were convinced that man, by the exercise of reason, could attain to some knowledge of that divine, supernatural framework within which Christian doctrine made sense.[3]

[1] There were exceptions, particularly in France; for these, see J. S. Spink, *French Free-Thought from Gassendi to Voltaire*, London, 1960, and E. A. Gellner, "French Eighteenth-Century Materialism", in *A Critical History of Western Philosophy*, edited by D. J. O'Connor, New York, 1964, pp. 275–95.

[2] Rom. 1:20.

[3] See *Religion and the Knowledge of God*, by Gustave Weigel, S. J. and Arthur G. Madden, Englewood Cliffs, N. J., 1961, pp. 157 f.

These thinkers would have been aghast at the suggestion that somehow the conclusions of faith and those of reason did not in the long run coincide. It would simply never have occurred to them that the two could diverge. The hey-day of confidence in reason's ability to penetrate to the ultimate, theistic structure of reality was of course the seventeenth and eighteenth centuries.[1] So great indeed was the confidence in rational religion that the pressing contemporary problem was to fit revealed knowledge, the insights gained by faith, into this massive rational framework. So much, it was felt, could be established by reason alone that it was not easy to persuade men that divine, supernatural revelation could add something worth having to rational religion. The apparent danger to which eighteenth-century theology was exposed was that revealed theology might become absolutely redundant. It was to make revelation relevant and meaningful within the framework of rational religion that Anglican thinkers like Bishop Joseph Butler (1692–1752) and William Paley (1743–1805) strove in their theological work.

How did seventeenth- and eighteenth-century thinkers erect this framework of theistic belief within which Christian faith and practice seemed to make sense? By means of certain arguments, proofs and demonstrations. We shall have to take a close look at two of these in particular, not only because the plain man readily understands them, but also because a great many sincere religious believers still regard them as convincing, and also because their validity is still defended in some conservative theological circles, Roman Catholic and Protestant. These arguments are called, firstly, the cosmological (or causal) argument for the existence of God, and secondly, the teleological argument for the existence of God (or the

1 For this period see, for example, G. R. Cragg, *The Church and the Age of Reason*, Pelican History of the Church, vol. 4, London, 1960; Leslie Stephen, *History of English Thought in the Eighteenth Century*, vol. 1, Harbinger Books, London, 1962; James Collins, *God in Modern Philosophy*, London, 1960; E. Gilson, *God and Philosophy*, Yale, 1941, chapter III, "God and Modern Philosophy"; A. C. McGiffert, *Protestant Thought Before Kant*, Harper Torchbooks Edition, New York, 1962; Basil Willey, *The Seventeenth-Century Background*, London, 1934, *The Eighteenth-Century Background*, London, 1940.

argument from design).[1] The first of these argues in this way. The world around us consists of things, events and phenomena. These might conceivably not have existed. They do exist because they have been brought into existence by other things, events and phenomena, which in turn might conceivably not have existed. This regression brings us to a first cause whose non-existence is inconceivable, if the existence of the individual members of the causal chain is to be intelligible. This great first cause of all things is identified with God, the creator of the universe. The second argument proceeds like this. When we observe the structure of the world around us we find in it unmistakable signs of order, of harmony and of beauty. The planets and the seasons revolve regularly; natural organisms such as flowers and eyes are fitted cunningly together in order to perform certain functions. And just as a beautiful and efficient human artefact means a human designer, so design, order and harmony on a cosmic scale must mean a cosmic designer or artificer, also identifiable with God.

We must notice two things about these arguments. The first is that many who are Christian believers feel them to be overwhelmingly persuasive, even if they do not formulate

[1] The so-called "eighteenth-century triad" of theistic arguments contained also the *ontological* argument for God's existence. This argument, formulated originally by St. Anselm of Canterbury, was utilized later by the philosophers Descartes and Leibniz. It attempts to prove God's existence by purely logical means, on the basis of a definition of God. If we accept Anselm's definition of God as "that being greater than which cannot be conceived", the ontological argument asserts that it is contradictory to conceive of God's non-existence, since existence is inherent in God's perfection. To use Descartes' form of the argument, the idea of God necessarily entails existence just as the idea of a triangle necessarily entails that the sum of its interior angles equals 180°. The classical criticism of the argument is Kant's, that "existence" is not the type of attribute that can be part of a definition. The idea of having one horn is necessarily part of the definition of "unicorn", but this does not mean that unicorns actually exist. Consequently, most modern philosophers and theologians regard the ontological argument as invalid. The classical formulations and criticisms of the argument have been re-printed in *The Existence of God*, edited by John Hick, New York, 1964, pp. 23–70. The argument has not been dwelt upon at length in this book mainly because it never became a burning issue between theologians on the one hand and philosophers and scientists on the other, as did the other two members of the triad. But see our discussion of analytic theological language in chapter 6, below, pp. 178 f.

them precisely in philosophical language. The second is that by means of such arguments, heavily supported by detailed illustrations, in the case of the argument from design, from the various sciences (especially biology), seventeenth- and eighteenth-century thinkers erected a theistic framework, a description and explanation of the universe as created, designed and sustained by an all-powerful God, transcendent over and independent of the cosmos, which he brought into being by his own will for the fulfilment of his own purposes. Theism, the belief in such a God, was the background against which man's earthly destiny was played out. It would be wrong to assume that these theistic explanations and description were uncriticized. There were, as early as the end of the sixteenth century, thinkers who cast doubt upon the theistic interpretation of the universe. Nevertheless, it is true that this philosophical theism, erected and defended by arguments like those outlined above, outlived and repulsed most of its critics until it was fatally undermined by the criticisms of Hume and Kant in the second half of the eighteenth century.

Let us consider first the criticisms which Hume brought against the cosmological argument.[1] We remember that the crux of that argument is that the cosmos as a whole demands belief in God as its ultimate cause. Hume took up the whole matter of causality.[2] He argued that when we assert that a certain phenomenon B must have been caused by another phenomenon A, we merely mean that all Bs we have observed coming into existence have been observed to have been preceded by As. Therefore when we *observe* another B we feel, on the basis of our past experience of Bs having been preceded by As, that there is a strong probability of this B having been preceded by an A. In other words, if I observe a chair and enquire about its origin, I may assert that it must have been constructed by a carpenter. But I can only mean by this that since all chairs in existence are in principle *observably* preceded by the work of carpenters, I have good grounds for

1 A useful compendium of Hume's writings on religion has been published in the Fontana library as *Hume on Religion*, edited by Richard Wollheim, London, 1963. In what follows we shall give references to the sections of Hume's works and, where possible, page-references to *Hume on Religion*.
2 *A Treatise of Human Understanding*, Book I, Part III.

making this assertion. In other words, my assertion about causality is based on *experience* and *observation*. But the entire universe is a very different matter from a manufactured article like a chair. I cannot, according to Hume, assert that the universe demands a God as its ultimate cause, because this would mean that since I have observed all other similar universes coming into existence preceded by the agency of a deity, it is very probable that this universe did likewise. This is nonsense, since a multiplicity of universes and causal deities are not conjoined in my past experience like chairs and carpenters, houses and builders, or watches and watchmakers. In other words, causal connections in Hume's view only hold between observable states of affairs, and whatever God is, he is hardly that. It is also obviously dubious to speak of the entire universe as being an observable state of affairs.

If Hume's analysis of causality is plausible, then the cosmo-logical argument is not so convincing as it appears at first sight. In this discussion of Hume, we have repeatedly used words like "observe", "observable", and "experience". This is important, because a philosophy like that of Hume which bases itself on observation and experience is called "empiricist", and Hume was of course one of the great exponents of philosophical "empiricism". To this philo-sophical standpoint we shall have occasion to return later. Hume's empiricism has an important bearing upon religious speculation. If truth depends upon observation and experience, how could we expect to find an ultimate cause of the cosmos, independent of it, since the coming into existence of the cosmos lies beyonds the limits of all possible experience and observation? Why should we not simply be content to say that we have no means of knowing anything at all about such matters? Why should we not regard these ultimate causes (if they exist) as forever concealed from us? This attitude of professing ignorance about ultimate meanings and causes is called "agnosticism", and to this attitude also we shall have to return later.[1]

We turn now to Hume's criticisms of the argument from design. We remember that the crux of that argument is the alleged similarity between the universe and a cunningly

[1] See chapter 6, below.

constructed machine like a watch.[1] It was just this alleged similarity which Hume challenged. He asserted that the universe as a whole resembles just as much a huge vegetable as a piece of clockwork.[2] If Hume's point is valid, then the argument from design is seriously weakened. For while our experience allows us to observe a piece of clockwork coming into existence through the agency of a clockmaker, we can never observe a flower coming into existence through the agency of a flowermaker; so our inference from cosmos to cosmic designer is undermined. Is the alternative to deliberate design then pure chance? Hume suggests that this is not inconceivable. He points to the cosmogony of the Greek philosophical school of Epicurus.[3] Suppose, said the Epicureans, that the cosmos consists from all eternity of an infinite number of atoms or particles, of a very great (but not infinite) number of shapes, sizes and weights, falling through infinite space in infinite time. These atoms will form every conceivable grouping and arrangement, rather like the patterns in a child's kaleidoscope. One of these groupings may enjoy a certain degree of stability; our contemporary universe may be nothing other than this relatively orderly grouping which in infinite time is only one of a myriad number of such groupings.[4] If this hypothetical cosmogony is at all plausible, the argument from design must be weakened.

We must note certain points about Hume's use of the Epicurean cosmology. First, it does not matter from his point of view if there is no observable and measurable evidence for this type of speculation. For there is no observable and measurable evidence for the argument from design either. There are (at

[1] The classic exposition of the argument from design in English, William Paley's *Natural Theology* (1802), compared the universe to a watch, but it is clear that the comparison was common in eighteenth-century theology. It was probably first used by Bernard Nieuwentyl in his book, *The English Philosopher*, London, 1718–19, and was used also in Abraham Tucker's *The Light of Nature*, 1768–78. See L. Stephen, *History of English Thought in the Eighteenth Century*, vol. 1, pp. 346–7.

[2] *Dialogues Concerning Natural Religion*, VI; in *Hume on Religion*, pp. 145 f.

[3] *Dialogues*, VIII; *Hume on Religion*, pp. 155–60.

[4] For an Epicurean view of the universe see Lucretius' *The Nature of the Universe* (*De Rerum Natura*), translated by Ronald Latham, Penguin Classics, 1951.

least) these two hypothetical explanations of cosmic origins with little, from the point of view of experience and observation, to choose between them. This means that the argument from design *proves* (in the logical sense of the word) nothing. It loses its convincingness and persuasiveness. Second, the lack of evidence for the Epicurean cosmology was only temporary. Abundant evidence for this type of explanation seemed to be forthcoming in the next century, the nineteenth. The Epicurean hypothesis denies the need for a consciously designing creator, and asserts that there is but one basic kind of reality, namely material particles. Although Hume put forward the Epicurean model only as a speculative alternative to the argument from design, a near-contemporary of his, the atheistic Baron Paul d'Holbach (1723–89) adopted such a model as the basis for a philosophical system which came to be known as materialism.[1] D'Holbach held that physical matter was the ultimate reality and that all else, including man's thinking, feeling and willing, must be explicable only in terms of the qualities of and changes and movements in such matter. The long-term significance of this movement was that in the nineteenth century it supplied the conceptual framework for experimental sciences like physics and chemistry, and later, the model for all experimental science, including geology and biology. Biological processes, including human activities like thinking, willing and choosing, were to have as ultimate explanations the shape and size of, and the processes in a physical structure, the brain. Such convictions found philosophical expressions within philosophical systems like determinism and naturalism.

In the nineteenth century the Epicurean hypothesis seemed to receive confirmation in the shape of scientific observations from a well-known source; from organic evolutionary theory associated with the name and researches of Charles Darwin (1809–82). Darwin's evolutionary theory contained two points of significance for philosophical thinking about religion. The first was that life (including man's life, thought and activities) had apparently arisen from inert matter, which was an apparent corroboration of the Epicurean theory. The second was that highly complex and efficient organisms had become

[1] *The System of Nature* (1770); see E. A. Gellner, *op. cit.*

such, not because of some cosmic planner, but because physical environment exerts such a fierce pressure that organisms have to adapt themselves, over staggeringly long periods of time, into complex and highly efficient structures, or perish! Thus the cosmos came to be regarded as the background for the process popularly known as "the survival of the fittest". If so, it appeared clear why there is not much evidence of simple, crude, apparently undesigned structures; these have perished in the struggle to survive. At the other end of the scale, the most highly adapted and complex structure we know is man himself, equipped with intelligence and foresight, making him amazingly independent of his physical environment. These developments are relevant to our theme for two reasons. First, they show that Hume's speculative alternative to the argument from design was eventually to find considerable support from experience and observation. Second, they demonstrate that this alternative explanation was one which seemed to dethrone man from that high, even unique, place which had been assigned to him within the Christian theistic framework, as the crown of and key to God's creation. In the second half of the nineteenth century man came to be seen as merely one item, an extremely complicated and absorbingly interesting one, within a physical cosmos of items all of which were in principle regarded as totally explicable by the natural sciences. This was a significant contributory reason why the crucial area of discussion between theologians and philosophers in the later nineteenth century was man himself, his status, nature and value. In the next chapter we must return to this dispute between theologians and philosophers centreing upon human nature.[1]

To return to Hume's criticisms of the argument from design, he made some further points which he thought weakened the inference from the structure of the cosmos to one, all-powerful designer.[2] He pointed, for example, to the facts of evil and suffering in the world. If we infer from the facts of beauty, harmony and order to a good God, what kind of inference do we make from the facts of ugliness, disharmony and chaos? Here we must remember that in the

[1] See below, pp. 79 f.
[2] *Dialogues*, V; *Hume on Religion*, pp. 138–43.

34

history of religions an important place has always been held by dualistic systems, such as Zoroastrianism or Manichaeism, which interpret reality within the framework of a struggle between a Good Principle and an Evil Principle.[1] Does this, for example, not represent a more accurate inference from the actual state of affairs in the cosmos than the inference proposed by the argument from design? Hume therefore suggests that more plausible inferences from the facts of suffering and meaninglessness might be that the universe is the work either of an aged, decrepit deity with failing powers, or of a young, inexperienced deity who has not yet reached the full development of his.

Again, it mattered little to Hume whether or not there is evidence for these hypothetical alternatives to the argument from design. The point to grasp is that if these hypotheses do not do violence to the facts, the argument from design is gravely weakened. In competition with these alternative hypotheses it loses its persuasive finality. And the sceptic appears to be within his rights if he asserts that in the light of Hume's criticisms the argument from design proves (in the logical sense of the word) nothing at all. Hume's criticisms of the argument from design, published in the *Dialogues Concerning Natural Religion*, were, in time, a shattering blow to the confidence of those who held that a rational examination of nature led to the firm conviction that the structure of nature demanded belief in a benevolent, all-powerful designer who could be identified with the God of Christian belief. It is the theological and philosophical consequences of this shattered confidence that are going to absorb our attention in much of the remainder of this book.

There are two sides to Kant's attitude to natural theology, one negative and the other positive, and both of these have important implications for modern and contemporary philosophical thinking about religion. We shall deal with these in turn. First, there is the negative side. Kant effected what has been called a Copernican revolution in philosophy, because he severely restricted the scope of man's certain, indubitable

[1] For Hume monotheism was neither the original nor necessarily the most rational form of religion; see Hume's *The Natural History of Religion*, edited by H. E. Root, London, 1956.

knowledge of the world.[1] He held that we can have no certain knowledge of things-in-themselves, of natural phenomena, events and entities. When we experience these, our minds give them shape, structure and relation; our minds do not discover a necessary pattern or order which is inherent in nature; rather, they impose patterns and groupings upon the things and phenomena which surround us in space and time. Indeed, we cannot do otherwise, because our minds are so constituted by certain categories or principles that we cannot but see reality, so to speak, through the lenses given by the inherent structure of mind. In a sense, therefore, our minds, partly at least, *constitute* reality. Let us take a concrete example of this which is relevant for the philosophy of religion, the example of causality, which we have already looked at in the light of Hume's philosophy. According to Kant's theory of knowledge (or epistemology), one of the innate categories or principles of mind is that of "cause-and-effect". We can no more dispense with this in our thinking than we can with mind itself.[2] We cannot but link events and things into causal patterns; in doing so, we impose an orderly pattern upon that which surrounds us in the world. But we cannot conclude from this that "every event must have a cause", that is, that causality is a necessary law holding universal sway in the realm of nature. The only certainty or necessity there is attaches to the fact that this is how mind is constituted and that human thinking must proceed along these lines.

The implication of this Kantian epistemology for speculative theology is immediately apparent. Let us look again at the cosmological argument for God's existence. The crux of that argument is that since every phenomenon must have a cause, so must the universe as a whole. If one accepts Kant's epistemology, the premise of the argument (every event must have a cause), falls to the ground.[3] As we have seen, necessity attaches to no constraining principle in the world

[1] In the *Critique of Pure Reason*, 2nd edition, 1787; we shall give page-references to the Meiklejohn translation published in the Everyman's Library, London, 1934.

[2] In Kantian terminology, it is *a priori*; that is, prior to all experience.

[3] *Critique of Pure Reason*, "Of the Impossibility of a Cosmological Proof of the Existence of God", pp. 352 f.

of nature, but only to the way in which mind shapes the data which it finds in nature. But there is another, and perhaps more serious difficulty.[1] The data upon which mind imposes patterns and connections are derived from objects and phenomena and objects *within the limits of space and time*, that is, from nature. But the causal argument for God's existence (and the argument from design) carries its inference from our experience in the space-time continuum to a point outside it, for the cosmic first cause (or designer) transcends nature.[2] It is precisely this way in which the theistic demonstrations move to a point outside all possible experience and observation which makes them invalid from the Kantian standpoint. How could one possibly experience or observe a transcendent first cause of things or a complete causal chain? Thus these two theistic arguments must lose their persuasiveness, if Kant's epistemology is held to be plausible.

Kant did not of course deny that reason could frame a notion of a first cause or a cosmic designer which could function as a useful hypothesis. But a hypothesis, by definition, lacks the evidence which makes its acceptance certain. And if there are competing hypotheses in any field the one which appears to command the most evidence commands acceptance. Moreover, we have seen from our examination of Hume's critique of the theistic demonstrations that more than one hypothesis is viable. Kant's conclusion then about the cosmological and teleological demonstrations of God's existence is that they must fail to convince, to persuade; that is, that they are, as *proofs*, invalid. When we add Kant's criticisms of the theistic arguments to those of Hume, it would be understandable if we concluded, with a great many philosophers and theologians, that these arguments in themselves accomplish nothing at all, and that they were in the long run completely undermined by the counter-arguments of these two thinkers. Certainly, historically speaking, the critiques of Hume and Kant have had an immensely powerful cumulative effect throughout the nineteenth and twentieth centuries in undermining confidence in the power of speculative reason to make

[1] *Op. cit.*, pp. 355–6.
[2] *Op. cit.*, "Of the Impossibility of a Physico-Theological Proof", pp. 361–7.

out a case for theistic belief, by making inferences from the existence and structure of the natural world. Unless this is appreciated, a great deal of what follows in this and succeeding chapters will be unintelligible.

We turn now to the positive side of Kant's attitude to natural theology. We remember that Hume had put forward as a speculative alternative to the argument from design a hypothesis which tended towards atomistic determinism. But Kant was too strongly impressed by the astounding capacity of matter to adapt itself and by man's startling uniqueness to be in the least attracted by a completely mechanistic explanation of the cosmos.[1] He therefore set out to exempt man from that causal interpretation which appeared to be apt for nature. Kant held that man's uniqueness was rooted in the fact that man was essentially a moral creature, and it was by concentrating attention upon man's moral experience that he not only heavily underlined man's uniqueness over against nature, but also opened up an important chapter in the history of philosophical thinking about religion. It is not going too far to say (as we shall argue in detail later) that in a sense we, in the second half of the twentieth century, are still living in the Kantian era of religious thought. We can grasp something of this Kantian revolution in philosophical theology if we recall Kant's dictum that he had "to deny knowledge in order to make room for faith". He had attempted to abolish all possibility of attaining objective, certain knowledge of God by means of philosophical argument and speculation, when he tried to dispose of the traditional theistic arguments.

---

[1] Kant's anti-mechanistic and anti-deterministic attitude comes out strongly in this passage: "It is quite certain that we can never get a sufficient knowledge of organized beings and their inner possibility, much less get an explanation of them, by looking merely to mechanical principles of nature. Indeed, so certain is it, that we may confidently assert that it is absurd for men even to entertain any thought of so doing, or to hope that maybe another Newton may some day arise, to make intelligible to us even the genesis of but a blade of grass from natural laws that no design has ordered. Such insight we must absolutely deny mankind"; quoted in John Dillenberger, *Protestant Thought and Natural Science*, London, 1961, p. 185. Cf. what Kant wrote in the Preface to the second edition of the *Critique of Pure Reason*, p. 20: "Criticism alone can strike a blow at the root of Materialism, Fatalism, Atheism, Free-thinking . . . which are universally injurious".

But he tried to establish the possibility of belief in God by means of a method which has had vast repercussions in modern and contemporary philosophical theology. This method was to put forward a *moral* argument for the existence of God, which proceeds along lines like these.[1] Duty comes to us in the form of a "categorical imperative". Such an imperative is not merely the product of our desire or inclination. It is "categorical" in contradistinction to "hypothetical"; it is absolute and unconditional. It could not conceivably follow the form, "You ought to do your duty *if*. . .", because this is reconcilable with, "You ought to do your duty *if* you have sufficient desire or inclination to do it", a proposition which is incompatible with any idea of duty. This second form would be that of a hypothetical imperative, such as, "You ought to use a hammer *if* [i.e. on the hypothesis that] you want to drive in nails." The hypothetical imperative concerns prudential, not moral, actions. Kant held that if this analysis of morality was acceptable, then the moral subject was bound, practically, to believe in three things—the freedom of the will, the immortality of the soul and the existence of God.

First, we deal with freedom of the will. It would, argues Kant, be ludicrous to feel obliged to do an action if in fact we were unable to do it. It would be fantastic to tell someone in poverty that he has a duty to donate a large sum to charity. In the words of the eighteenth-century dictum, "ought implies can". Therefore genuine morality implies and demands moral freedom. Note the implication; this freedom at once detaches man, partly at least, from the realm where things are causally interpreted. In other words, the genuine moral agent transcends nature. Second, we deal with the immortality of the soul.[2] The genuine moral life consists of man's repeated attempts to conform his will to the wholly good will. There is for Kant a Highest Good (*Summum Bonum*), which comprehends and embraces those particular good ends which man aims at in his moral experience, and from which these several lesser goods derive their significance. In spite of his repeated

[1] *The Critique of Practical Reason*, trans. by T. K. Abbott, 6th edition, London, 1909, Part One, Book II, chapter II, pp. 206–46.
[2] *Op. cit.*, pp. 218 f.

attempts, man never quite arrives at his destination, he suffers reverses and failure, he falls short. To the end of his earthly existence the final achievement of this Highest or Supreme Good eludes his grasp. Therefore man must have faith in, he must live in the expectation of, a life beyond this one where this supreme achievement, at which he has been aiming in vain during his earthly life, is possible and actual. That is, Kant believes that morality demands that we believe in the immortality of the soul.

Third, we deal with the existence of God.[1] Kant was aware that the pursuit of virtue, the moral life, does not always lead to happiness, and that the pursuit of happiness does not necessarily lead to the achievement of virtue. Kant held that this insight leads the moral agent to belief in a God who properly correlates these two, happiness and virtue. Further, Kant makes use of the insight that man is unique in living simultaneously in two dimensions, that of nature and that of morality.[2] Man is bound to enquire about the relationship between these two. For example, is the constitutive, determinative sphere that of nature? Has man been flung into a jungle which is apathetic towards his pursuit and achievement of moral values and ideals? Or, on the other hand, is the natural order somehow sympathetic towards his moral development? Kant felt that questions like these must lead the man who takes the moral life with utter seriousness to regard nature as the creation of a deity who is concerned with man's moral progress and fulfilment, and with the final correlation of virtue and happiness. The moral life, lived in utter seriousness, must involve the moral agent, according to Kant, in practical everyday belief in such a God.

This sketch of the Kantian moral argument for the existence of God has been given only in the briefest outline. At this point we must make certain preliminary and tentative comments upon it which are important for our theme. First, strictly speaking, it is incorrect to call Kant's argument a "proof". As an argument it "proves" nothing really. If one is opposed to the conclusion, namely theistic belief, it

[1] *Op. cit.*, pp. 220 f.
[2] In Kantian terminology, the *phenomenal* and the *noumenal* spheres.

is possible to challenge almost every stage of it.[1] It would be more correct to describe it as an "invitation", in which we are invited to share with Kant his understanding of the moral life and the feelings and longings and frustrations that accompany it, and to investigate practically, in our everyday living, whether this understanding does lead us in the direction of theistic belief. Kant was quite clear that one could derive from his argument nothing like objective, mathematical certainty. It could only give everyday, practical certitude. That is, he realized that the existence of God and the immortality of the soul were not publicly demonstrable, observable and verifiable states of affairs. The certitude of morally based belief only comes privately to the moral agent who takes the attempt to live according to moral imperatives with utter seriousness, and who presses through in faith to the practical implications of his attempt. Thus the moral argument differs qualitatively from, say, the cosmological and teleological ones. The seventeenth- and eighteenth-century defenders of these held that reason alone enabled any rational man to demonstrate God's existence publicly from the existence or structure of nature. Kant's argument was that belief in God was a private matter resulting not only from the exercise of reason but also of the will.

Our second comment follows from the first. The Kantian God appears to be merely an implication or function or aspect of morality. For Kant, God rounds off, completes and fulfils morality. He is clear that there is no possibility of combining our moral awareness of God with our scientific knowledge of the world into a metaphysical picture of a God-created and God-controlled cosmos. He distinguishes carefully between, on the one hand, the knowledge gained by the empirical investigation of nature within space and time (which he calls "theoretical knowledge"), and, on the other, the practical implications (which Kant calls "postulates") of morality, namely freedom, immortality and God. These two types of knowledge must be carefully distinguished, and it is illegiti-

---

[1] Kant's argument has been thoroughly criticized, rather woodenly and unimaginatively, by C. D. Broad in *Five Types of Ethical Theory*, London, 1930, pp. 139–42.

mate to combine them into a theistic world-view.[1] From the point of view of religious belief, a certain danger is clear; it might be felt that Kant's postulates, for example God, are merely luxurious and sophisticated extensions of morality of such a tenuous kind that they might conceivably be given up without noticeable loss or inconvenience. That is, Kant's ethics might easily be transformed into a form of moral humanism.

Kant was insistent that there was no question of religion (in the form of a divine lawgiver or a system of divine rewards and punishments), functioning as the presupposition of morality or the motive for moral action. All rational men know by reason alone what their duty is and the knowledge that something is their duty is sufficient reason for them to perform it.[2] "Duty for duty's sake" is an accurate enough summary of Kantian morality. To be fair to Kant, he was convinced that we *must* believe in God and in immortality, because in the struggle of the moral life there is a strongly felt need for assurance that we can attain to moral perfection, and that nature is such that we are not positively hindered from such attainment. In short, we need to be assured that in our moral striving we are not chasing after a chimera. The moral venture is such that it requires something to bind together and reinforce our scattered moral inclinations, orienting them in the proper direction; and this something for Kant is God.[3] Thus Kant wrote in the *Critique of Judgment* that his moral argument "only establishes the Being of God sufficiently for our moral destination, i.e. in a practical point of view".

In view of this we must ask questions like these: is it not

[1] *Critique of Practical Reason*, pp. 231 f.: "How is it possible to conceive an Extension of Pure Reason in a Practical point of view, without its knowledge as speculative being enlarged at the same time?" Cf. Gottfried Martin, *Kant's Metaphysics and Theory of Science*, Manchester, 1955, pp. 158–9: "God is not an object of the mathematico-scientific knowledge which is brought to bear on the causal flow of events in space and time."

[2] Kant held that man is morally "autonomous"; that is, since he is immediately aware of moral demands there is a sense in which man is "a law unto himself". But "autonomous ethics" also implies that ethics, so far as motive and the knowledge of duty are concerned, is independent of any alleged special revelation by a divine legislator.

[3] See James Collins, *God in Modern Philosophy*, London, 1960, pp. 193 f.

then a relatively short step to affirming that it is merely the *idea* of God which has value? To put this another way: Is it not the vital thing, according to Kant, to have an awareness or consciousness of God?[1] If so, could this not lead in the long run to the view that God only exists *within* or *for* the moral consciousness, or that in some sense God's existence is merely willed by the moral agent? Clearly if these questions are to the point, further questions would have to be asked concerning the extent to which the Kantian conception of God can usefully function as the basis for Christian theism, and whether the Kantian approach to God's existence could possibly do justice to the God of the Bible and of the Creeds. These questions are by no means academic ones formulated in order to occupy the philosopher of religion. They are fundamental questions which must be tackled by anyone who tries to make sense of belief in God. Moreover, as we shall see in the next chapter, important developments in nineteenth-century philosophy and science made it inevitable that these questions thrown up by the Kantian approach to God should be burning issues between theologians and philosophers. Nor did the nineteenth century supply final answers to them; our own century has clearly inherited them from the nineteenth, and they are still in the forefront of discussions between theologians and philosophers in the nineteen-sixties.[2] To these questions in different forms we shall have to return later.

Our third comment is this: we ought not to be put off by the rather quaint, eighteenth-century expression which Kant gives to the argument in the *Critique of Practical Reason*. It is sometimes tempting to dismiss the argument as the product merely of his rigid moralism, said to be derived from his Scottish-Prussian ancestry. It is equally tempting to be amused, for example, by Kant's quaint eighteenth-century demand for the correlation of virtue and happiness. These temptations should be held in check because, as we shall see in our third

[1] We do not need to agree with the rather cruel remark of the philosopher Herder that Kant's God is merely a nail which he used in order to hold together a morality which was falling to pieces.

[2] See, for example, our discussion of the approach of R. B. Braithwaite to religious belief, pp. 184 f. below.

chapter, the Kantian argument is capable of almost infinite translation, reformulation and restatement. Nineteenth- and twentieth-century theology has amply demonstrated that a moral type of argument for religious belief has a truly amazing variability and vitality. Since the end of the eighteenth century, Kant's argument has been regarded, if not as a model, as an inspiration for those seeking to find God within the sphere of morality.

Our fourth and final comment is this: it has often been said that Kant stands to the history of modern philosophy in a relationship something like that in which Copernicus stands to the history of modern science, so great has his influence been. Kant himself referred to the "Copernican revolution" that he was trying to bring about in philosophy, and posterity has borne out his claim to be justified. In 1897 the neo-Kantian thinker Auguste Sabatier wrote this: "Thinkers may today be divided into two classes: those who date from before Kant, and those who have received the initiation and, so to speak, the philosophical baptism of his critique. These two classes of minds will always have much ado to understand each other."[1] Sabatier was a Protestant theologian and was thus assessing Kant upon his effect on theology, which has been immense. We must bow to the judgment of a great systematic theologian who was also a distinguished disciple of Kant, Julius Kaftan, who described Kant as the philosopher of Protestantism.[2] Kaftan did not merely mean by this that Kant, in his opinion, dealt the death-blow to that speculative picture of the universe within which even today Roman Catholic theologians work out the divine purpose for man.[3]

[1] *Outlines of a Philosophy of Religion Based on Psychology and History*, Harper Torchbooks Edition, New York, 1957, p. 276.

[2] See his *Truth of the Christian Religion*, trans. by George Ferries, Edinburgh, 1894, vol. i, pp. 351 f.

[3] One of the greatest twentieth-century Roman Catholic theologians, Professor Karl Adam, wrote this about Kant in 1929: "The individualism of the Renaissance, the dismemberment of man and his relations in the age of Enlightenment, and finally the subjective idealism of Kant, whereby our minds were taught to relinquish the objective thing, the trans-subjective reality, and to indulge in boundless subjectivism: these influences tore us from the moorings of our being, and especially from our true and essential basis, that humanity which produces, supports and enfolds us", *The Spirit of Catholicism*, The New Ark Library, London, 1959, p. 39. "After Kant

That is doubtless true, but Kaftan meant more than that.

Kant's importance for Protestantism is that in the post-Kantian period a great many theologians have tended to define their presuppositions in sympathy with his formal theological attitudes. The overall tendency has been to accept from Kant, and, incidentally, from Hume, the futility of trying to construct by speculative reason a picture of the natural universe as God-governed and God-designed. They have also tended to follow Kant in approaching belief in God from the standpoint of man's unique inner life and experience. To put this another way, Kant confessed himself overawed by two things, "the starry heavens above and the moral law within". Many Protestant thinkers have tended to follow Kant in holding that "the starry heavens above" (i.e. physical nature) can tell us precious little for certain about God's being and activities, but that man's unique values, strivings and drives may tell us a great deal. It would therefore not be an exaggeration to say that from the beginning of the nineteenth century until the present day many Protestant thinkers have followed a theological "Kantian pattern". Much of what follows in succeeding chapters will examine the ways in which this Kantian pattern has influenced theology in the modern period.

We are now perhaps in a position to recapitulate and summarize. Why have we devoted so much space to this treatment of the attitudes of Hume and Kant to philosophical thinking about religion? We have already hinted at an answer — their effect upon subsequent theologians. But there is another very cogent reason. If, in the nineteen-sixties, we were to investigate the writings of philosophers about contemporary attitudes to and estimates of religous belief, we should find that these contain copious references to the discussions to be found in Hume and Kant. We should find that contemporary philosophers, when they write about religion, find it impossible to avoid the views of these two

and his school had made the transcendental subject the autonomous law-giver of the objective world and even of the empirical consciousness itself . . . then the whole consciousness of reality became afflicted with an unhealthy paralysis" (p. 10). "The Catholic has no sort of passion for autonomy and self-glorification. From this point of view, as well as from others, Kant's 'moral autonomy' is a product of Protestantism" (p. 240).

thinkers. It is therefore clear, as we argued earlier, that it is hardly possible for any of us to understand the exciting contemporary dialogue between religious believers and philosophers unless we have some notion of the attitudes of Hume and Kant to belief. We should lack a key enabling us to enter into the dialogue which is really the subject of this book.

Even in our very brief survey of their thought we can see emerging themes, attitudes, lines of thought and tendencies which their philosophical successors were to take up and develop, often with significant implications for religion. Let us recapitulate and note some of these themes and tendencies, because they set the stage for the subsequent dialogue between faith and philosophy. First, in the work of both we see the philosophical attitude of *empiricism*. "Empiricism" is derived from a Greek word meaning "experience". In philosophy it denotes roughly the point of view which holds that all our knowledge is derived from our experience, usually our sense-experience, of things and processes in space and time. Hume, we remember, threw out the causal type of theistic reasoning because, never having *experienced* other similar universes coming into existence through the agency of deities, we are not entitled to conclude that ours had done so. Similarly, he dismissed the argument from design; having likened our cosmos to a gigantic vegetative organism, he pointed out the impossibility of *experiencing* or *observing* the design of comparable organisms. We recall also that Kant had strictly limited the scope of reason to things and phenomena within the *observable* and *experienceable* world of space and time, and that this had made him take up a very sceptical attitude to the theistic arguments. In different ways these two thinkers helped to advance the empiricist tradition. Empiricist philosophy of course ascribes great prestige to science and to scientific method; it is a notable British philosophical tradition numbering among its exponents four great British philosophers, Locke, Berkeley, Hume and Mill. Since Hume (and largely because of his influence), empiricism has been strongly influential in Anglo-Saxon philosophical circles, and in twentieth-century England a significant philosophical school has been called "Logical Empiricism".[1]

[1] See below, pp. 198 f.

Closely linked with empiricism is another philosophical attitude called "Positivism".[1] Positivism ascribes an absolute prestige to experimental science; it insists that the scientific methods of experiment, observation, prediction and measurement are ultimately the *only* methods of accumulating knowledge. Positivists too look back to the work of Hume with admiration and gratitude. This philosophical standpoint, which became powerful in the middle of the nineteenth century, explicitly tries to discredit philosophical speculation and rational theology. A powerful school of positivism, all of whose tenets are by no means dead today, held sway in the nineteen-twenties and thirties, namely Logical Positivism, associated in Britain with the name and writings of Professor A. J. Ayer.[2] As we shall discover, the influence of Hume's work, including his work on religious belief, has been potent within this school of thought.

Third, in Hume's discussion of rational theology, we can see emerging, in germ at least, a philosophical position (not unconnected with empiricism and positivism), which we may call "naturalism". Naturalism considers that the totality of things and events which we call "nature" is the totality of all things and events whatever. Naturalism denies the need of any ultimate explanations of nature in terms of "supernature" or the "supernatural". It absolutely denies that nature requires explanation in terms of a divine dimension or by reference to a transcendent realm of values or to minds which are not wholly explicable by reference to natural substances or forces. The Epicurean hypothesis, considered by Hume as an alternative explanation to the one based on the teleological argument, is of course thoroughly naturalistic. Naturalism logically implies atheism, and while Hume was no atheist, his nineteenth-century naturalistic successors emphatically were.[3] One but not the only form of naturalism was "materialism", which holds that ultimately there is one basic ingredient of reality, physical matter. Materialism involves the view that all living organisms, including humans, are fundamentally material bodies. What some call "minds"

[1] See below, pp. 78 f.
[2] See below, pp. 192 f.
[3] See below, pp. 76 f.

47

or "souls" are fundamentally only rather startling qualities inherent in this material. Again, the Epicurean hypothesis is clearly materialist, and we have already noted the existence of eighteenth-century philosophical materialism associated with the name and work of D'Holbach. It was a philosophical standpoint which was to appear attractive to many during the second half of the nineteenth century.

Fourth, we must note the importance of Kant's attempt to salvage religion from the onslaught of empiricism, positivism and naturalism. Kant had exempted man from an exhaustive explanation in a causal, physicalist fashion. Man was undoubtedly a part of nature, but his moral experience meant that he was more than, that he transcended nature. His moral freedom, for instance, guaranteed that he was no mere thing determined by causal necessity. He was distinguished from nature also by his morally-based drive to believe in God and in his own immortality. We have noted that this approach to religion involved the danger of the transformation of religion into secular humanism. It tended towards the confinement of God within the private moral consciousness; towards, to put it differently, belief in a God who, if morality were to receive a non-Kantian interpretation, might be regarded as too tenuous to deserve significant belief. In short, Kantian ethics with its religious postulates might well be transformed, without noticeable loss, into a highly moral but quite secular humanism. Again and again we shall see post-Kantian theology move sharply in this dangerous direction. We have come to the end of our survey of the significance of the thought of Hume and Kant for the rational basis of religious belief. As we proceed, we shall see that in the ways just described these two set the stage for the dialogue and the conflict between theologians and philosophers throughout the nineteenth and twentieth centuries. During this period theologians have tried to come to grips with and overcome the sceptical and negative elements inherent in their thought. And more often than not, we shall discover, they tried to do so by a method not unlike that suggested by Kant himself, who had in his own lifetime tried to overcome the religious scepticism inherent in his own philosophical system.

Chapter Two

THE SIGNIFICANCE OF THE
NINETEENTH CENTURY

IN 1793, a few years before the beginning of the nineteenth century and eleven years before his death, Kant set down what he felt to be the content and value of Christianity, which followed from his rehabilitation of theism solely on ethical grounds. He did so in his treatise, *Religion Within the Limits of Reason Alone*.[1] Kant's attitude to official, ecclesiastical religion is well illustrated by the following anecdote. On the annual occasion when the university of which he was a professor, the University of Königsberg, processed from the university buildings to the town church for its church service, Kant used to detach himself from the academic procession just as it was about to enter the church, and went home.[2] Nor did he ever participate in services of Holy Communion. In other words, official ecclesiastical religion was, strictly speaking, unnecessary for the person who was highly developed morally. Nevertheless, in his *Religion* Kant conceded that there were functions which it could valuably perform.

In the *Religion* he expressed the view that for him religion is nothing more than the recognition of all our duties as divine commands. Therefore all theological terminology ought to be translated into moral. The heart of genuine religion is duty done for the sake of duty. Human evil for Kant is the mysterious tendency within mankind not to perform moral actions for the proper reason, namely duty alone. The Christian religion is valuable solely because it assists mankind to overcome this evil tendency. Christ, for example, functions as *the* moral ideal of mankind, because although surrounded by a frightening array of opposing influences and temptations, he loftily ignored them for the sake of what he took to be his duty. Thus Christ, merely as ideal or example, calls to moral

[1] See the Harper Torchbooks Edition, New York, 1960.
[2] Karl Barth, *From Rousseau to Ritschl*, London, 1959, p. 151.

man to transcend the everyday world of interlocking cause and effect, the sphere of earthly influences, threats, attractions and distractions, in order to ascend to the world of morality, the realm of duty for duty's sake.

Moreover, moral man can be further assisted and confirmed in dutifulness, according to Kant, by joining in fellowship with men engaged in the same moral task, a fellowship sternly devoted to the promotion and propagation of pure, that is, absolutely disinterested morality. This fellowship Kant roundly equates with the historic Christian Church. Different branches of the Church are, it is true, at odds with each other. But this is so, insists Kant, only because the confession of each contains differing degrees of the (ideally) unadulterated religion of morality. These differences, Kant was sure, would largely disappear if these communions would translate their credal tenets into moral doctrines, thus revealing their inner nature. So too with all that goes on within the Church. Once it is realized that everything without exception must serve purely moral ends and none other, all ecclesiastical activities would be seen in calm and rational perspective. Only harm can come of the not uncommon failure to perceive that all religious machinery, for example, ecclesiastical laws, ceremonies and services, must serve purely ethical ends. Indeed, undue emphasis placed on such ceremonials and services in themselves can lead to the hideous idea that God's favour or acceptance can be won by offerings made to him in church! The Kantian God can have nothing to do with this; he exists for one reason alone, the strengthening of human wills for the performace of duty for duty's sake.

Kant's 1793 treatise on religion contains two further ideas which we must note particularly carefully. The first is the Kantian view that the interpretation of Scripture must be strenuously and exhaustively moral. The second is that what is claimed to be official church doctrine must be carefully scrutinized, sifted and sorted. A clear distinction between what is doctrinally essential and inessential, between what is primary and what is only secondary, must be made. By this distinction Kant meant bluntly that which is relevant to conduct and that which is not. The first is central and the second only peripheral. This distinction within doctrine was to influence significantly, as we shall see, much nineteenth- and twentieth-century theology. To turn finally to the devotional life of the Christian, Kant could only find a place for prayer (or anything which approximated to it, such as contemplation or meditation) in so far as it fosters and strengthens the dutiful life; this can be its only justification. Indeed, towards the end of his life he expressed the view, which logically follows from his other theological views, that moral progress made prayer seem increasingly futile.

This Kantian re-interpretation of Christianity throws up a list of questions which are difficult for even a mildly orthodox Christian. In 1793 Kant came into collision with Prussian religious orthodoxy, and was forbidden by King Frederick William II from writing anything further on theological subjects.[1] The reasons for this prohibition are not in the least obscure. Is Kant's version of Christianity not excessively, even grotesquely, moral? Can one, as easily as Kant appeared to think, reduce the historic Christian faith to a mere way of life? The Christian may well be aghast at the remnant that is left of the historic faith after Kant's re-interpretation. For example, Kant seemed to imply that Christ was a mere man whose significance is purely ethical, in contradistinction to the historic view that Christ is qualitatively more than human, and in a unique super-moral sense in a unity with God. Christ seems to have been reduced to a human Ideal or Example. More seriously, He seems to exist only in the moral agent's mental image of Him. His function is apparently reduced to that of an evocative and inspiring pictorial representation. It follows from this that there can no longer be room in Kantian Christianity for the conception of a contemporary living and victorious Christ, redemptively active in Church and world.

The Christian Church's only justification and function, according to Kant, are ethical. No longer can there be room for atonement and redemption in their traditional senses, and there can be no room whatsoever for propitiation and sacrifice. There is minimal scope for personal prayer and devotion. The adoration and worship (lit. *worth-ship*) of God in the classical sense are out of the question. Scripture and doctrine

[1] K. S. Latourette, *A History of Christianity*, London, 1954, p. 1052.

have been shrunk into what can influence behaviour. No longer could it be said that doctrine *describes* reality, which is indeed a staggering change. The distinction between the primary, moral and the secondary, non-moral dimensions in Scripture and doctrine opened the way for the rejection of much that for seventeen centuries had been regarded as essential truths of faith. Within Kantian Christianity there is too an apparent lack of need for what Christian theology calls "grace", both in the sense of the utterly undeserved gift of God to a mankind unable to help itself, and of the continuous, gratuitous working of God's spirit in human life. Kantian Christianity sets forth a way of life; but in it there is little place for joy, ecstasy, gratitude, self-giving, mystical self-forgetfulness, and the affections we find both in the New Testament and in the lives of the saints. It is a way of life involving stern, grim, austere, unflinching devotion to duty, to which is subordinated all else in heaven and on earth.

This does not mean that Kant's account of the Christian religion is incorrect. Much of what he said about Christianity is valuable, true and full of shrewd insight. Many religious and theological systems could only benefit from an acquaintance with his thought. His intensively ethical emphasis is powerful both as an astringent and a corrective. Christ is the great ideal of human life. The Christian Church must promote a way of life. Prayer must have moral fruits. What we mean is that there is a great deal more to Christianity than Kant's account would have us believe. Christ is more than a moral ideal or example. The purpose of the Church is not limited to the spread of moral attitudes. There is more to prayer than ethical self-improvement. Our difficulties with Kant concern not so much what he said as what he left unsaid, or what he felt unable, because of his negative attitude to natural theology, to say. His account of religion in general and Christianity in particular stands like a huge question-mark over the threshold of the nineteenth century. His religious thought set down a pattern which some theologians followed. It fixed certain limits which others had to overcome. It formulated a set of questions to which theologians had to find answers. Herein lies its importance. To some significant nineteenth-century developments we must now turn.

Before we actually look at any nineteenth-century theology, we must first make a few comments about the character of the century as a whole and our approach to it. The nineteenth century has often rightly been compared in significance to one of the great determinative eras in the history of the Church, like the fourth, the thirteenth or the sixteenth centuries. It was a convulsive and highly complex century which saw the emergence, sometimes only germinally, of most of the significant movements, tendencies and theories which have formed the background and starting-points for much of our twentieth-century living and thinking. Such movements were political, philosophical, scientific, social, economic, psychological and theological. Intellectually speaking, the century was both exciting and complex. Unless we have some idea of the theme which engrossed its attention we will not easily follow many of the discussions which have occupied our own century. Two church historians, Dr. Kenneth S. Latourette and Dr. Alec Vidler, have christened the nineteenth century a "Revolutionary Age" and an "Age of Revolution" respectively.[1] Since "revolution" means a fundamental and sometimes violent change from one state of affairs to another, these labels aptly describe the nineteenth century from the side of theology. The explosion which sparked off the revolution in philosophical theology was of course the critical empiricist treatment of natural theology of the second half of the eighteenth century, which we outlined in our first chapter. No longer could the old theistic picture of the cosmos be taken for granted, and no more could religious belief be expounded on the same basis. Hence the emergence of the new state of affairs of the nineteenth-century revolution. Another recent writer significantly describes nineteenth-century theology as "experimental".[2] He uses the word in two senses. First, in the sense of involving the *testing* of new, untried ways of doing theology. Second, in the sense of basing these on inner *experience*. The nineteenth century's theological

---

[1] See K. S. Latourette, *Christianity in a Revolutionary Age*, vols. 1–5, London, 1959–63, and Alec R. Vidler, *The Church in an Age of Revolution*, London, 1961.

[2] A. D. Galloway, in the introduction to *Basic Readings in Theology*, London, 1964, p. 10.

significance was, as we shall see, that it was concerned with new theological experiments which stressed the unique awareness and experience of man, the way, in fact, pioneered by Kant himself.

Theologically speaking, therefore, it is apt to describe the nineteenth century as "the century of religious experience". It was the century when there was stressed in theology above all else the value and unique inner life of man. It was the era when theology, whether it was always conscious of doing so or not, tended to follow a Kantian pattern, in turning away sceptically from philosophical arguments for theistic belief, based upon inferences from the existence or structure of nature, in favour of the fundamentals of religion implicit in the experience, feelings or moral drives of human beings. Nineteenth-century theology can thus be characterized by saying that it had an anthropological or humanistic starting-point, and sometimes an excessively anthropological or humanistic quality throughout. What this means will become clearer as we proceed, but we would do well to keep this remark in mind as we do so. We have already noted the complex character of the nineteenth century from the point of view of the history of ideas. It follows that there can be no question of providing even the barest outline of nineteenth-century theological thought, a task whose completion would require at least several bulky volumes. All that we can hope to attempt in this chapter is a glance at several key-figures and a few typical movements and tendencies in order to illustrate those themes which absorbed the thinkers of the century and which our own century has inherited from the nineteenth.

The briefest account of nineteenth-century systematic theology would be gravely deficient without some treatment of the theologian who not only initiated but dominated it, Friedrich Ernst Daniel Schleiermacher (1768–1834), Professor of Theology in the Humboldt University of Berlin. As every student of theology knows, Schleiermacher "did not found a school but began an era".[1] And one of his contemporaries prophesied that "from him a new period in the history of the Church will one day take its origin".[2] Theological

[1] Karl Barth, *From Rousseau to Ritschl*, p. 306.
[2] A. Neander, quoted by Barth, *loc. cit.*

genius apart, Schleiermacher's great historical significance derives from several factors. First, he was the first great Protestant post-Kantian theologian. There is evidence that he first studied Kant's works as early as 1785, when he was only seventeen years old.[1] He was an undergraduate at the University of Halle in 1787 when it was turmoiled over the implications of the critical philosophy of Kant.[2] "Since Socrates was in Athens there has, perhaps, been no more eventful period in which a young man could be baptized into philosophy."[3] In trying to assess Schleiermacher's merits, a distinguished scholar warns us that ". . . we must . . . bear in mind . . . the straits into which theology had been driven by Kant's philosophy of religion".[4] This much is clear: Schleiermacher knew intimately the writings of Kant and his academic disciples; he realized that the pressing theological task of his day was to take Kant seriously and to answer him.[5] We shall see below how he attempted to do this.

Second, Schleiermacher lived in an age when there was a danger of Christianity's being dismissed by educated people as irrelevant and meaningless. The title of his first important book, addressed to an audience of educated, sophisticated Berlin sceptics, reflects that this danger was uppermost in his mind: *Addresses on Religion to the Cultured Amongst Its Despisers*. Rudolf Otto has told us that Schleiermacher's theological programme was no less than to "lead an age weary with and alien to religion back to its very mainsprings", in an age when religion was threatened with oblivion and superannuation.[6] Early nineteenth-century man had learned from the thinkers of the eighteenth how to be humane, aesthetically minded, and, significantly, from Kant, how to be moral without

[1] W. A. Johnson, *On Religion: A Study of Theological Method in Schleiermacher and Nygren*, Leyden, 1964, p. 8.

[2] J. A. Chapman, *An Introduction to Schleiermacher*, London, 1932, pp. 20 f.

[3] *Op. cit.* p. 22.

[4] Barth, *op. cit.*, p. 308.

[5] Schleiermacher wrote to his father when he was twenty-one years old, in 1789, to say that he had read and studied all of Kant's works, Johnson, *op. cit.*, p. 11.

[6] In his introduction to *On Religion: Speeches to its Cultured Despisers*, Harper Torchbooks Edition, trans. by John Oman, New York, 1958, pp. vii–viii, to which all future page-references will be given.

necessarily being religious. Consequently, religion seemed superfluous. It appeared to have been driven into a corner.[1] This was, in outline, the situation that faced Schleiermacher just before the turn of the century.[2]

In Schleiermacher's theological programme we must concentrate on three important themes. First, there is his attempt to negate and correct Kant and Kant's theological predecessors. Second, there is his attempt to transcend Kant's conception of religion. Third, there is his ultimate failure to escape very far beyond the limits which Kant had laid down. We must glance briefly at each of these in turn. First, we deal with Schleiermacher's attempt to reverse the tendencies of Kant and Kant's predecessors. We recall here that Kant (preceded by Hume) had demonstrated that nothing certain could be known about a cosmic first cause or designer because such a notion lay beyond the limits of reason and all possible experience. Their scepticism shattered the widespread assumptions of seventeenth- and eighteenth-century natural theologians, and thus drove religious belief into a critical situation. These theologians had inferred from the existence and structure of the cosmos to a Highest Being prior to, above, behind and beyond the cosmos, apart from whom the cosmos must apparently remain inexplicable. But Kant had brought back the notions of God and immortality to complete and reinforce his ethical system. This was briefly the situation with which Schleiermacher had to deal at the end of the eighteenth and the beginning of the nineteenth centuries. He did so in his *Speeches on Religion*, the first edition of which was published in 1799, only six years after the appearance of Kant's *Religion Within the Limits of Reason Alone*.

Schleiermacher makes it plain that he shares with his sceptical Berlin audience their antipathy both for the abstract, Highest Being deposed by the Kantian critique and for the

[1] *Op. cit.*, p. ix.

[2] "Like Origen among the older theologians [Schleiermacher] sums up in his own person all the different tendencies which before him had existed only in opposition, and the genius by which he was able to reduce the clamorous hosts to order and unity has enabled him to present an ideal for the future, the importance of which no criticism in points of detail can obscure", W. Adams Brown, *The Essence of Christianity*, Edinburgh, 1904, p. 175.

miserable Kantian God who reinforces and binds together an ethical system. He derides the idea of "the Highest Being . . . exalted above all personality, as the universal, productive, connecting necessity of all thought and existence,"[1] the God defended by theological rationalism and deposed by Kantian criticism. For Schleiermacher Kant was tilting at a windmill, because this Being was not the God of authentic religion at all; ". . . whosoever insists . . . that the Highest Being thinks as a person and wills outside the world, cannot be far travelled in the region of piety".[2] The rationalist theologians and their critics had formed a ludicrously narrow and inadequate conception of God. "The usual conception of God as one single being outside of the world and behind the world is not the beginning and end of religion."[3] This is "only one manner of expressing God, seldom entirely pure and always inadequate".[4] Schleiermacher knew that the criticisms of Kant and the Kantians had done their work, but this did not greatly worry him. "In your ornamented dwellings, the only sacred things to be met with are the sage maxims of our wise men, and the splendid compositions of our poets. Security and sociability, art and science have so fully taken possession of your minds that no room remains for the eternal and holy Being that lies beyond the world."[5] This much is clear, the Highest Being whose existence had been defended by the rationalists of the Age of Reason and doubted by Kant is for Schleiermacher merely the conclusion of an argument or of a philosophical demonstration, and as such his demise should not seriously impoverish authentic religion.

Further, Schleiermacher agreed with the "despisers of religion" in their scorn for the Kantian God "brought back through the backdoor of ethics". "Nor shall I say how religion is a faithful friend and useful stay of morality, how, by its sacred feelings and glorious prospects, it makes the struggle with self and the perfecting of goodness much easier for weak man."[6] He holds that the cultured despisers of

[1] *Speeches*, p. 95.
[2] *Ibid.*, p. 99.
[3] *Ibid.*, p. 101.
[4] *Loc. cit.*
[5] *Ibid.*, p. 1.
[6] *Ibid.*, p. 18.

Kantian religious belief are right in not embracing Kant's theology and in not instructing others in it in order to attain to moral perfection: "How could you, who are called to educate others and make them like yourselves, begin by deceiving them, offering them as holy and vitally necessary what is in the highest degree indifferent to yourselves, and which, in your opinion, they can reject again as soon as they have attained your level."[1] Further, he points out that "to recommend religion by such means would only increase the contempt to which it is at present exposed".[2] If Schleiermacher's description is to be trusted, it seems that the Kantian rehabilitation of religion on ethical grounds had already, before the close of the eighteenth century, succumbed to those very dangers we had noted were inherent in it. "You seem to say," he wrote to the cultured despisers, "that . . . morality can be quite moral without . . . being pious."[3] The religious postulates of morality had proved, strictly speaking, to be unnecessary, and Kant's ethical system had apparently degenerated into humanism.

As for the immortality which Kant held was required by ethics, Schleiermacher joins the cultured despisers of religion in scorning this also: "A weak tempted heart must take refuge in the thought of a future world. But it is folly to make a distinction between this world and the next. Religious persons at least know only one. If the desire for happiness is foreign to morality, later happiness can be no more valid than earlier . . ."[4] "To wish to transport religion into another sphere that it may serve and labour is to manifest towards it also great contempt."[5] Religion, says Schleiermacher ironically, "must render a special service! It must have an aim; it must show itself useful! What degradation! And its defenders should be eager for it!"[6] He therefore dismisses ethically-based theism: "It were better that such utilitarians should be

[1] *Ibid.*, p. 19.
[2] *Loc. cit.*
[3] *Ibid.*, p. 29.
[4] Ibid., p. 20; compare the rejection of the notion of the after-life as a reward by another nineteenth-century thinker, Ludwig Feuerbach, below pp. 72 f.
[5] *Loc. cit.*
[6] *Loc. cit.*

submerged in the eternal whirlpool of universal utility . . ."[1] "High renown it were for the heavenly to conduct so wretchedly the earthly concerns of man . . . For such a purpose religion does not descend from heaven."[2]

Very little can be hoped for, according to Schleiermacher, if religion bases itself solely on metaphysical or moral demonstrations; "belief must be something different from a mixture of opinions about God and the world, and of precepts for one life or for two. Piety cannot be an instinct craving for a mess of metaphysical and ethical crumbs."[3] It is clear that theology must go beyond these two; ". . . it seems time to approach the matter from the other end, and to begin with the clear-cut distinction between our faith and your ethics and metaphysics, between our piety and what you call morality."[4] Schleiermacher continues in this way: "And yet, however high you go; though you pass from the laws to the Universal Lawgiver, in whom is the unity of all things; though you allege that nature cannot be comprehended without God, I would still maintain that religion has nothing to do with this knowledge, and that, quite apart from it, its nature can be known."[5] The late Professor H. R. Mackintosh well summed up the understanding of religion which Schleiermacher had to overcome and transcend in these words: "In the recent past, it must be remembered, religion had come to be identified with a group of moral doctrines about God and the world, touched with a spirit of petty teleology, while in the austere view of Kant it had virtually been made equivalent to a single aspect of morality."[6]

Thus Schleiermacher attempted to negate and correct the

[1] *Ibid.*, p. 21; Schleiermacher's use of the terms "utilitarian" and "utility" is interesting. Many sceptical philosophers have had some regard for religion due to its alleged social utility. We are reminded of the celebrated remark of David Hume that religion may be criticized, but "not before the servants". John Stuart Mill, the utilitarian philosopher, defended the retention of religion on the grounds of its social usefulness in his essay, *The Utility of Religion*. For our discussion of the defence of religion on the grounds of its moral and social usefulness, see below, pp. 181 f.

[2] *Speeches*, p. 21.
[3] *Op. cit.*, p. 31.
[4] *Ibid.*, p. 34.
[5] *Ibid.*, p. 35.
[6] *Types of Modern Theology*, London, 1937, p. 43.

notions of religion prevalent in Kant and in Kant's predecessors. He does so, first, by stressing that the God of the rationalist theologians, dethroned by Kant's critique, is a very nebulous, precarious, abstract and distant deity, detached from the world, appearing dubiously at the end of a philosophical proof. He is quite adamant that this "God" is not the God of authentic Christian faith. Second, he insists just as strongly that the God of Kantian moral theism is just as precarious and nebulous. This God is a prop, functioning temporarily for moral neophytes, but dispensable as soon as the moral life achieves adult stature, rather like the cripple's crutch which he can hurl gladly on to the rubbish-dump as soon as he can walk unaided. These lines of thought which Schleiermacher develops over against seventeenth- and eighteenth-century theological conceptions possess no merely antiquarian interest. They are of major importance in the history of modern theological thought, and we shall have to return to them later. For example, we find one contemporary writer suggesting that the God over whose "existence" theologians and sceptical philosophers still squabble is perhaps the God of seventeenth-century rationalism, the God dethroned by Kant and ignored by Schleiermacher and his school.[1] There are still many insights in Schleiermacher of great relevance for the contemporary philosophical assessment of religion.

Second, we must deal briefly with Schleiermacher's attempt to transcend, to go beyond the eighteenth-century notion of religion. Whatever religion is, insists Schleiermacher, it is not merely a mixture of natural science, metaphysics and ethics, which the seventeenth and eighteenth centuries had supposed it to be.[2] It has often been linked with these of course, but they do not constitute its essence.[3] It is true that even the Scriptures contain metaphysical and moral conceptions, but it is a mistake to suppose that these are their principal contents.[4] The essence of religion is to be found in "the

[1] J. A. T. Robinson, *Honest to God*, London, 1963, p. 40.

[2] *Speeches*, p. 30.

[3] *Ibid.*, p. 33; to find the "essence of religion" or the "essence of Christianity" was to become one of the major tasks of nineteenth-century theologians. Ludwig Feuerbach, Adolf von Harnack and W. Adams Brown all wrote books with the title, *The Essence of Christianity*.

[4] *Speeches*, p. 34.

immediate consciousness of the universal existence of all finite things, in and through the Infinite, and of all temporal things in and through the Eternal".[1] For Schleiermacher, true religion "is an affection, a revelation of the Infinite in the finite, God being seen in it and it in God".[2] True piety is "a surrender, a submission to be moved by the Whole that stands over against man".[3] The truly religious life is "the first contact of the universal life with an individual".[4] The knowledge which it involves "is immediate, raised above all error and understanding".[5] H. R. Mackintosh gives us an anthology of phrases used by Schleiermacher which illustrates the richness and many-sidedness of his conception of religion: "Thus, religion consists in man's becoming conscious of his own limitations, of the fortuitous nature of his life as his being runs its course and silently disappears in the Infinite. It is his giving up all audacious pride, and regarding all individual things, himself included, as being necessarily what they are. It is to live in the endless nature of the Whole, to perceive and divine with quiet reverence the place assigned to each and all. It is to have sense and taste for the Infinite, to lie on the bosom of the universe and feel its boundless life and creative power within our own. It is to drink in the beauty of the world and be drenched through and through with its spirit. It is devoutly to overhear the All in its expressions and acts, to let oneself be swept away by its influence as we contemplate the wonders of its workings, to discover and love the Spirit pervading the cosmic whole."[6] Although in the *Speeches* Schleiermacher describes the essence of religion by various terms (feeling, intuition, sense, taste and so on), when he came to write his large, very influential text-book of dogmatic theology, *The Christian Faith*,[7] he selected the term "feeling" (Ger. *Gefühl*) as basic, and elaborated it by calling it "the feeling of absolute dependence".[8]

[1] *Ibid.*, p. 34.
[2] *Loc. cit.*
[3] *Ibid.*, p. 37.
[4] *Ibid.*, p. 43.
[5] *Loc. cit.*
[6] *Types of Modern Theology*, pp. 45–6.
[7] Trans. by H. R. Mackintosh and J. S. Stewart, Edinburgh, 1928.
[8] *Das Gefühl der schlechthinnigen Abhängigkeit.*

It is obvious that Schleiermacher here is reacting strongly against and trying hard to transcend eighteenth-century and Kantian conceptions of religion. The God of Schleiermacher, far from being the unstable, nebulous end-term appearing at the end of a philosophical syllogism, is designated by him "the the World, Universe, the One and Whole, the Eternal World, the Heavenly, the eternal and holy Destiny, the lofty World-Spirit, the divine Life and Action of the All".[1] That is, the God of Schleiermacher interpenetrates, pervades the entire world. The world is interspersed and shot through with the divine. God is inescapable in all everyday life-situations. He is so close to man's consciousness and so integrated within man's experience that he is almost identifiable with them. To substantiate this, Schleiermacher points to the universality of religion in history and in the world. This religion, with all its qualitative variety and its different expressions, realizes itself in the great world-religions, of which Christianity, although the greatest, is but one example. At heart, all religions are the expression of the same feeling, awareness, consciousness, experience, intuition, sense, call it what we will. It is this sublime feeling or awareness which is the essence of religion, an awareness which precedes and lies at a deeper level in man than discursive reason or moral awareness. It is this feeling which gives rise to philosophy and ethics. From it religion derives its drive and its vitality. Nor is Schleiermacher's God a prop or crutch temporarily required by the man who either lacks moral stamina or who wants to make sense of moral experience, a prop which he may kick away when he is done with it. For Schleiermacher religion does not appear on the outer edges of morality. It is no mere sub-compartment of ethics. Schleiermacher makes a valiant, and, within limits, successful attempt to give religion an origin, status and validity independent of natural science, metaphysics and ethics. For him religion flourishes at the centre of man's being and bears fruit in all kinds of human experience.

What then of theology linked with philosophical argument, as in the seventeenth and eighteenth centuries, and with

[1] Mackintosh, *Types*, p. 50; cf. Schleiermacher's *Speeches*, pp. 26–118, the second speech.

ethics, as in Kant? Schleiermacher realizes that he might be accused of making a separation between religion on the one hand, and, on the other, philosophical knowledge and ethics. Hence he writes to the cultured despisers: "Such a separation of knowledge and piety, and of action and piety, do not accuse me of making."[1] Religion indeed does involve knowledge, because the religious believer can become an object to himself. He can contemplate, investigate, and describe his own religious feelings and affections. The results of such investigation and analyses are theological ideas and principles.[2] But Schleiermacher does not omit to warn his audience not to "forget that this is scientific treatment of religion, knowledge about it, and not religion itself".[3] It follows therefore that all theological discourse, formulations, creeds and dogmas are always secondary. They are derived from reflections upon religious experience itself; but the "contemplation presupposes the original activity".[4] Nor, says Schleiermacher, "can the description be equal to the thing described".[5] From this it is of course a short step to the startling suggestion that religious doctrines are but the formal descriptions of the affections of the religious consciousness. Hence we have this revolutionary theological assertion by Schleiermacher: "Make sure of this, that no man is pious, however perfectly he understands these principles and conceptions, however much he believes he possesses them in clearest consciousness, who cannot show that they have *originated in himself* and, being the *outcome of his own feelings, are peculiar to himself.* Do not present him to me as pious, for he is not. His soul is barren in religious matters, and his ideas are merely suppositious children which he has adopted, in the secret feeling of his own weakness."[6] Beside this we may place the following assertion: "Now the religious ideas which form those (religious) systems *can and must be nothing else than* such a description (of the emotions of piety), for religion cannot and will not originate in the pure

[1] *Speeches*, p. 38.
[2] *Ibid.*, p. 46.
[3] *Ibid.*, p. 47.
[4] *Loc. cit.*
[5] *Loc. cit.*
[6] *Loc. cit.*, italics mine.

63

impulse to know."[1] Schleiermacher thus admits that there is religious knowledge; but it is secondary to and derived from religious experiences, emotions and affections. This experiential approach of Schleiermacher to theology had momentous consequences for nineteenth- and twentieth-century Protestantism. It tended in the long run towards the position that the method of theology *par excellence* was to describe and make explicit in words and concepts the implications of the inner consciousness of the believing Christian, and, in certain extreme disciples of Schleiermacher, to the position that the entire contents of the Christian faith could be *totally derived from* an analysis of the feelings, emotions, attitudes, hopes, fears, expectations and drives of the authentic believer. This tendency, initiated by Schleiermacher, had very far-reaching consequences indeed for the whole of modern theology.

Nor would Schleiermacher countenance any breach between religion and ethics. He thus addresses the cultured despisers: "If your ethics are right, and [the pious man's] piety as well, he will not, it is true, acknowledge any action as excellent which is not embraced in your system."[2] But building an ethical system is not his business. Besides, there is a fundamental difference between ethics and religion: ethics involves activity, the manipulation, regulation, mastery and control of life. But religion involves passivity, "a surrender, a submission to be moved by the Whole that stands over against man".[3] Only by distinguishing between itself and ethics can religion keep its necessary passivity and thus its essential character pure. Nevertheless, the distinction must not be made too wide; "I do not mean," writes Schleiermacher, "that, for example, a man might have religion and be pious, and at the same time be immoral. That is impossible."[4] In these ways then, Schleiermacher tried hard to go beyond and transcend theological conceptions current in the seventeenth and eighteenth centuries and in the writings of Kant.

Third, we must look at Schleiermacher's ultimate failure, in his account of the Christian faith, really to escape very far

1 *Ibid.*, p. 48, italics mine.
2 *Ibid.*, p. 37.
3 *Loc. cit.*
4 *Ibid.*, p. 38.

beyond the limits which Kant had set when he rehabilitated religion on the basis of the moral consciousness. Essentially the point we wish to make is this: Kant had denied man *objective*[1] knowledge of God by examining and making inferences from the natural cosmos. For Kant, physical nature was opaque to God's existence and activity. But he had allowed man an *inter-subjective*[2] conviction of God's reality within the limits of moral experience. Schleiermacher agreed enthusiastically with the Kantian point of view that nature was indeed opaque to the reality of a God conceived of as a thing, entity or function located above, beyond or outside the cosmos, whose existence was held to be necessary in order to explain the construction, motion or maintenance of physical nature. The demise of such a God under the blows of Kant neither embarrassed nor disarmed Schleiermacher. On the contrary, he welcomed the situation. For the demise allowed the true character of the God of religious experience to be seen with startling clarity,[3] as the ultimate, absolute character of everyday reality when it is penetrated by religious feeling, intuition and insight. Schleiermacher never renounced, writes H. R. Mackintosh, "the right he claimed so firmly to urge that with a personal God outside the world, religion as such has nothing to do".[4] This right was to cause a great deal of trouble for those whom Schleiermacher influenced during the nineteenth and twentieth centuries. Moreover, the long-term effect of Schleiermacher's approach to theology was to confine God strictly within the limits of the religious consciousness; not, as in Kant, locating him on the outer, blurred edges of moral experience, but, and this is to Schleiermacher's everlasting credit, at the centre and heart of man's everyday awareness. It is to Schleiermacher's credit that he enormously widened and enriched Kant's concept of experience. Nevertheless, ultimately he could not escape the accusation that he also had confined God within the limits of consciousness, and in

[1] This term is used here to mean "publicly verifiable or demonstrable".

[2] This term is used here to mean that there are convictions which men share only by virtue of their being subjects of similar (moral) experience.

[3] We are reminded here of Kant's dictum that he had to abolish knowledge in order to make room for faith. The dictum could also have been Schleiermacher's.

[4] *Types*, p. 51.

consequence had denuded the historic faith of elements and dimensions essential to it.

Schleiermacher re-interpreted and reformulated Christianity, in the light of the eighteenth-century critique of theism and of his concept of religion outlined in the *Speeches,* in his dogmatic treatise, *The Christian Faith.*[1] This has often rightly been compared, in significance and influence, with the *Institutes* of Calvin.[2] Schleiermacher's book was vastly influential in European theological circles throughout the nineteenth century and into the first decade of the twentieth, and in the United States later than that. And some contemporary theological commentators hold that there is taking place now a revival of interest in Schleiermacher. It is for reasons like these that Schleiermacher has been named "the father of modern Protestantism". We must now glance at Schleiermacher's account of Christianity in *The Christian Faith.* According to Schleiermacher, religion is universal because religious experience and awareness are universal. Out of this universal religious consciousness spring the great world-religions, of which Christianity is one. Christianity's origins and uniqueness are to be sought in its historic founder, namely Christ.

By saying this Schleiermacher has advanced far beyond the conceptions of Christianity prevalent during the preceding one hundred and fifty years. The defenders of theism during the period 1650–1800 had given the impression that theism had originated in the abstract, quasi-mathematical reflections of scientists and churchmen on the structure and function of the natural order. Belief in God had tended to be identified with a set of explanatory propositions to which rational men must give their assent. This is true of Kant's conception of religious belief also.[3] The crux of the matter is that the seventeenth and eighteenth centuries were, by and large,

[1] The full German title was *Der christliche Glaube nach der Grundsätzen der evangelischen Kirche zusammen dargestellt, The Christian Faith, According to the Principles of the Reformed Church, Systematically Set Forth.*

[2] "In the opinion of competent thinkers *The Christian Faith* of Schleiermacher is, with the exception of Calvin's *Institutes,* the most important work covering the whole field of doctrine to which Protestant theology can point", editors' preface, *The Christian Faith,* p. v.

[3] This matter is taken up and explored in our fourth chapter below.

fundamentally uninterested in history as a sphere of knowledge and a source of information.[1] The philosophers, theologians and scientists of this period, the period when the modern natural sciences were born, were overwhelmingly and understandably interested in "nature" as *the* sphere of knowledge and *the* source of truth.[2] This turned out to be, as we shall see below, disastrous and crippling for theology in the post-Reformation period. Schleiermacher's definition of and emphasis upon Christianity as a *postive historical religion* with a historic founder marks at least the beginning of modern philosophical and theological movements reacting against this pernicious "anti-historicalness" of the Age of Reason. Schleiermacher's stress on christology marks a break-through into a modern rehabilitation of Christian belief.

Closely linked with this stress on history is Schleiermacher's stress on the utter centrality of Christ, who is for Schleiermacher supremely the *Redeemer* of men. He is so because his consciousness, his awareness, is absolutely flooded with thoughts of God. Christ is unique because no other religious founder or prophet has had his awareness so completely saturated with the consciousness of the reality of God. It follows from this that the difference between Christ and other men (a difference which many theologians hold to be the basic concern of Christian theology) could hardly be absolute. The difference between Christ, and, say, Jeremiah could only be that Jeremiah's awareness was not so highly saturated with thoughts of God as the awareness of Jesus. Doubtless this is true; nevertheless, the christological issue between historic Christian faith and the theology of Schleiermacher is whether there is more to this difference between Christ and other men than Schleiermacher allowed to be the case. To put this another way: Schleiermacher defines Christ the Redeemer in terms of *function*; Christ's consciousness is absolutely God-saturated and his function is to communicate to his followers this pure, undimmed, and untarnished awareness of God, an awareness which redeems men from all sinfulness and

[1] See Alan Richardson, *History Sacred and Profane*, London, 1964, I, "The Crisis of the Eighteenth Century", pp. 17–53.

[2] Basil Willey, *The Seventeenth-Century Background*, and *The Eighteenth-Century Background*.

unworthiness. Doubtless this is true; no Christian believer would wish to deny it. Nevertheless, the question must be asked: Does not historic Christianity assert that there is more than a difference of *function* or *office* between Christ and other holy men, a difference which can only be described as a difference of *being*?

When Christians down the ages have been compelled to formulate who and what they meant by Christ, have they not felt themselves obliged to say first what Christ *does*, and then what Christ *is*, and in so doing have been forced to find language which, although clearly inadequate to its task, indicates that Christ was not merely human, that He was more than natural? That is, that His origins and nature are not wholly explicable in terms of those natural, psychological and historical factors which are perfectly apt for assessing the theological significance of Jeremiah or St. Paul? The answer to these questions is clearly yes; if so, it might be argued that Schleiermacher's initial, fundamental stress on religious feeling and consciousness prevented him from giving an account of Christ which goes beyond the limit of feeling, consciousness, awareness. The result is that Christ is portrayed as a man; a very special and even a unique man, but a man nevertheless. This point is important. In his christology, Schleiermacher clearly transcended eighteenth-century conceptions of Christ as simply an ethical teacher and prophet, imparting to men universal moral precepts with great clarity. He clearly tried also to transcend the Kantian conception of Christ, where the only difference between Christ and men was His unique adherence to duty in the face of frightful forces distracting Him from it. Schleiermacher had widened, deepened and enriched Kant's whole approach to Christianity. Yet it appears that whereas Kant had said that Christ's uniqueness resides merely in His unique moral consciousness, Schleiermacher said that Christ's uniqueness resides in his God consciousness. This is one of the reasons for our saying that Schleiermacher failed to escape far beyond the limits which Kant had set, and also that ultimately his theology followed a "Kantian pattern".

We are now perhaps in a position to isolate two criticisms which are invited by Schleiermacher's approach to religion and to Christianity. The first concerns the absolute primacy which he ascribes to religious feeling, consciousness, inner experience. In the long run, his position seems to be that our belief *must be restricted to what we can feel and experience*. This appears to be fair comment upon his reiterated conviction that doctrine is merely a description, an analysis or a making explicit of the contents of the religious awareness. Now this begs the question: Are there genuine elements in Christian belief which cannot be directly experienced or felt in Schleiermacher's sense? If there are, it follows that his version of the Christian religion must lack elements and dimensions previously regarded as essential. An examination of Schleiermacher's version of Christianity demonstrates that his fundamental stress on experience as normative led him inevitably to discount or reject themes and doctrines which had been regarded as constitutive of the Christian view of things. One example of this is Schleiermacher's attitude to the doctrine of the Trinity; although he did assent to this, it is obvious that he did not regard it as fundamental, because such a doctrine could not be derived from a reading of the religious consciousness of the believer.[1] The doctrine of the Trinity was for him in no sense a "doctrine of faith".[2]

It has also been contended that Schleiermacher had little taste for the traditional Christian doctrine of eternal life.[3] Thus Schleiermacher writes in the *Speeches*: "The true nature of religion is . . . immediate consciousness of the Deity as He is found in ourselves and in the world. Similarly the goal and the character of the religious life is not the immortality desired and believed in by many—or what their craving to be too wise about it would suggest—pretended to be believed in by many. It is not the immortality that is outside of time, behind it, or rather after it, and which still is in time. It is the immortality which we can now have in this temporal life; it is the problem in the solution of which we are for ever to be engaged. In the midst of finitude to be one with the infinite and in every moment to be eternal is the immortality

---

[1] See *The Christian Faith*, pp. 738 f.
[2] *Op. cit.*, p. 741.
[3] *Op. cit.*, pp. 717 f.; cf. Mackintosh, *Types*, p. 80.

of religion.''[1] Such believers "desire an immortality that is no immortality. They are not even capable of comprehending it, for who can endure the effort to conceive an endless temporal existence? Thereby they lose the immortality they could always have, and their moral life in addition, by thoughts that distress and torture them in vain''.[2] Now no doubt this is to emphasize one element in Christian teaching, the fact that Christian believers *have* eternal life now in the present.[3] Nevertheless, traditional Christianity has always held beliefs about *future* immortality which differ from the feelings of timelessness and eternity characteristic of much religious and mystical experience.[4] In other words, Schleiermacher's re-interpretation of Christianity tended to be also a transformation of it. His over-emphasis on feeling and consciousness as the basis of all religion meant a certain reduction in the scope and content of the traditional Christian faith. This is what Hugo Meynell means when he characterizes Schleiermacher's version of Christianity in the *Speeches* as "aesthetic reductionism", while Kant's in the *Religion* is labelled "moral reductionism".[5] A considerable number of Protestant attempts to re-interpret the faith since Schleiermacher have undeniably followed Schleiermacher's programme and have invited similar criticisms.

The second criticism that Schleiermacher's theology invites underscores the extent to which he did not really escape far beyond the limits set by Kant. Kant's "God", we found, was an idea performing a function in the moral consciousness, and as such we described it as rather nebulous and unstable. Such a "God" might easily be dispensed with if His moral function was no longer considered necessary. A curiously similar criticism might be brought against Schleiermacher's theology if we substitute for the Kantian "moral consciousness" his "religious consciousness". Schleiermacher was adamant that this was the only dimension within which God was to be sought, and not (as in the case of seventeenth-century theolo-

1 *Speeches*, p. 101.
2 *Ibid.*, p. 100.
3 Mackintosh, *Types*, p. 80.
4 Hugo Meynell, *Sense, Nonsense and Christianity*, London, 1964, p. 110.
5 *Op. cit.*, pp. 72 f. and 90 f.

gians) the dimension of nature, or (as in Kant) the dimension of morality. The only realm with which the theologian is concerned is that of consciousness, feeling, awareness, intuition, inner experience. Hence his insistence that God is not a being beyond, behind or above the world, and his conviction that doctrine is, in the last analysis, a description of the contents of the religious consciousness. The danger is clear; Schleiermacher might be understood as saying that God has His existence only *within* the consciousness or experience of the believer, and that it is futile to seek his existence elsewhere. If this is what Schleiermacher was driving at, granted that man's consciousness is given a natural, non-religious interpretation, it is conceivable that Schleiermacher's God might vanish as abruptly as Kant's! In other words, if Schleiermacher's religious man could be given an adequate natural (i.e. non-religious) interpretation and explanation, the consequence might be the transformation of theology into anthropology, religion into humanism.

We do not mean that Schleiermacher's theology actually succumbed to these dangers, although, due to the notorious ambiguity of some of his writings, they are capable of interpretation in these dangerous directions. Despite his major theological achievement, he did initiate an era in the development of theology in which these dangerous tendencies were latent and in which they worked themselves out in rather alarming ways. So great is Schleiermacher's perennial importance that various subsequent attempts at theological reinterpretation follow, either implicitly or explicitly, the basic lines of his theological venture and seem to critics to become involved in difficulties rather similar to those encountered by Schleiermacher's nineteenth-century disciples. This is one of the reasons why we have given Schleiermacher's theological reconstruction so much attention in our survey of theological trends in the nineteenth century. It is not going too far to say that whoever does not grasp the way in which Schleiermacher approached his task and the difficulties which this method encounters will have great difficulty in understanding subsequent and contemporary discussion of theological issues.

In our survey of nineteenth-century theological trends we

must now turn to the work of Ludwig Feuerbach (1804–72), a thinker important not only in himself and on account of those upon whom he is a decisive influence, but because his thought illustrates perfectly, if in an extreme manner, the working out of those alarming tendencies which we observed were latent in the thought of Schleiermacher.[1] It is true that Feuerbach worked out his theological ideas in the light of the philosophy of religion of Schleiermacher's Berlin colleague G. W. F. Hegel (1770–1831), but there is sufficient fundamental similarity on theological issues between Schleiermacher and Hegel to allow us to regard Feuerbach's theological ideas in the light of the *type* of theology which is to be found in the writings of Schleiermacher. In 1841 Feuerbach published his book *The Essence of Christianity (Das Wesen des Christentums)*,[2] in which he set forth a radical re-interpretation of Christianity which he thought to be the logical outcome of the type of thought to be found in Hegel and Schleiermacher. According to Karl Barth, Feuerbach "sought to take Schleiermacher and Hegel seriously, completely seriously, at the point where they concurred in asserting the non-objective quality of God. He wanted, that is, to turn theology, which itself seemed half-inclined towards the same goal, completely and finally into anthropology; to turn the lovers of God into lovers of men, the worshippers into workers, the candidates for the life to come into students of the present life, the Christians into complete men; he wanted to turn away from heaven towards the earth, from faith towards love, from Christ towards ourselves, from all, but really all, supernaturalism towards real life."[3]

In what ways did Feuerbach wish to transform theology

[1] Much has been made of Feuerbach's approach to religion in J. A. T. Robinson's *Honest to God*.

[2] Translated by George Eliot, Harper Torchbooks Edition, New York, 1957; this edition has an illuminating introductory essay by Karl Barth. Interesting treatments of Feuerbach's thought are readily available in Karl Barth, *From Rousseau to Ritschl*, pp. 355–61; H. R. Mackintosh, *Types of Modern Theology*, pp. 121–30; James Collins, *God in Modern Philosophy*, pp. 239–49; "The Copernican Turn of Theology", by Jacob Taubes, in *Religious Experience and Truth*, edited by Sidney Hook, New York, 1961, and Edinburgh, 1962, pp. 70 f.

[3] *From Rousseau to Ritschl*, p. 355.

into anthropology, the science of God into the science of man? According to Hegel and Schleiermacher, the absolutely unique quality of man is that he engages in sublime thought and reflection (Hegel), that he has sublime feelings and intuitions (Schleiermacher). Feuerbach's question is: Why consider these to be evidence pointing away from and beyond man to a sublime being above and beyond nature? Why should the sublimity not adhere to man and to man alone? Why should the sublime and the ineffable, what man erroneously calls "God", not be man's own sublime capacities and potentialities, which he falsely *projects* on to an imaginary supernatural being? The term "God" is useful as the focal point of all those sublime human hopes, dream, aspirations and drives produced by human history. "God" is thus, for Feuerbach, the quintessence of all excellence that has been felt, thought, hoped, dreamed and intuited since the human species began. "God as the epitome of all realities or perfections is nothing other than a compendious summary devised for the benefit of the limited individual, an epitome of the generic human qualities distributed among men, in the self-realization of the species in the course of world history."[1] Feuerbach therefore does not regard theological statements as false; falsehood only comes into the picture when man is deluded into thinking that what theology describes is not man himself, but some non-existent supernatural deity! He wishes to retain theological language and descriptions; but he insists that the object they apply to is man and not God. Hence the transformation he demands of theology into anthropology, of the doctrine of God into the doctrine of man, of religion into a sublime and ineffable humanism. In doing so, Feuerbach believed that he was logically developing the theological approach of Hegel and Schleiermacher.[2]

Feuerbach moved through the entire range of Christian doctrines, translating each one into its humanistic or anthro-

[1] Quoted from Feuerbach's *The Philosophy of the Future*, p. 28, by Barth in his introductory essay to *The Essence of Christianity*, p. xvi.

[2] Barth tells us that Feuerbach "owes to Schleiermacher his best insights", and that Feuerbach confessed that "Schleiermacher's Berlin Church of the Trinity remained 'holy ground' throughout his entire life", *op. cit.*, p. xxviii.

pological equivalent. Thus, the incarnation meant for him the literal transformation of God into man, theology into anthropology. The Christian belief in miracles points to the valuable power of fantasy in the human mind that human desires are capable of fulfilment. The sacraments of Baptism and Holy Communion are ceremonials enshrining human belief in the curative powers possessed by nature. Christian belief in the Holy Spirit is really the projection, the objectification of the human creature's inner groaning for the fulfilment of his most cherished aspirations. Prayer is man's contemplation of himself in the light of his capacities and needs. And, most important of all, "God" is the unified projection and objectification of all past and present human desires, aspirations, drives and longings for perfection and excellence.[1] But God has no objective existence above, beyond or behind the world. Neither science nor philosophy has need of God as an explanatory principle or factor.[2] God can only properly be said to exist *within* human thoughts, feelings and hopes. To interpret God in this way means the abolition neither of religion nor Christianity. The man who does so sees them in their real light and in doing so undergoes an experience of liberation. This liberation consists in man's coming to regard religion merely as the sphere of his own development towards perfection, as the dimension which calls to him to assume the attributes of divinity, hitherto wrongly attached to a supernatural deity. Religion's task is simply to challenge man to attain to his true, perfect self.

Feuerbach is classed as a philosophical naturalist, and his thought as naturalistic. That is, he considered the totality of

[1] Feuerbach's approach here represents the beginning of nineteenth-century psychological naturalism, see pp. 90 f. below. James Collins, *God in Modern Philosophy*, p. 241, tells us that Feuerbach "employs the psycho-genetic method to break down the claim of Christian theology . . . to be concerned with independent reality. Psychogenesis is a technique for tracing the doctrine of God back to certain drives of human nature itself. The theistic mind thinks that it is dealing with the real order, whereas it is only engaged in objectifying the human aspirations and images which constitute the stuff of religion." In short, Feuerbach reduces "theism to our subjective religious dispositions".

[2] This is of course the outcome of the critique of the theistic arguments by Hume and Kant.

things and processes which we call "physical nature", which are studied in the natural sciences, to be the totality of all things and processes whatever. This is the necessary correlate of his rejection of all "supernaturalism". As Feuerbach wittily put it in a German aphorism, *"Mann ist was er isst"* ("Man is what he eats"). We note this because naturalism, as we shall see below, was a philosophical standpoint destined to become crucially important later, and was to evoke significant philosophical and theological reactions in the second half of the nineteenth century and in the opening years of the twentieth. We note also Feuerbach's conviction that traditional supernaturalistic religion erred gravely in diverting human attention and energy away from man to a (non-existent) God, from this world to another, from this life to the next. God benefited at man's expense. "To enrich God, man must become poor; that God may be all, man must be nothing."[1] Conversely, the demise of the supernatural, other-worldly deity means for Feuerbach the enrichment of man and his reinstatement at the centre of things. Feuerbach thus became one of the precursors of nineteenth-century atheism, and *The Essence of Christianity* was of course avidly read, digested, quoted, and its arguments developed by both Engels and Marx. This demonstrates how a certain tenet of the theologies of Kant, Hegel and Schleiermacher, the non-objective character of God's existence, could easily be developed and exploited in directions which all three of them would clearly have abhorred.

Kant had tried to show how nothing certain could be known of a transcendent causal and designing deity who existed independently of the world. But he had been convinced that at least the *idea* of God was necessitated by the moral consciousness. Schleiermacher had a little too readily agreed that the dethronement of a transcendent God independent of the cosmos made little difference to genuine Christian spirituality. Schleiermacher's God appeared to many of his interpreters and critics to exist only *within* man's sublime feelings and intuitions. We suggested earlier that the deities of both Kant and Schleiermacher were far too loosely attached to objective reality. What appears to have happened in

[1] *The Essence of Christianity*, p. 26.

Feuerbach's case is that he tried to develop this trend and adamantly denied that God any objective existence at all, that He was any more than a useful focal point for human aspirations. In making this denial, Feuerbach thought that he was drawing out the logical implications of his predecessors' thought. In the long run, historically, the results of his work were naturalism and atheism.[1] Feuerbach's theological importance is perennial; his version of Christianity stands like a huge question-mark over humanistic or anthropocentric theologies, over all attempts to base religious belief *solely* on human needs, drives, hopes, feelings and aspirations. The contemporary interest of theologians in him is justified, because his thought functions still, as Barth puts it, as "a thorn in the flesh of modern theology".[2]

Feuerbach was a naturalist, and it is to the two philosophical attitudes of scientific naturalism and positivism that we must now turn. Scientific naturalism claimed that all the salient features of the universe can be explained or interpreted in natural, observable and measurable terms. It identified all of reality with physical nature, and assumed the non-existence of anything above, beyond or behind nature. Historically, it assumed different forms; sometimes it was materialistic, in which reality was ultimately equated with the solid, billiard-ball atoms of nineteenth-century physics, a theory which also involved determinism, and the denial of the freedom of the human will. But naturalism was not necessarily materialistic, since many naturalistic philosophers identified reality with cosmic energy, or something of the kind.[3] Different forms of naturalism tended to model themselves on different scientific disciplines, whether physics, biology or psychology.

The most famous type of naturalism, associated with the name of Ernst Heinrich Haeckel (1834–1919), held that all reality is substance, and that *all* human activities, physical, emotional, aesthetic, moral and spiritual, are merely manifestations of processes within substance, nothing more. It is

[1] In *God in Modern Philosophy* James Collins significantly deals with Feuerbach, Marx and Nietzsche in his chapter on the emergence of atheism.

[2] Introduction, *The Essence of Christianity*, p. xxiv.

[3] John Macquarrie, *Twentieth-Century Religious Thought*, London, 1963, p. 96.

significant, from our point of view, that Haeckel adamantly denied the truth of the three fundamental religious doctrines which Kant had tried to rehabilitate on moral grounds—the freedom of the will, the immortality of the soul and the existence of God. Haeckel was an extreme interpreter of Charles Darwin (1809–82), whose experimental and observational work in biology had appeared to demonstrate that man, as one of the species of physical nature, had come to be what he is through the operation of certain natural laws. Darwin's views, though they themselves did not necessarily lead to atheistic views, were seized upon by thinkers like Haeckel in Germany and Thomas Henry Huxley (1825–95) in England, as experimental corroboration of an exclusively naturalistic and thus overtly atheistic interpretation of the universe.

Another point about this evolutionary naturalism must be noted. Earlier we observed that Hume had opposed the traditional argument from design by the Epicurean cosmology —the hypothesis that reality may owe its apparently designed appearance to kaleidoscopically altering combinations of physical particles. This *naturalistic* hypothesis seemed, in the light of the work of Darwin and his philosophical interpreters, to have received significant suport from science. One of the significant repercussions of evolutionary naturalism was therefore to discredit anew the older natural theology—the attempt to establish God's existence and the existence of a super-sensible, supernatural realm by means of speculative inferences from the natural order, such as the causal argument or the argument from design. If the Humean and Kantian criticisms had delivered a cripppling blow to such arguments, evolutionary naturalism now seemed to have killed them stone dead, a fact of which theologians were forced to take account. One other question with which naturalistic interpreters of reality had to deal was the phenomenon of religion itself. By and large, they attempted to give an explanation of the origins of religious beliefs and practices without reference to a supernatural deity or dimension. They tended to offer a set of interpretations of religion in which it was depicted as having evolved "naturally" from primitive man's fears, hopes, plans and aspirations.

Closely associated with philosophical naturalism was the

standpoint of scientific positivism. Positivism is the view "that since all genuine knowledge is based on sense experience and can only be advanced by means of observation and experiment, metaphysical or speculative attempts to gain knowledge by reason unchecked by experience should be abandoned in favour of the methods of the special sciences".[1] Nineteenth-century positivism was closely associated with the name of the French thinker Auguste Comte (1798–1857), the celebrated founder of the so-called "Religion of Humanity". Comte held that there had been three successive stages in the history of the human mind's quest for knowledge; he denigrated and rejected the first two of these, the theological and the metaphysical, in favour of the third, the positive[2]—the method of the positive or empirical sciences, in which laws are framed on the bases of experiment, prediction and observation. Comte exhibited a marked antipathy for traditional religious supernaturalism, and an almost fanatical faith in and reverence for human reason, especially as it was manifested in nineteenth-century experimental science. Accordingly, he advocated the scientific reconstruction of society based upon knowledge of the laws of human development—he is thus credited with being the founder of modern sociology. Comte combined with his sociological interests a new type of religion in which man, rather than a supernatural deity, was worshipped.

The positivism of a thinker like Comte has a bearing upon our theme for two reasons. First, it seemed to underline Hume's anti-theistic critique. Hume, in rejecting the validity of the traditional theistic proofs, had, in his strong emphasis upon *observation*, *experience* and *experiment*, exhibited a strongly positivistic attitude to knowledge. Thus nineteenth-century positivism, like naturalism, appeared to confirm the implausibility of the traditional theistic arguments, a fact which had, as we shall see below, a marked effect upon the type of theology which sprang up in reaction against it. Second, positivism has by no means a purely antiquarian interest for theologians and philosophers. Two vastly important philosophical movements of the twentieth century, namely logical

[1] *Concise Encyclopaedia of Western Philosophy and Philosophers*, edited by J. O. Urmson, London, 1960, p. 322.
[2] "Positive" is here used in the old sense of "factual", "practical".

positivism and logical empiricism, have strong affinities with nineteenth-century positivism. We shall deal with these in our sixth chapter below.

We now turn to a consideration of one of the major theological movements of the second half of the nineteenth century, which originated partly at least as a reaction against naturalistic and positivistic philosophy, the theology associated with the name of Albrecht Ritschl (1822–89).[1] Since Ritschlianism was a theological movement powerful in Europe until the nineteen-twenties, and until later in the United States, Ritschl's thought really brings us into the twentieth century. It possesses contemporary significance because it has been suggested that one of the great contemporary theological schools, that of Rudolf Bultmann, has been decisively influenced by Ritschlian thought, and that Bultmann's theological approach can only be fully appreciated in the light of the teaching of the great nineteenth-century theologian.[2]

Ritschl's attitude to the Christian religion can only be appreciated if we view it against the background of certain contemporary philosophical movements, naturalism, positivism and neo-Kantianism. We have already sketched the naturalistic and positivistic standpoints, and there is no doubt that Ritschl reacted strongly against the understanding of *man* inherent in naturalism. The late H. R. Mackintosh was of the opinion that the Ritschlian theological system "was thought

[1] Valuable treatments of Ritschl's theological approach are available in H. R. Mackintosh's two papers, "The Philosophical Presuppositions of Ritschlianism" and "The Development of the Ritschlian School", printed in *Some Aspects of Christian Belief*, London, 1923, and in his *Types of Modern Theology*, chapter V; W. Adams Brown, *The Essence of Christianity*, Edinburgh, 1904, chapter VII; John Dillenberger, *Protestant Thought and Natural Science*, London, 1961, chapter VII; John Macquarrie, *Twentieth-Century Religious Thought*, London, 1963, chapter V; Karl Barth, *From Rousseau to Ritschl*, London, 1959, chapter XI. It must be pointed out that what we offer in this present chapter is only a brief survey of the contact-points between Ritschl's thought and philosophy, and not an account of Ritschl's systematic theology in all its variety and richness. Ritschl was a very great and prolific systematic theologian, and some of his systematic theology is available in English in his *The Christian Doctrine of Justification and Reconciliation*, trans. by H. R. Mackintosh and A. B. Macaulay, Edinburgh, 1900.

[2] See, for example, Paul Althaus, *The So-Called Kerygma and the Historical Jesus*, Edinburgh, 1959, pp. 82 f.

out by a sincere believer in the truth of religion, with his back to the wall and his face to the advancing forces of materialistic science".[1] John Dillenberger warns us that "we should not be misled by the fact that Ritschl . . . seldom directly referred to Darwin and Darwinism. The concern of the liberal tradition with the nature of man stemmed directly out of the final blow that the materialistic interpretation of man—which was implied in Darwinism even if it was not confined to it—had delivered to theology".[2] Adams Brown describes Ritschl's approach to his theological task thus: "In Ritschl we see the effort to reinstate Christianity upon the unique pedestal from which it had been cast down . . . by an appeal to considerations the force of which the positivist himself must recognize."[3] And Mackintosh has elsewhere described Ritschl as "the champion of personality and moral values at odds . . . with contemporary naturalistic pessimism".[4] In other words, if positivisim and naturalism had the last say, Ritschl saw clearly that man might well be reduced to the stature of one tiny, and perhaps negligible, item amongst the myriad items of which nature is composed. If nature is ultimate reality, and man simply a part of nature, it is a short step to the conclusion that man is but one interesting little organism in a huge world of organisms.

To preserve the uniqueness of man, believing man especially, in the face of philosophies which appeared to threaten him with near-extinction, was one of the driving-forces behind Ritschl's theology. And since scientific positivism had closed the doors to knowledge to all but scientific experimenters, observers and interpreters, making phrases like "theological knowledge" and "religious knowledge" contradictions in terms, Ritschl felt compelled to work out a valid theory of religious knowledge which could stand on its own feet, independent of scientific enquiry. For these reasons, we find over and over again in Ritschl's work terms like "man's spiritual supremacy over nature", "man over nature", "the threat of nature" and "the supremacy of spirit over nature".

[1] *Some Aspects of Christian Belief*, p. 152.
[2] *Protestant Thought and Natural Science*, p. 251.
[3] *The Essence of Christianity*, p. 227.
[4] *Types*, p. 150.

The Christian view of the world, writes Ritschl, "assures to spirit its pre-eminence over the entire world of nature".[1]

The third driving-force behind Ritschl's theology was of course the philosophical movement known as "neo-Kantianism." From about 1860 there occurred in German circles an intense interest in the thought of Kant and its relevance for all kinds of academic disciplines. Ritschl had the full relevance of Kant's work for religion pointed out to him by one of his colleagues in the University of Göttingen, the holder of the Chair of Philosophy, Herrmann Lotze (1817–81), who can be described as an early neo-Kantian. From Kant, as interpreted by Lotze, Ritschl accepted the view that reason was impotent to penetrate to "things-in-themselves", and thus also the Kantian conclusions about the invalidity of the traditional arguments for God's existence. Consequently, throughout the later part of his career especially, Ritschl raged against the influence of speculative philosophy on theology, distinguishing sharply between the "God" of philosophical theism and the God of the Bible, the God and Father of Christ. Like Schleiermacher before him, Ritschl insisted that the demise of the "God" of metaphysical speculation, the functional God who exists over, above and independently of the natural order, makes no difference to authentic Christian faith. Ritschl was therefore thoroughly Kantian in holding to the impotence of speculative reason to establish the existence of a deity or of a supernatural, supersensible realm of divine essences or spiritual beings. Like Kant also, Ritschl felt obliged to abolish knowledge in order to make room for faith.[2]

Ritschl also took up a strongly Kantian position in his positive view of religion. Kant, we noted, wishing to exempt man from the mechanistic, deterministic explanation which seemed apt for the realm of natural phenomena, the realm studied by the empirical sciences, had heavily stressed man's uniqueness over against nature as a moral agent, whose moral striving obliged him to believe in his freedom and immortality, and in God's existence.[3] Ritschl followed this Kantian pattern probably more closely than any other post-Kantian theologian.

[1] *The Christian Doctrine of Justification and Reconciliation*, pp. 209–10.
[2] H. R. Mackintosh, *Some Aspects of Christian Belief*, p. 125.
[3] See above, pp. 38 f.

He felt that he must do so because in his time "nature", interpreted and depicted by naturalists and positivists, had taken on, from the standpoint of man as a creature of unique value, a sinister, threatening and destructive appearance. Authentic religion is born, therefore, not in mystical or theoretical contemplation, but in the conflict which man experiences going on between himself and nature. Ritschl put it in this way: "The religious view of the world, in all its species, rests on the fact that man in some degree distinguishes himself *in worth* from the phenomena which surround him and from the influences of nature which press in upon him."[1] "In every religion what is sought, with the help of the supernatural spiritual power reverenced by man, is a solution of the contradiction in which man finds himself, as both a part of the world of nature and a spiritual personality claiming to dominate nature. For in the former rôle he is part of nature, dependent upon her, subject to, and confined by other things; but as spirit he is moved by the impulse to maintain his independence against them. In this juncture, religion springs up as faith in superhuman spiritual powers, by whose help the power which man possesses of himself is in some way supplemented, and elevated into a unity of its own kind which is a match for the pressure of the natural world."[2]

In other words, feeling himself under the relentless, threatening pressure of nature, man, terrified of his own demise as a person of moral *worth* or *value*, finds his being flooded by faith in a being who transcends brute nature, guaranteeing man's spiritual *worth* and enabling him to realize his moral *values*. This being, for Ritschl, is God: "Knowledge of God can be demonstrated as religious knowledge only when he is conceived as securing to the believer such a position in the world as more than counter-balances its restrictions. Apart from this *value-judgment of faith* there exists no knowledge of God worthy of this content."[3] Ritschl insisted that all discourse about God should be confined to the form of *value-judgments*. That is, in making statements such

[1] *The Christian Doctrine of Justification and Reconciliation*, p. 17, italics mine.

[2] *Ibid.*, p. 189.

[3] *Ibid.*, p. 212, italics mine.

as "There is a God", or "God exists", or "I believe in God",
I must be clear that I am referring ultimately to the *value*
or *worth* which God has for my personal being and its moral
fulfilment, hideously threatened as it is by a blind, impersonal,
destructive nature. The Ritschlian form of the human dilemma
is "Believe or perish!"

This definition of religion as the solution of the conflict
between the claims of moral value and the relentlessness of
nature determines Ritschl's conception of the Christian faith.
The significance of Jesus, for instance, is to be seen in what
he did, in his actions within the sphere of history. The
historical Jesus, by giving himself up unreservedly to all
that sinful society could inflict upon him, in perfect love for
and trust in God, reveals God as a being who is, from the
human point of view, absolutely worthy of being trusted and
loved, in the face of the most appalling, chilling circumstances.
Without Christ's life of perfect obedience and faithfulness
the real nature of God would have remained obscure and
unknown, and men sunk in ignorance, unbelief and sin. The
work of Jesus is therefore unique and indispensable.

It follows that those who accept and follow Jesus reap the
benefits of his actions; they are assured in their relationship
with Him of God's love and trustworthiness in the face of
hideous natural forces opposing and threatening them. In
Christ, their ignorance of God's true nature is abolished;
in Him they experience reconciliation with God. The
followers of Jesus in community constitute the Christian
Church, which as a body participates in the work of Jesus, in
His relationship with God, and also in His spiritual supremacy
over nature. The Church founded in history with Jesus as her
Lord continues His work of drawing men into that unique
redeeming and liberating relationship with God which His
work inaugurated. The Church is therefore a kingdom or
realm of moral ends and values whose subjects are assured of
that supremacy over nature displayed and won by the work
of Jesus, and thus of the attainment of their full moral stature
in spite of the fiercest opposition from nature.

Ritschl is clear that Jesus' work points towards his divinity.
Since God has been defined solely in terms of "worth",
"value", "supremacy over nature" and the like, and since

Jesus *alone* can impart to men the assurance of value and their supremacy over nature, He shares by virtue of his work in the divine "essence", and so it is permissible for us to confess the divinity of Jesus. And since Jesus *alone* in his trust and obedience has revealed man gloriously triumphing over nature, He is the ideal man; or, as Mackintosh puts it, He is "the archetype of moral personality".[1] This very brief and inadequate sketch of Ritschl's approach to religion in general and Christianity in particular may help us to come to some sort of philosophical estimate of it. First of all, we must be generous enough to admit that Ritschl accomplished a very great deal indeed. In an age when pessimism, materialism, naturalism and positivism threatened to reduce man's status and significance to vanishing-point, Ritschl's powerful defence of man as a unique moral personality linked to a transcendent realm of values did much to inspire a theological generation in its task of defending man as a spiritual being called to find his real, authentic self in a realm transcending brute nature. Nor did Ritschl do so by means of thin, abstract argument. His *Justification and Reconciliation* is a rich, elaborate attempt to link together the main New Testament themes with the spiritual needs and drives of his contemporaries, as he saw them. Without doubt he put new life into Christian concepts for his own generation. Ritschl's thought was thus to fertilize the last quarter of the nineteenth century and the first quarter of the twentieth. Grateful as we must be for his achievement, we must now go on to ask critically how his thought appears to the philosopher. In other words, what are its preconceptions, fundamental principles and tendencies? Are these acceptable? Let us try to answer these questions, linking up our answers with our earlier discussions.

The most interesting way to approach these questions, and the way which makes the issues stand out clearly, is to compare Ritschl's account of Christianity towards the end of the nineteenth century with that of Kant in *Religion Within the Limits of Reason Alone*, towards the end of the eighteenth. There are curious similarities between the two. It is true that Ritschl's account is much broader, fuller and richer, and very much more biblical. It is also true that Ritschl places a

[1] *Types*, p. 162.

greater emphasis on grace, on the divine condescension to an imperfect humanity, and thus on liberation and redemption. Nevertheless, fundamental similarities remain. Among these is the definition of God almost wholly in ethical terms. Within Ritschlian as within Kantian Christianity it is hard to say anything more about God—indeed, we are forbidden to say anything more—than that he performs a moral *function*. He prevents man from sinking without trace into the abyss of mechanical nature. Ritschl's conception of Jesus, not unlike Kant's, concerns almost wholly his moral obedience and his *function* as moral ideal and archetype. Ritschl's conception of the Church is curiously rather like that of Kant—a society or community with a moral function to perform; to assist men in their struggle against nature, and thus to achieve their true moral selves. In Ritschl as in Kant there is a rather disconcerting moral grimness and sternness which is disconcerting; Mackintosh rightly says of Ritschl's theology that "we do not easily think of it as stimulating the reader to joy unspeakable and full of glory".[1] Most fundamental and obvious of all, there is a similarity in the unequivocally anthropological, humanistic, moral approach of them both. From that anthropological (or, better still, anthropocentric) standpoint of Ritschl stem most of the criticisms that have subsequently been brought against his theological system.

We must now consider two fundamental criticisms that can be brought against Ritschl's position. The first concerns the significance which he ascribes to Jesus. H. R. Mackintosh makes a criticism of Ritschl's christology which is rather similar to criticisms which we have already made of the christologies of Kant and of Schleiermacher.[2] If Jesus' significance is confined to the unique *moral* function which he exercises on behalf of men, then, says Mackintosh, "we cannot easily pass by the assertion that in no sense is there an impassable gulf between Christ and us".[3] "On such terms," Mackintosh continues, "it is hard to see how, except presumably in degree, He is to be distinguished from prophets or

---

[1] *Types*, pp. 173–4.
[2] See above, pp. 52 and 68.
[3] *Types*, p. 165.

other pious men."[1] And he goes on to show that this basic christological weakness has two corollaries: first, that he can have little to say about Christ's pre-existence, and, second, less about his contemporary redeeming activity, which he seems to interpret as "a prolongation of the effects of His historical existence,"[2] or "the posthumous result of what He did in the first century".[3] In other words, the philosopher will want to know, in the case of Ritschl as in the cases of Kant and Schleiermacher, whether this type of ethical *reinterpretation* of Christianity does not in the last analysis turn out to be a *transformation*.

The second criticism to be examined concerns Ritschl's adamant assertion that *all* theological statements must be value-statements.[4] This is so fundamental to the whole Ritschlian enterprise that it must be looked at most carefully. Two important points about Ritschl's assertion ought to be kept in mind. Ritschl is only able to make out a theological case on the basis of "value" or "worth" if man and nature are in irresolvable conflict, if nature exerts a relentless pressure threatening man with oblivion. Only if this is the case does talk of values and value-judgments possess relevance and point. But what if the nature-man conflict should disappear? Would not the relevance of value-judgments and so of God disappear also? Mackintosh has stated bluntly that in Ritschl's view "since religion arises to solve a contradiction—between man and nature—and depends for its very life upon this opposition, the reconciliation of the opposing terms would sound the death knell of faith. In the limiting case of a perfect harmony between the spirit of man and its natural environment the need for devotion would have disappeared."[5] He goes on to argue that in Ritschl's view man's union with God is "but a mere necessity of his present unfortunate situation".[6] And in another place he asks pertinently if in Ritschl's conception of religion "there is anything that radically distinguishes religion from civilization, which also in its own

[1] *Ibid.*, p. 166.
[2] *Ibid.*, p. 163.
[3] *Ibid.*, p. 164.
[4] With this criticism read our discussion of Bultmann, below pp. 171 f.
[5] *Some Aspects of Christian Belief*, pp. 135–6.
[6] *Loc. cit.*

way is the conquest of nature, the realization of man's free sway over the world? On Ritschl's terms the attitude of man to the cosmos is made central and all-determining, not his attitude to God".[1]

These are issues our attitude to which radically determines our estimate of Ritschlian Christianity, and of many twentieth-century re-interpretations of Christianity. It is clear that there are possibilities of a reconciliation between man and nature. An aesthetic interpretation of and attitude to nature is clearly possible in literature, in poetry and in the arts. In such cases, nature may assume a friendly and benevolent countenance, but the conflict between man and nature, and presumably the religion which springs up to resolve it, may disappear. There is no permanent need for nature to be portrayed by philosophy as it was depicted by naturalists like Haeckel. Philosophical fashions, like other fashions, can change rapidly, and the "forbidding nature" of nineteenth-century deterministic pessimism was to be no more permanent than nineteenth-century physics. As soon as philosophers cease to portray nature as the relentless oppressor of man, pressing him down until he becomes indistinguishable within the interlocking mesh of cause and effect, the pressing need for value-judgments and for value-religion must decrease proportionately.

A theological approach like Ritschl's has also to answer awkward questions concerning the process called nowadays "secularization", which is one of the major theological problems of the nineteen-sixties. We have noted Mackintosh's suggestion that the Ritschlian type of religious approach has to compete with "civilization". This opens up interesting lines of thought. Our twentieth-century civilization has applied almost all its resources to the task of subduing nature. This has been attempted by biological, economic, agricultural, psychiatric, medical, climatological and other techniques. And the mind boggles at the staggering possibilities now being suggested, and not only by science-fiction writers, of man's future existence in an environment completely sealed off from the changes and chances, in short, from the *relentless pressure* of nature. Of course, such an exist-

[1] *Types*, p. 151.

87

ence will throw up acute problems and difficulties. But we must consider these possibilities in the light that they cast upon our problem of the impermanence of the nature-man conflict.

Within the area of religion itself, here too contemporary civilization has been applying its resources to help man cope with his personal life. Organizations are coming into existence whose aim is to assist man to cope with acutely difficult personal problems, without appeal to supernatural forces or agencies or the like. We have heard Barbara Wootton describe the process whereby in our civilization the priest has come to be effectively replaced by the psychiatrist. We have read Dietrich Bonhoeffer's description of modern psychotherapy as one of the "secularized off-shoots of Christian theology".[1] Without trying to give a theological evaluation of the process of secularization, we can say that it does at least cast light on how the nature-man contradiction is in process of being resolved in our time. Nature is no longer feared as a relentless, smothering foe, and human values are being retained and pursued without much appeal to supernatural forces and factors. There is therefore truth in Mackintosh's description of Ritschl's God as "the needed prop of ethical aspiration, the trustee of our moral interests".[2] The point we have been trying to make in our discussion of secularization is that in our contemporary world this kind of prop is in danger of being discarded and replaced by temporal structures, and the trustee of being dismissed and replaced by this-worldly guarantors.

---

[1] *Letters and Papers From Prison*, Fontana Edition, London, 1959, p. 107. Bonhoeffer also gave a sketch of a book which he never lived to write, *op. cit.*, pp. 163–6, "Outline for a Book": in it he had intended to point out how much traditional religion had been based upon the insuring of life against accident and misfortune, and the minimization or elimination of danger. Its goal had been to make man independent of nature. But technical organization had displaced the spiritual techniques which were formerly used to conquer nature, so that the factors which threaten man's existence are now no longer natural but organizational. Actually, one important contemporary theological school, the existentialists, realize this, and in their work the dangers which threaten man's authentic life are portrayed as deriving from contemporary technological mass-society. See our fifth chapter below.

[2] *Types*, pp. 150–1.

We move on to the second point that must be made about Ritschl's fundamental conviction that all theological statements must be in the form of value-statements. Ritschl's position shows a tendency towards that translation of theological statements into anthropological ones that we observed in the context of Feuerbach's work. That is, in the long run the Ritschlian approach tends towards the transformation of itself into ethical humanism. Ritschl would have approved of the opinion expressed by the Reformer Philipp Melancthon (1497–1560), that we can know God only in His "saving benefits", not as He is in His "essence". That is, our knowledge of God is wholly dependent upon His effects upon us, by the value or worth that He has for our souls.[1] We may not say anything descriptive or factual about God as a being existing in His own right, independently of our drive towards the realization of values.[2] We only refer in theology to the ways in which God is related to this drive. Now this appears to be a rather risky thing to say, because it appears to be not far from saying that "God" is somehow only an aspect or dimension of human life, which is what Kant had appeared to say, and what Feuerbach emphatically did say. It appears to be not far from holding that out of all the factors of which man's spiritual experience is composed, the key-factor, the factor without which the entire structure would collapse is "God", who exercises a consolidating, cohesive and reinforcing function, thus protecting man's moral and spiritual integrity from the intimidating advance of an impersonal, blind, mechanical nature. But it is dubious if God can be adequately defined merely in terms of a function so limited as this.[3]

One of Ritschl's American disciples, W. Adams Brown, defended Ritschl against such criticisms brought by A. E.

[1] As a Lutheran, Ritschl was also doubtless influenced by Luther's limitation of theological knowledge to God and Christ as they are *pro me* (for me) or *pro nobis* (for us), and not as they are "in themselves".

[2] The technical way of putting this is to say that we are unable to make *ontological* statements about God; we may talk about him only in *anthropological* statements.

[3] Another obvious influence on Ritschl here is Kant, with his denial that "pure reason" can penetrate to "things-in-themselves", and his assertion that human knowledge is limited to "appearances". Thus, we cannot know God's essence, only his effects on us.

Garvie in his book *The Ritschlian Theology*.[1] Garvie suggested that Ritschl could be interpreted as meaning that God was a mere imagination, invented by man in his need to console himself with the dream of deliverance. Brown rightly points out that Ritschl defines God in terms of "the power and the will to deliverance without which man must be helpless . . . a power making himself felt in helplessness, and who, if He did not so help, would not be God".[2] But Brown goes on to give the show away. He points out that for Ritschl, "the qualities which the philosophers have grouped under the head of absoluteness, infinity, impassibility, aseity, incomprehensibility and the rest, are of all others *the most indifferent to the religious consciousness*. Whether God be, metaphysically speaking, absolute or not is a matter of trifling importance, *providing He delivers man from his sorrows and saves him from his sins*".[3] In other words, Ritschl appears to limit God to those redemptive functions which he exercises within man's consciousness of value, thus leaving himself open to the charge of the philosopher that he has reduced the content of the conception of God which had always been entertained in Christendom, and also that he has confirmed the nineteenth-century tendency towards the transformation of religion into an enlightened ethical humanism.

In the light of Feuerbach's naturalization of the theological systems of Hegel and Schleiermacher in terms of man's projection of his inner drives, needs and aspirations on to a God who is really the product of these, it is easy to see how the Ritschlian conception of religion is specially vulnerable to this type of psychological naturalism. John Macquarrie points out that one of the early American psychological naturalists, James Henry Leuba (1867–1946), had Ritschlian thinkers in mind when he began to explain religion merely in terms of latent psychological forces and moral drives. Such Ritschlians, appealing only to inner experience, "have to contend with psychology, which carries the scientific method into the inner experiences of the soul". According to Leuba,

[1] London, 1899, pp. 186 f. and 267.
[2] *The Essence of Christianity*, p. 237.
[3] *Loc. cit.*, italics mine; cf. *The Christian Doctrine of Justification and Reconciliation*, pp. 226 f.

these inner experiences only "show how belief in God has arisen from the gratification it provides for affective and moral needs".[1] This neatly makes the point towards which our discussion has been tending. When we consider Ritschl's account of religion in general and Christianity in particular as having their roots *merely* in the realm of values, we immediately want some assurance that our religious beliefs, attitudes and practices have foundations which transcend our inner consciousness, needs or aspirations. We want some evidence obtained, say, from a divine revelation or from an examination of history, or something of the like. In fact, as we shall see, the twentieth century has witnessed significant attempts to find some such foundations, and thus to protect Christian faith from those naturalistic attacks against which some nineteenth-century theological movements were so vulnerable.

We are now perhaps in a position to take stock of our survey of some nineteenth-century theological trends, and to summarize some results which may help us to get the period into focus. Although we have sometimes been critical of much of the theology we have looked at, we must be fair, keeping in mind how much thinkers like Schleiermacher and Ritschl had been able to accomplish, which is not always acknowledged by their critics. Both worked in situations which were, from the theological point of view, fairly desperate. Schleiermacher began his work immediately after the empiricist onslaught on theism which occurred during the latter part of the eighteenth century. Ritschl and his colleagues also had their backs to the wall, facing the tides of positivism, naturalism and determinism, which appeared to them to be sweeping human personality away into oblivion. In these hard circumstances both accomplished a very great deal indeed. Over against the theological conceptions of the previous two centuries, they tried to show that the God of Christian belief is not a mere X who appears precariously outside the world, at the distant end of some philosophical syllogism. For them God was firmly integrated within human experience in the world. God's reality and activity was for them immediately present at the centre of human living and striving, not mediated by a piece of tortuous reasoning. This was indeed an advance

[1] *Twentieth-Century Religious Thought*, p. 105.

over the previous two centuries and therefore up to a point a neutralizing of the scepticism of a thinker like Hume.

Although, as we have shown, it was possible to attempt a naturalization of their conception of religion, we must be clear that they did not share the assumptions (for they were no more than that) of the naturalists. Behind their formal theologies there is the firm conviction that man's total nature, fashioned by the divine creator, should exhibit, in its feelings, deepest intuitions, aspirations and drives, marks of that image in which it had been created. In other words, they would have reversed the logic of the naturalists. These sublime thoughts, affections and drives are caused by God, and not He by them! We must note also that the Schleiermacher-Ritschl tradition represented an impressive overcoming of and advance over many theological conceptions current in the previous two centuries, in so far as they tried to show that historic Christian belief did not originate in the cloistered speculations of metaphysicians and men of science, but rather that it was linked closely with a historical founder and with a positive historical revelation and redemption. This distinction that they so clearly made between the conceptions of rationalistic philosophical theism, on the one hand, and the insights of historic Christianity, on the other, led of course to twentieth-century attempts to secure the independence of genuinely *Christian* belief from philosophical criticism.[1]

Our survey of the nineteenth century began with Kant's moral re-interpretation of Christianity, and the century shows marked signs of his influence. In the first place, it exhibited a lack of interest in, if not a positive antipathy towards, *metaphysics*.[2] It looked with disdain on the pre-Kantian theistic arguments and proofs. This was true of both Schleiermacher and Ritschl. Consequently, these trends did not regard belief

[1] For this theme, see especially our fourth chapter below.

[2] The term is used here to mean the attempt to reduce to a system of first principles our knowledge of the universe as a whole, using not merely the methods of the empirical sciences, but of appealing also to the plausibility inherent in the satisfying intellectual system as a whole. Its content thus includes but also transcends what is given in experience. In this sense, the older theistic demonstrations, those criticized by Hume and Kant, were metaphysical.

in a God independent of man and the cosmos as essential to authentic Christian faith.

Secondly, the starting-point of much nineteenth-century theology was humanistic, anthropological. Its central interest was, as it was Kant's, human nature.

Thirdly, it frequently showed signs of a tendency to slide in the direction of a high-minded ethical humanism. The most alarming example of this was the work of Feuerbach, but other theologians exhibited this tendency in greater or less degree.

Fourthly, these theological systems have been fairly widely criticized for having reduced the scope and content of the traditional Christian faith. Most obviously, this has come out in their definition of God merely in terms of the humanly valuable functions he exercises, or in finding the significance of Christ merely in his function as example, ideal or archetype.

Fifthly, many nineteenth-century theologians have been widely criticized on their alleged weakness on the sinfulness of human nature. The man upon whom their interest was focussed battled fiercely for human values, and thus appeared not to grovel in self-abasement. Schleiermacher hardly doubted that God's revelation is almost completely continuous with the natural man's religiousness. Ritschl seemed to assume that the unredeemed man's ignorance of God's nature is completely co-extensive with all that the Bible calls sin.

Sixthly, the God of much nineteenth-century theology inevitably appeared (especially to its critics) to be the apotheosis, the deification of nineteenth-century man. It is easy to see why, if God performed a mainly ethical function. He inevitably appeared as the glorious sum total of contemporary man's values, ideals, aspirations, ambitions and visions, and Christ equally inevitably appeared as the archetype of nineteenth-century religious and moral man. If God had not been conceived in this way, it would not have been so easy for Feuerbach to describe him as a projection or reflection. This explains why it is not uncommon to find nineteenth-century theologians being accused of having worshipped a "bourgeois" God, and of having forgotten the Bible's insistence upon the glaring unlikenesses between man and God.[1]

[1] Cf. especially our discussion of Karl Barth in the fourth chapter below.

93

Seventhly, these theologians displayed a lack of interest in and even an antipathy for dogma as a description, explanation or analysis of realities existing independently of the human realm. The sphere of "dogma" was limited to the making explicit of the insights of the believer.

Eighthly, there was in this period a heavy stress on Jesus as ethical teacher, prophet and example, and a parallel stress on the Synoptic Gospels at the expense of the remainder of the biblical canon, particular the Old Testament and the Pauline literature.

We have now come to the end of our survey of some nineteenth-century theological trends. Some insight into these trends is essential for anyone who wishes to make sense of recent and contemporary theological discussion. The nineteenth century laid down many of the main lines along which subsequent theologians have attempted to overcome the religious scepticism which was generated by eighteenth-century empiricism. As we shall see below, our own twentieth-century theology has very largely consisted of extensions of nineteenth-century lines of thought and reactions against them.

Chapter Three

THE MORAL ROUTE TO THEISTIC BELIEF

IN Germany the theological world was dominated by more or less Ritschlian theologians until the beginning of the third decade of the twentieth century. Amongst such theologians were Wilhelm Herrmann (1846–1922), Adolf von Harnack (1851–1930) and Julius Kaftan (1848–1926). These theologians were Ritschlian in standpoint in that they rejected speculative, metaphysical attempts to establish the framework of a religious world-view, and stressed instead man's inner, practical drive towards moral values. The Ritschlian school is important for our understanding of the relations between faith and philosophy in the twentieth century partly, but not only, because, as we shall see in the next chapter, it was mainly against Ritschlian types of theology that there occurred after the First World War the explosive revolution associated with the names of Søren Kierkegaard and Karl Barth. Nevertheless, the exploration of the relationship between man's moral experience and his religious convictions was not confined to Ritschl and his disciples. Since Christianity is classified as "ethical monotheism", and since ethical considerations appear on practically every page of the Bible, it is not surprising that in every century theologians and philosophers explore anew the relationship between the moral and the religious, between ethics and theology. This is true also of our own century, in which the relationship has continued to absorb the interest of philosophers of religion, despite Barth's protest against any link-up of secular ethics and Christian theology. To an examination of a few of such explorations we now turn.

In order to clear the ground, we must first indicate what we do not mean by the type of moral theism which we are about to investigate. First, we do not mean by it the not uncommon ground view that religious beliefs are valuable, if not indispensable, because they supply powerful psychological

95

motivation for the performance of duty.[1] This may very well be true, but it overlooks the fact that logically the religious beliefs in question may be groundless, and yet able to supply motive power for dutifulness. Second, we do not mean that the concrete demands of conscience can be simply identified with the "commands of God", and thus be taken as proofs of God's existence or activity. As we shall see, such a naif view of the matter is indefensible, and involves insuperable difficulties. Third, we do not mean by it that some kind of religious belief is necessary in order for persons to act morally. On the contrary, we shall defend the view that plain men, including unbelieving and non-religious plain men, can discern the difference between right and wrong and can act dutifully. The type of moral theism we put forward here concerns the full justification or interpretation, or the implications of the everyday moral experience of everyman. We emphasize this point because there are religious thinkers who assert that without some divine revelation the plain man is unable to make moral distinctions, and without divine grace is unable to act dutifully.

The kind of moral theism we wish to examine here has been neatly summarized by John Hick. It is not an argument at all in the strict sense of the word; it is certainly not a proof in any quasi-mathematical sense. It is "the claim that anyone seriously committed to respect moral values as exercising a sovereign claim upon his life, must thereby implicitly believe in the reality of a trans-human source and basis for these values, which religion calls God".[2] Hick continues: "To recognize moral claims as taking precedence over all other interests, is, in effect, to believe in a reality, other than the natural world, which is superior to oneself and entitled to one's obedience."[3] It is important to note Hick's use of the term "natural world". As we shall see, moral theists are unanimously anti-naturalistic in the sense that they react sharply against any identification of reality with nature, with that slice of reality singled out for study by the natural, experimental sciences.

[1] See Hastings Rashdall, *The Theory of Good and Evil*, Oxford, 1907, vol. II, pp. 256 f.
[2] J. Hick, *Philosophy of Religion*, Englewood Cliffs, N. J., 1963, pp. 27–8.
[3] *Loc. cit.*

The first thinker whose views we consider is the late W. R. Sorley, who in his *Moral Values and the Idea of God*[1] explored the relationship between man's moral experience and religious beliefs. One of the presuppositions of Sorley's argument for theism was his intense "anti-naturalism". He was in fact impressed by the whole approach to philosophy of the neo-Kantian Herrmann Lotze, the Göttingen colleague of Ritschl, who had, we recall, put Ritschl on to the track of the notion of value as the pathway to religious truth. Sorley was clear that nineteenth-century naturalism, in identifying reality with physical nature, had made a hideous error. It had attempted to work out a view of reality in which there could hardly be room for moral values, since they are incapable of investigation by the methods of the physical sciences. Sorley wished us to ". . . take experience as a whole, and . . . not arbitrarily restrict ourselves to that portion of it with which the physical and natural sciences have to do".[2] He wished our entire interpretation of reality to "have ethical data at its basis and ethical laws in its structure".[3] Scientific naturalism had gone wrong with its naif assumption "that we have first to find out the true nature of things, and that the rule and end for conduct will then be plain".[4] The success of the physical sciences depends of course upon the strict limitation of their subject-matter. Nevertheless, such limitation involves ignoring or disregarding the entire ethical aspect of reality, an aspect which is quite fundamental in life.[5] "Morality," writes Sorley, "is a factor in experience; ethical ideas have a place in consciousness. Our theory of reality as a whole must take account of these things; and the question concerns the difference which they make in our final view of the world and in the arguments which lead up to that view."[6]

Sorley held that our moral experience led us to the view that moral awareness is impinged upon by an objective moral ideal; objective in the sense that our recognition of its absolute

---

[1] 3rd edition, Cambridge, 1935.
[2] *Moral Values and the Idea of God*, p. 7.
[3] *Loc. cit.*
[4] *Op. cit.*, p. 8.
[5] *Op. cit.*, p. 21.
[6] *Op. cit.*, p. 22.

validity does not confer validity upon it. It exists, Sorley insisted, independently of moral agents, in "the mind of God".[1] Nor did Sorley hold it possible to regard moral values as analogous with physical laws or mathematical relations. These are only aspects of the natural order which enquiring minds recognize "to be there". Moral values are different; their operation cannot be observed in natural events, sequences and phenomena. They have to do with the lives of persons, and their validity does not depend either upon their being completely grasped by thought or their being fully actualized in the obedience or characters of moral agents. That is, they transcend both intellect and will; men strive to apprehend intellectually and to realize practically an ideal which is greater than their comprehension and their obedience. Thus Sorley held it to be inconceivable that the moral ideal should have its existence wholly within man's material environment (nature), or in the minds or characters of any individual or society of individuals. His conclusion is that the moral ideal must exist in a trans-human and super-human mind, which is the creative ground of the moral and non-moral orders. For Sorley, this mind is the mind of God.

Before we leave Sorley, we must note his language. He was writing in 1918, and to us his language appears as rather quaint. But he was deliberately using the language of philosophical idealism, stressing his lack of sympathy with that mounting attack on idealism which was fashionable during the first few decades of the twentieth century. We might also conclude, with many contemporary analytic philosophers (whose work we shall examine in our sixth chapter below), that Sorley's language was not merely quaint, but impossibly imprecise and unclear. But we must remember that he had sharply demarcated the moral from the natural sphere, ethics from the natural sciences. He made it clear that ethics, for him the science of values, must work out its own peculiar categories and terminology in order to do justice to moral experience. There is no reason to expect that such language and terminology should possess the precision and clarity typical of mathematical and physical discussions. Despite the vagueness and imprecision of his language, Sorley's central

[1] *Op. cit.*, p. 351.

98

intention is clear: he wanted to say that distinctively moral experience is such that it can only be adequately described as the exertion by values of a claim upon the moral agent from without. There is a sense in which they grasp him, and not he them. Their objectivity leads Sorley to claim that these values are rooted in the trans-human source which he calls God.

The next thinker to whose views we turn is the late Donald M. Baillie (1887–1954), who also put forward views about morality's function as the pathway to theistic belief, in a chapter of his *Faith in God*.[1] Baillie points out that in the struggle between belief and scepticism which took place in the nineteenth century, many thinkers turned instinctively towards moral conviction as the great reality which could not be shaken in the midst of the contemporary intellectual and spiritual storm; thinkers like F. W. Robertson (1816–53), Lord Tennyson (1809–92) and Robert Browning (1812–89). These were not, significantly, academic philosophers like Lotze, Ritschl or Sorley. Baillie uses evidence from the case-book material of the great American psychologist of religion Edwin M. Starbuck to show that in the United States in the same period, the experience and conviction of duty survived the blasts of philosophical criticism. A moral path to religious belief was also commended by, for example, George Tyrrell (1861–1909), Baron Friedrich von Hügel (1852–1925), John Henry Newman (1801–1890) and John Middleton Murry (1889–1957). Baillie argued on the basis of this evidence that in some way our modern world was driven by peculiar intellectual circumstances to find faith through moral conviction. He was also of the opinion that the moral route to theism was specially significant because it was to be found not only in the writings of scholars such as Kant and Ritschl, but also in the lives and reflections of simple Christian believers.

For Baillie, the essence of religious faith is our "conviction that our highest values must and do count in the whole scheme of things", that they "reveal the very meaning and purpose of the universe, that love is at the heart of all things".[2] It is "but

[1] London, 1927 and 1964, chapter V, "Faith and Moral Conviction"; page-references are to the 1964 edition.
[2] *Faith in God*, p. 176.

of this germinal conviction that the whole rich harvest of religious belief grows".[1] He confesses himself dissatisfied with the vague language which his convictions force him to use, but sees no alternative to using it, if he is to do justice to man's moral experience. Baillie distinguishes his brand of moral theism from those consisting of inferences, like Kant's "moral argument" for God's existence. We only come to grasp and understand values in being faithful to them in life-situations. The more we understand them, the more they come to be seen as the revelation of a divine purpose. The more moral values are sought, the more clearly it is perceived that they are "real", that they reflect an infinite goodness which transcends individual moral agents. He also makes it clear that his type of moral theism must not be confused with the argument that urges that God's existence can be inferred as the cause of a psychological function called "conscience". He is aware that conscience is conditioned by social, traditional and environmental factors. This conditioning makes any simple transition from the fact of conscience to the fact of God highly questionable. The moral conviction upon which Baillie wishes to build lies at a deeper level than any theory about the origin and conditioning of a psychological function.

Baillie parts company with Kantian inferential arguments for God's existence because he holds that in moral experience we have a direct and immediate knowledge of religious reality.[2] He holds that "faith in God is a very part of our moral consciousness without which the latter becomes meaningless".[3] Moral conviction "tells me not simply something about myself or about the action indicated, but about the very meaning of the universe".[3] Presumably he means that the qualities of ultimacy, absoluteness and unconditionality inherent in moral obligations reflect the ultimate, absolute and unconditional goodness at the heart of reality. He bluntly disagrees with those (e.g. Bertrand Russell) who think it illegitimate to proceed from ethical judgments to descriptions of the nature of the universe.[4] Russell indeed exemplifies the

[1] *Op. cit.*, p. 177.
[2] *Op. cit.*, p. 182.
[3] *Loc. cit.*
[4] *Op. cit.*, pp. 183 f.

view which Sorley had rejected, that the primary task of the thinker is to reach a true description of things in general and *only then* raise ethical considerations. In this view (which is really a type of scientific naturalism), ethical considerations are peripheral to man's intellectual task. But, as we have seen from our consideration of Sorley, Russell's view here is arbitrary in the sense that it depends upon the way in which Russell has personally chosen to evaluate the moral as compared with the natural sphere. At an early stage in his career Russell held that "the good" was a simple indefinable concept which had no reference to existence. At a later stage he came to hold the view that "good" and "evil" had no objective reference whatsoever, but were merely the products of human wishes and desires. But on this theory, Baillie argues, ethical judgments *do* refer to something in existence, to what is desired or wished by human beings.[1] He insists that if Russell's views are sound it is impossible to see how we can continue to talk of "morality". If morality is held not to lead to a religious viewpoint, then it becomes simply a label for a mass of arbitrary, subjective desires; in short, it becomes meaningless.[2]

Baillie makes it clear that every human being, *qua* human, even if he doubts God's existence, is capable of choosing rightly in the conviction that what is chosen is worth it intrinsically. If he tries to make final sense of his moral convictions, if he tries to set them in a meaningful context, he must come to the assurance of God. He comes, that is, to see the moral quest in the context of a moral order which reflects the character of its creator and originator. Thus religious faith is implicit in moral experience and obedience. Moral experience in its ultimate, unconditional dimension contains the germ of religious belief. With this conviction Baillie has to reconcile the fact that many who take morality with great seriousness appear to have no religious beliefs. He insists nevertheless that when all religious beliefs are doubted, and even rejected, unswerving loyalty to one's moral values, understood as exercising an absolute, unconditional claim upon one's life, preserves the germ of religious belief of which

[1] *Op. cit.*, p. 184.
[2] *Op. cit.*, p. 185.

we have spoken. Thus Baillie praises those "agnostics" (in a theological sense) who go on striving for moral values even when unable to accept dogmas which assure them that these values reflect "the ultimate nature of things". It is impossible to deny that all men whose lives reflect moral faith implicitly and perhaps unconsciously possess also religious faith, in germ at least.[1] Not that he concedes that such implicit faith is identifiable with Christian faith in its maturity, or that it is unnecessary for this germinal faith to be clothed in the garments of a concrete living religion. Religion is more than morality, and requires for its fruition beliefs, ideas and worship.

Baillie amends some of his earlier terminology. He feels that it is not quite right to say that faith is *based upon* moral experience, indeed that faith is *based upon* anything. This shows why it is so difficult to produce a convincing moral "argument" for theism; there is no argument which leads *from* moral experience *to* anything. Rather Baillie wants to say that "the germ of faith is *present* . . . in the moral conviction".[2] He can therefore define faith, as he admits, dangerously, as "what everyone knows, if only he is willing to know it".[2] But when any attempt be made to describe what is given in faith, resort must be had to inadequate symbols which may cause the greatest perplexity. Nevertheless, conceding this perplexity, moral faith does demand that "these values are somewhere perfectly realized".[3] Baillie is clear that this "faith" is but a "mustard-seed" requiring for its germination and fruition the proper environment, "the experience of life, the fellowship of the Church, the inheritance of the saints".[3] This is the inner meaning of faith, whether that of the simple charwoman or the learned theologian.

We consider now the moral path to theism traced by the late Professor A. E. Taylor, a thinker of a type more strongly intellectualist, even Kantian, than Baillie.[4] Not unlike Lotze, Ritschl and Sorley, Taylor appealed to "extra-biological evidence", by which he meant "the notorious facts of the

[1] *Op. cit.*, p. 193.
[2] *Op. cit.*, p. 194.
[3] *Op. cit.*, p. 195.
[4] See especially his *Does God Exist?*, The Fontana Library, London, 1961.

moral life of mankind".[1] Thus Taylor also was very anti-naturalistic in his philosophical approach; he deplored the quite arbitrary limitation of reality to physical nature, the subject-matter of the natural sciences. In particular, he deplored the misuse of the word "fact".[2] Man's convictions about right and wrong are just as *factual* as man's biological and procreative life. Moreover, moral convictions permeate all human activities; they are neither secondary nor peripheral, as some philosophical standpoints would lead us to believe. For instance, if a gigantic change in our climate occurred, this would entail huge changes in our way of life. But if we were to adopt the moral attitudes implicit in Nazi racialism, an equally huge overhauling of our way of life would become necessary.[3] It is therefore ludicrous to suggest that natural factors or movements are somehow more *factual* or *real* than moral ones. Even those who hold that "rightness" and "wrongness" are nonfactual cannot themselves help using genuinely moral categories; for example, when they inform us that it is "wrong" to blame someone for *wrong*-doing on the ground that what we call "wrong" is sheer fancy, or that "moral" distinctions are arbitrary preferences. Morality appears to be inevitable for all, including moral sceptics. Man's making of moral distinctions is therefore as much a *fact* as any other activity, and a complete picture of the universe must take it fully into account.

As to motives, Taylor is clear that there can be no other proper motive for dutifulness than dutifulness itself. Genuine moral behaviour implies that "you ought simply because you ought".[4] Thus Taylor did not shrink from saying (although he admits that the language is seventeenth- and eighteenth-century) that moral distinctions are "immutable and eternal".[5] He means that they are valid "independently of the thoughts and wishes of any of us".[6] Nor does he shrink from mathematical language; one can no more wish away or think away the moral character of an action than one can wish or think a

[1] *Op. cit.*, p. 96.
[2] See below, pp. 205 f.
[3] Taylor's book was first published in 1945.
[4] *Op. cit.*, p. 100.
[5] *Op. cit.*, p. 102.
[6] *Op. cit.*, p. 103.

crooked line straight. Taylor also considered that inherent in moral judgment was the consciousness of desert, good or ill.[1] Men feel it rational or natural that good deeds require a different kind of desert from ill. From his understanding of moral experience Taylor draws conclusions not dissimilar to those drawn by Sorley. Human intelligences and wills have only come to apprehend the moral law gradually, piecemeal. At our stage of development we have not uncovered all the implications of morality. The moral law transcends our understanding and grasp of it and its implications. If this understanding is correct, in what sense may we describe it as "valid"? Taylor held that it made sense to speak of it as valid if there is a trans-human and super-human intelligence "which has not, like our own, to make acquaintance with it piecemeal, slowly and with difficulty, but has always been in full and clear possession of it, and a will which does not, like our own, often set it at naught, but is guided by it in all its operations."[2]

Taylor's argument now makes an important move, from the sphere of morality to the sphere of nature. If moral facts are primary, if they can be regarded as significant clues to the nature of reality, moral reflection may lead us to view nature as a whole geared to a moral purpose, the production, fulfilment and attainment of moral personalities. If this conclusion were reached, Taylor believed that it allowed us to regard nature as having been created with this moral end in view, which in turn leads towards faith in "one God . . . almighty, creator of heaven and earth and of all things visible and invisible".[3] But Taylor went further; if reflection on our moral experience convinced us that *the* end for which nature is created is the attainment of moral personality, then the concrete occurrences which frustrate such attainment, such as early deaths, accidents and other tragedies, bring us into a dilemma which, in Taylor's view, can only be resolved by faith in the existence of a sphere not subject to those vicissitudes which appear to frustrate nature's supreme end.[4]

Taylor openly points out the condition of the force of this

[1] *Op. cit.*, p. 103.
[2] *Op. cit.*, p. 107.
[3] *Op. cit.*, p. 108.
[4] *Op. cit.*, pp. 108–9.

argument. It is the truth of his conviction that "the law of right and wrong is as much part and parcel of the structure of the universe as the law of gravitation or the law of conservation of energy".[1] If this assumption is untrue, his argument must fail. Like Baillie, Taylor is clear that the moral pilgrimage that leads to religious belief is one of faith; but he insists that it is a rational one. But it is not a particularly easy one. Every individual sooner or later encounters situations and circumstances which tempt him to believe that reality is unreasonable. In such cases, Taylor prescribes that moral agents should hesitate before taking such circumstances as typical of and as clues to the nature of our total experience. Taylor's position here is not dissimilar to Baillie's on practical loyalty. His conception of the moral path to belief is a speculative one which yet makes room for practical, activist elements.

A less speculative and more activist conception of the moral path to religious belief is to be found in the work of Dr. Geddes MacGregor.[2] MacGregor starts from a consideration of authentic interpersonal relationships. He considers that there are fundamental differences between our relationships with things and our relationships with persons, and insists upon these being carefully distinguished. He too, therefore, like the other thinkers we are considering in this chapter, can be described as anti-naturalistic. The distinctive attribute of the interpersonal relationship is that in it the members trust the will of each other.[3] This trust is directed towards the conviction that both wills acknowledge a set of absolute, unconditional values. If this were not so, the relationship would be inauthentic, short-lived, unstable. This trust is involved, for example, in marriage. The vows which people marrying make to each other, in the words "for better, for worse", indicate that the keeping of the vow is to be independent of circumstances.[4] If marriage is to be worthy of the name it must be essentially a tri-partite business, requiring not merely two partners, but also a standard of unconditional value, acknowledged by both.

[1] *Op. cit.*, p. 110.
[2] *Introduction to Religious Philosophy*, London, 1960, pp. 262 f.
[3] *Op. cit.*, p. 263.
[4] *Op. cit.*, p. 264.

In the moral life, properly understood, we also experience an absolute, unconditional demand being made upon us by another person. In this sense, it can be said that in our moral experience "we encounter God".[1] Not, MacGregor insists, that we make an inference from our experience to the conclusion, "God exists." Rather, God is an inalienable and inescapable element *in* our moral experience. When, in practical everyday life, the moral agent commits himself unreservedly to the pursuit of moral values, only then can encounter with God, the unconditional and absolute, take place. God is not to be met with beyond or outside or above the moral life. He is to be encountered *within* it.[2] When values are pursued desperately, the moral agent discovers that he has been struggling with and against God. MacGregor has little sympathy with the idea that God, as the Other, is to be met in some other-worldly, supramundane sphere, whether that of theoretical or mystical contemplation. To the contrary, the moral route to belief involves "plunging into the stream of life itself and entering into the deepest involvement with the values that confront us, exercising our wills to the utmost . . ." God is encountered only "in the very extremity of the battle".

The final thinker whose views we consider in this brief survey is H. H. Farmer.[3] Farmer holds that a full account of our moral experience in all its dimensions requires us to notice three factors. First, that the values we strive after are related to the will in a relation he calls "unconditional-oughtness".[4] He means that genuinely *moral* obligation is not conditional upon our personal wants, needs, desires and so on. Moral obligations "thrust themselves into the midst of our ordinary likes and dislikes, wants and preferences".[5] Farmer rejects the view, one that we must discuss fully below, that what we call "unconditional-oughtness" is ultimately derivable from certain natural processes, for example, social pressures. His

[1] *Op. cit.*, p. 265.
[2] *Op. cit.*, p. 266.
[3] See especially his *Towards Belief in God*, London, 1942, and *Revelation and Religion*, London, 1954.
[4] *Towards Belief in God*, p. 192.
[5] *Loc. cit.*

view is that unconditional-oughtness can only be adequately accounted for by positing a dimension of being which cannot be derived from the sphere of nature, nor wholly explained in terms of natural forces and factors. For Farmer, this dimension is that of God. He concedes the force of the objection that there appears to be no good reason for identifying this dimension with that of the God of religion. His reply to it is that the bare idea of God is closely connected with the idea of unconditional moral demand, although it must be admitted that the idea of such a demand does not logically entail the idea of God.[1] He is really appealing to the close connection between religion and morality.

Second, Farmer holds that moral experience contains an element of *paradox*, and that a full account of such experience must do justice to this. One side of the paradox is the fact that moral agents are aware of the objectivity of moral values, in the sense that they cannot be identified with mere inclinations. Evidence for this is the fact that moral subjects rationally discuss moral issues. If moral drives were identifiable with mere tastes it would rightly be felt that rational discussion of or discrimination between them was time-wasting.[2] The other side of the paradox is that while our ability to discuss moral issues shows that such values are in some sense "real", absolute moral obligations disclose to us that in another sense such values are "not yet real", in the sense that we are obliged to "realize" them in the world. The paradox is that moral values appear "real" in one sense and "yet unrealized" in another, a paradox which is particularly problematical. Farmer rejects one obvious way of getting rid of the paradox, by adopting the view that moral values can be described as real in exactly the same way as mathematical truths are real.[3] The difference is that the mathematician is a passive spectator or observer of an inert aspect of morality. But the moral agent is no detached observer of things. His values, unlike the mathematician's truths, press in upon him, so to speak, drawing him towards themselves, thrusting themselves into his day-to-day existence, demanding realization and actualiza-

[1] *Op. cit.*, p. 196.
[2] *Op. cit.*, pp. 196–7.
[3] Cf. our discussion of Sorley, pp. 97 f. above.

tion. In short, they are active, not inert. The paradox is not so easily got rid of in this way.

When an unprejudiced moralist really comes to grips with this paradox and tries to incorporate it in his thought, he may be led to somewhat odd conclusions. As an example, Farmer points to the work of the German metaphysician Nicolai Hartmann (1882–1950). Hartmann was an "ontologist", that is, a philosopher interested in the problem of "being". As such, Hartmann insisted that being is multi-dimensional, that reality is stratified, constituted by various layers. There are higher and lower strata, each stratum possessing its own categories of description and understanding, proper only to itself. In his ethical approach, Hartmann adopted a method very similar to that of the philosophical school of *phenomenology* and of its leader Edmund Husserl (1859–1938). It is hard to describe this method briefly, but we can say that phenomenologists approach consciousness and reality *descriptively*, freeing themselves as far as possible from presuppositions, assumptions and prejudices, which they attempt to "bracket off". They are interested in letting the "phenomenon itself" speak for itself. When Hartmann adopted this phenomenological approach to ethical questions, he attempted to give a descriptive account of the moral consciousness and what is "given" to it. He thus became convinced of the existence of an order of moral values, and in trying to describe how these are related to the moral consciousness, he was compelled to use rather odd language.

He asserted the existence of timeless moral essences which press upon the human mind for their actualization. Farmer points out that Hartmann ascribed to these essences "a sort of *personal* interest in, and activity towards, their own realization in human life".[1] While he was not a believer, Hartmann advocated a faith of a kind, "faith of a unique kind, differing from trust between man and man, a faith which reaches out to the whole of things".[2] Why did Hartmann use this curious language? Perhaps the answer is to be found in the funda-

[1] Quoted in *Towards Faith in God*, p. 199.
[2] *Ethics*, vol. III, p. 330, quoted in J. Macquarrie, *Twentieth-Century Religious Thought*, p. 269.

mentals of his philosophy. If reality is multi-dimensional, and each dimension requires its *own* proper categories and terminology, ethics is obliged to work out a special language suited to its own phenomena and subject-matter. This is so because, as Hartmann points out, the categories of one stratum of reality may not be used to understand another stratum. Presumably Hartmann would have agreed that one should not expect ethical terminology to be derived from the jargon of, say, the natural sciences, or that it should necessarily possess the clarity or precision of mathematics. The categories of the dimension of nature are not apt for describing the phenomena of the moral consciousness. Farmer is willing to acknowledge the impressiveness of Hartmann's description of the moral consciousness, taking account, as it does, of the paradox of which we have spoken. Nevertheless, he feels that once the paradox is fully acknowledged, theism, which makes the affirmation of good behind all things, and which calls upon man for co-operation in the realization of good, is much more intelligible and illuminating. He believes that of all theories that can be put forward to do justice to this paradoxical element in moral obligation, theistic belief does this better than any other.

Third, there is yet another paradoxical element in moral experience which requires to be dealt with. One side of this paradox is that the plain man can make no sense of moral obligation unless he be considered to some degree free to accept or reject moral commands.[1] The other side is that moral experience, in Farmer's view, entails believing in the ultimate supremacy of moral over all other considerations, in short, in "the ultimate triumph of moral values".[2] If a moral agent really thinks otherwise, "the springs of moral energy begin to dry up". The heart of the paradox is that two things must be held together: man's freedom and the inevitability of the victory of goodness. Farmer holds that only theism does this satisfactorily, because of its belief in a God who, while respecting the personal dignity and freedom of persons, yet guarantees through His power and wisdom that in the end

[1] *Op. cit.*, pp. 200–201.
[2] *Op. cit.* p. 201.

goodness will be vindicated. For Farmer, this God is the God of Christian theism.[1]

Farmer returns to the same theme in his 1950 Gifford Lectures, *Revelation and Religion*.[2] Here he makes the point that through the history of philosophy and theology there runs a firm strand of thinking which focusses attention upon man's awareness of a realm of eternal values, an awareness which is central to man's religious quest.[3] This strand can aptly be called *Platonic*. He is clear, as were thinkers like Lotze, Sorley and Taylor, that this strand is anti-naturalistic in tendency. It regards the moral values cherished by man, not as peripheral elements in reality, but as "ultimate constitutive and creative factors" in it.[4] *The* human task, which sharply distinguishes man from the processes of nature, is reverence for and actualization of moral values in the world. Farmer makes the point, and his view invites comparison with those of D. M. Baillie, that many holding this view would regard man's progressive awareness of such values as not merely one element amongst others in religion, but as in some way the essence of all religion.

In order to make his meaning clear Farmer uses a term borrowed from the work of the great Marburg phenomenologist of religion, Rudolf Otto (1869–1937), the German *Ahnung*, which denotes roughly "faith-perception", a feeling or awareness which grasps "a reality . . . overshadowing and interpenetrating the immediately given world".[5] Farmer again returns to the business of his language and terminology; the reality laid hold of in moral experience is not "expressible in clearly defined concepts". Farmer admits that the religion reached by such a moral route is exposed to a certain danger. It may have an extremely vague and nebulous character. But it does not, argues Farmer, need to succumb to such a danger. It can stress the way in which values, by pressing in upon man's awareness, point through to God's self-disclosure. Farmer would agree also that such a moral argument for

1 *Op. cit.*, p. 202.
2 Chapter VI, pp. 113 f.
3 *Op. cit.*, pp. 125–6.
4 *Op. cit.*, p. 126.
5 *Op. cit.*, p. 127.

theism as he defends has another weakness. It may not establish belief in God as "personal". It may indeed, as Farmer
says, point merely to a "few somewhat pallid abstractions".[1]
It is true that a thinker like Hartmann goes no further than to
describe values in vaguely personalistic language. Nevertheless,
Farmer holds that such an argument is theologically valuable
only if it is linked up with distinctively Christian belief about
revelation, which alone discloses the *thou-ness* of the God of
Christianity.

We are perhaps now in a position to summarize and draw
some conclusions from the views of those thinkers whose work
we have just surveyed. The following points appear to be
important. First, the core of these moral arguments for
theism seems to be that the ultimate, unconditional, absolute,
underived and transcendent attributes of the values we
encounter in experience reflect and point to their ground in
an ultimate, unconditional, absolute, underived and transcendent God. It is true that this claim does not carry us all the
way to the personal God of Christian belief.[2] Hartmann's
thought is a reminder of this, but even so, against this we
must set the fact that he felt compelled to use personalistic
language in describing values and their relationship to man.
Nearly all the thinkers we have surveyed feel the difficulty.
Baillie, for instance, carefully says no more than the "germ" of
religious faith is present in moral experience, a germ which
requires for its germination the atmosphere of revelation and
the Church. Farmer also feels the difficulty, but argues that
Christian revelation is *required* to make intelligible the description of moral experience he puts forward. Perhaps we might
say that if we accepted the analysis of morality sketched above
it would put us in the odd situation of having to believe in a

[1] *Op. cit.*, pp. 130.
[2] John Hick says of the moral argument that ". . . it cannot be presented
as a strict proof of God's existence" because "even if moral values are
acknowledged as pointing towards a transcendent ground they cannot be
said to point all the way and with unerring aim to the infinite, omnipotent,
self-existent, personal creator who is the object of biblical faith", *Philosophy of Religion*, p. 28. And W. G. Maclagan, in his *The Theological Frontier
of Ethics*, London, 1961, wishes to identify the whole range of moral values
with God, but feels considerable hesitancy about ascribing "personality"
to God.

floating realm of moral essences or values which impinge upon human consciousness, a situation which points through to distinctively Christian revelation, with its witness to a God as the source and ground of these values. If so, the objection should not be insuperable.

Second, we have noted that these thinkers are all, implicitly or explicitly, *anti-naturalistic* in the sense that they dissent from the identification of reality with nature, the object of the natural sciences. Reality is multi-dimensional, and the dimension of morality must be neither discounted nor dismissed as peripheral in our account of things. This conviction stems historically from thinkers like Kant and Lotze, and in neo-Kantian theologians and philosophers took the form of a protest against nineteenth-century naturalism. In this context, Sorley is strongly Lotzean. Taylor is vigorously anti-naturalistic, insisting upon the *factuality* of moral ideals and distinctions. MacGregor asks us to distinguish carefully between our relationships with things and those with persons. Farmer, following Hartmann, regards moral values as the "ultimate constitutive and creative factors" in reality, a view which is at the furthest possible remove from scientific naturalism.

Third, these thinkers may be described in varying degrees as "non-intellectualist". They try to cover themselves against the criticisms to which a moral argument like that of Kant is vulnerable. We do not find in their work abstract demonstrations or proofs, moving through logical steps from premiss to conclusion, as in a geometrical theorem. Rather, we find appeals being made to and claims made for what is given to each of us in our moral experience. Combined with this we find a strong "activist" strain. They make much of personal, practical loyalty and commitment to the day-to-day realization of values. Baillie, for instance, appeals to the experience of the plain man and the simple charwoman, of poets and artists as well as academic philosophers and theologians. He speaks of the germ of faith present in the moral experience of everyman. MacGregor takes as his starting-point ordinary interpersonal relationship, marriage in particular, and insists that God is encountered in the everyday and the mundane. Even in the most intellectualist of them, Taylor, whose moral argument could be described as Kantian, we find appeals to "moral faith", to commitment and loyalty. An implication of this is the superiority, religiously speaking, of such a starting-point to that of the older seventeenth- and eighteenth-century natural theology. There the starting-point was of course an interest in the origins and structure of nature. And an appreciation of its arguments presupposed a certain metaphysical facility. This older natural theology reflected also the predominant interests of the scholars and intellectuals of the period, in the methods and results of the natural sciences. Over against this natural theology, moral arguments for theism have this in their favour; they search for evidence in the ordinary, everyday moral experience of everyman, not in the specialized, rarified interests of a few.

Fourth, we make a point of great importance, one which we shall have to develop in detail in our next chapter. It concerns the nature of the relationship between knower and what is known. Suffice it to say this here. In moral experience, a passive observer or spectator does not stand over against a dead, inert, unresponsive object or collection of objects which are penetrated, grasped and understood by the intellection, controlled manipulation and activity of the observer. This appears to be the relationship between knower and what is known in the natural sciences, an essentially *subject-object* relationship. But it is a different matter in moral experience. Even an agnostic like Hartmann, when dealing with moral phenomena, felt compelled to speak of moral values taking "a personal interest in" and "acting towards" moral agents, "pressing upon" the human will. Hartmann did so because of his view that each layer of reality had to find and use its own categories of understanding, categories inapplicable to inferior layers. He would probably have prohibited the use of the categories of the natural sciences in ethics. MacGregor interprets moral experience as involving a demand being made upon us by another person, by God. In the moral life we find ourselves struggling with and against God.

In the thought of Farmer also, we find moral obligations described as "thrusting themselves" into the midst of our everyday living. They differ from mathematical truths in that they "press upon" persons, drawing them towards themselves. They are active, not inert. If this description of moral experience is acceptable, it makes a great difference for our theory of knowledge (epistemology). The relationship between knower and known cannot be a subject-object one, as in the empirical sciences. It must be a "subject-subject" one, or to use more modern terminology, an "I-Thou" one, in so far as values "take the initiative", "press upon" man, and "act towards" him. Values ought to be described as "subjects" and not as inert "objects". We shall explore the "subjectivity" of God in our next chapter.

Fifth, the God sought after in moral arguments for belief is religiously superior to the God whose existence was sought after in the older natural theology, the God of the causal and teleological proofs, the God of seventeenth- and eighteenth-century deism, dethroned by the criticisms of Hume and Kant. This latter deity, Descartes' "Author of Nature", the impersonal first cause, prime mover or cosmic architect, appeared to have constructed the universe, set the cosmic machine in motion, and thereafter took no interest either in it or its inhabitants.[1] We recall the insistence of Schleiermacher and Ritschl that so far as distinctively *religious* belief is concerned, the demise of such a deity at the hands of philosophical critics is of little moment. But the God of the moral theists is found at the heart of everyday moral experience, not at the conclusion of a dubious and tedious philosophical syllogism. And far from being conceived as aloof from the world and from the lives of humans, he is deeply involved in the development, striving and final attainment of his creatures. It was partly this insight that Kant was aiming at when he confessed that he had to abolish knowledge to make room for faith, an insight developed in various ways by Schleiermacher, Ritschl and the thinkers whose views we have surveyed in this chapter.

We must now consider three types of objection that can be brought against the theistic interpretations of morality we have outlined. The first concerns the possibility of giving a naturalistic account of the origins of moral awareness. The second concerns the difficulties involved in maintaining that nature is somehow sympathetic rather than apathetic to moral attainment. The third concerns the satisfactoriness or otherwise of

[1] See the fourth chapter below.

the language used in these interpretations, an objection which can only be fully evaluated in the light of our discussion of language in our final chapter. To deal with the first objection, we note that attempts can be made to explain the genesis of moral consciousness in terms of certain natural forces and factors, particularly social and psychological ones. In this way it is conceivable that ethics might become a department of sociology or psychology. If so, it would be hard indeed to describe moral distinctions as given, objective, underived, ultimate and the like. It is easy to sketch such an attempt. It might be said that persons, living in a social context, are under constant pressure to perform socially praiseworthy actions and to refrain from socially blameworthy ones. Society clearly tends to frown upon adulterous actions precisely because if adultery were universally practised and tolerated the stability and welfare of social groups would be threatened. Similarly, society tends to praise and encourage honesty and integrity precisely because in the long run such virtues tend to stabilize and strengthen social structures. Thus, if a *wholly* sociological account of morality were achieved, it might be possible to translate all moral terminology without remainder into sociological. For "good" and "evil" as applied to actions and attitudes we might read "social" and "anti-social". Our estimation of "virtues" and "vices" would depend *wholly* on how they were related to the common weal.

Alternatively, or complementarily, ethics might be transformed into a branch of psychology. An account might be given of the formation of conscience *wholly* in terms of the interdevelopment of the "id" and the "super-ego" in infancy and early childhood, as we find in the developed psychoanalytic theory of Sigmund Freud (1856–1939). The operation of moral judgments would then be considered in terms of the operation of a mechanism formed during the infantile experience of being encouraged to perform certain types of action and of being prohibited from performing others. Such sociological and psychological interpretations might be supported by other considerations. For example, much might be made of differences that exist in ethical opinion between people in the same society, or in different societies, or in the same society at different historical periods. Do not such differences make it impossible for us to describe moral distinctions as absolute, ultimate or objective?

What ought the theologian's reaction be to these lines of thought? There is a danger of the religious believer reacting in a highly emotional way, hysterically denying the effects of society and environment on moral experience. Such a reaction is indefensible. There is no reason why sociologists and psychologists should not throw light upon morality. Theologians and moral philosophers have no monopoly in the moral sphere and cannot forbid trespassers' right of entry. Indeed, the theologian ought to welcome the exploration and illumination of moral thinking by his colleagues in the medical and social sciences. Nevertheless, there are certain points that he is bound to make.

First, he must make the point that in our own age, when immense adulation is paid to the fruitfulness of the methods of empirical sciences like physics and chemistry, certain of the social sciences, in order to be regarded as "scientific", have tended to emulate excessively the presuppositions of the purely "natural" sciences. This encourages the tendency towards the *exhaustive* explanation of all human phenomena and areas of experience in terms of objectifiable, observable and measurable forces and factors. To do so is not at all "scientific". It is in fact extremely unscientific. It is to make the metaphysical assumption made by scientific naturalism, the assumption of the identity of reality with physical nature. And this assumption (it is no more than that) is one that was rejected by the theists considered in this chapter. Second, the theologian must insist upon the distinction between the "conditioning" and the "creation" of the moral awareness. Now clearly our moral thinking is *conditioned* by a great many factors. But is quite another thing to suppose that moral experience is purely the *creation* of these factors. While we acknowledge that the performance of some actions can be accounted for merely in terms of social pressures, others clearly cannot. It is a commonplace that many moral agents, the nineteenth-century anti-slavery campaigner William Wilberforce being a somewhat dramatic example, have acted throughout their lives according to conscience in a way contrary to the well-being and stability of society (Slavery, which Wilberforce regarded as unequivocally immoral, was an integral part of the economic basis of his society.) Clearly more than social factors were involved.

Of course, it may be objected that psychological conditioning also played a part. But here again it is clear that this cannot provide anything like a satisfying, let alone an *exhaustive* explanation. Paul Tillich points out that psychological and social pressures may provide the occasion for the making of moral judgments, but do not at all produce the *unconditional* dimension of the moral imperative.[1] Tillich says of such pressures that no matter how strong they may be "they are themselves conditioned, and it is possible to contradict them and to be liberated from them, as, for example, from the father-image or from the socially produced conscience".[2] This is particularly obvious in the case of the psychogenetic explanations of conscience. Mature persons often criticize the "outrageous" and "unreasonable" demands of an oppressive super-ego in the light of the pronouncements of a reasonable, healthy conscience. This shows that there is a great deal more to the making of moral judgments than environmental pressures transmitted through infantile experience. In other words, there is a vast difference between *conditioning* and *creating*, and it is indefensible to confuse these. Our moral reflection, in which we sift and criticize the concrete commands of conscience, discriminating between them and conditioned prejudices, is possible only because we are able to look at them in the light of the unconditional, the ultimate, the underived, the given. If not, we would be automata, determined by forces and drives which we could neither understand, evaluate nor control. In the words of Tillich, "one can, of course, discard every particular content (of the moral imperative) for the sake of another, but one cannot discard the moral imperative itself without the self-destruction of one's essential nature and one's eternal relationship. For these reasons, the attempts to undercut the unconditional character of the moral imperative by psychological arguments must fail."[3]

[1] Paul Tillich, *Morality and Beyond*, London, 1964, pp. 27 f.; Tillich's book is very relevant to the theme of this chapter.
[2] *Op. cit.*, p. 27.
[3] *Loc. cit.*

Third, we deal with the question of the differences which appear to exist in ethical opinion, differences which divide man from man and nation from nation. Here again the believer who holds that morality points towards religion should beware of allowing such considerations to stampede him into regarding moral distinctions as merely arbitrary. It is true that differences of ethical opinion do appear to divide our world. But it is clear that these differences mostly reflect not differences in the criteria of rightness and wrongness, but differences of opinion as to what the *facts* are upon which moral judgment is passed. To take a concrete example, acute differences of opinion have often been noted between American Christians and European Christians as to the rightness or wrongness of the use of thermonuclear weapons against two Japanese cities in 1945. Even a superficial examination of the arguments used by both parties (allowing that one is naturally inclined to justify the actions of one's own country) shows how the real issue is *factual* rather than *ethical*. The American argues that if this action had not been performed there would have been excessive losses of military personnel in a needlessly protracted war, that the Japanese showed no signs of capitulating, that in the long run the action taken saved a greater number of lives than it destroyed, and so on. We find his European co-religionist disagreeing with him; arguing that Japan was really on her last legs and that the war was bound to come to an end very quickly, that the Japanese were trying to sue for peace through Switzerland, and so on. The argument really is, "Granting that such-and-such was the case, the proper action was X." If we try to analyse apparently ethical disagreements in this way, it is amazing how clearly it emerges that factual disagreements lie behind them and produce them.

Of course it is possible to search out or imagine cases where the facts are not in dispute, for example, cases involving euthanasia, and where ethical agreement appears beyond reach. Again we should beware. Perhaps here also a hidden factual issue is involved; one's ethical judgment is not made independently of the answer one gives to the question: "What is a human being, a machine, a superior animal, a child of God?" But apart from these considerations, we should still beware. Even if we were forced to concede the existence of instances where there could be no question of a dispute over facts and where ethical agreement appeared unobtainable, this should not allow us to conclude that moral distinctions are arbitrary, temporary and subjective. For there can exist also seemingly irresolvable divergences of judgment in *rational* matters. Now clearly such divergences do not lead us to the conclusion that reason is one psychological function amongst others created by a set of sociological and psychological factors. That is, we do not conclude that the pronouncements of reason are arbitrary, subjective fancies. Rather, we look more closely at the issues involved and try to ascertain where the divergence occurs with a view to reaching agreement. Ethical disagreements are not radically different. For moral agents believe that ethical matters can be *discussed* rationally. If one man says, "I like dishonesty", and another, "I have no taste for dishonesty", and if their conditioned and arbitrary likes and dislikes are the only issues involved in the disagreement, rational discussion is futile. But in fact persons do enter into ethical discussions with a view to subsequent agreement, being utterly if unconsciously convinced that moral awareness possesses an inalienable, unconditional, ultimate and underived dimension, which is the presupposed norm of such discussions, and without which they would be inconceivable.

We now take up the second objection to moral arguments for theism, which concerns the difficulties involved in regarding nature as somehow sympathetically geared to moral accomplishment. The objection is that man's natural environment appears at times not only morally neutral but also hostile to man and his moral development. We have come across this kind of objection to theism before — Hume, in criticizing the argument from design, had pointed to suffering and evil as evidence against belief in God.[1] And those theists whose views we have outlined above were not unaware of the problem, since it is one with which believers have grappled since the composition of the book of Job and earlier. A. E. Taylor, for example, held that while reflection on moral experience leads us to regard nature as geared to moral purposes, nevertheless the occurrence of tragedies demands of us faith in a sphere of existence not subject to such vicissi-

[1] *Dialogues*, Part XI; cf. p. 34 above.

tudes, and that sooner or later we are all tempted to believe in the amorality of reality because of the occurrence of events which appear to cripple human development. And H. H. Farmer considered that our interpretation of morality involves us in reconciling somehow man's moral freedom (which allows him to opt for evil and consequently suffering) and our conviction that moral values will ultimately triumph, a paradox which Farmer considered to point towards belief in God.

This brings us to one of the oldest and most stubborn problems in the philosophy of religion, that of suffering and evil.[1] Although the limits of this book do not permit us to enter upon anything like a full discussion of the problem, we may yet make the following points which are relevant in the context of our discussion of morality. Essentially the problem is the reconciliation of the divine almightiness and benevolence with the occurrence of apparently uncontrolled evil and suffering. "The forces of nature, whose behaviour we can by science in some slight measure predict and control, are obviously without compassion or purpose . . . The pretensions of religion to prove the existence of an all-merciful, all-powerful, benign deity fly in the face of fact. If there be evil, there can be no God—and evil there is."[2] The classical Christian response to such an objection to religious belief (usually called a *theodicy*) has taken the form of showing that the facts of evil and suffering are not by themselves sufficient to rule such belief out of court. Briefly, we can make the following points.

First, the existence of a certain amount of real moral freedom implies that persons can choose courses of action which cause suffering to others. Logically, it appears that the only way this could be avoided would be to cancel such moral freedom. This would entail the transformation of moral

[1] For this discussion I am indebted to certain modern treatments of the problem, especially J. Hick, *Philosophy of Religion*, pp. 40–47, Ninian Smart, "Omnipotence, Evil and Supermen", printed in *God and Evil*, edited by Nelson Pike, Englewood Cliffs, N. J., 1964, pp. 103–112, and Alvin Plantinga, "The Free Will Defence", printed in *Philosophy in America*, edited by Max Black, London, 1965, pp. 204–220.

[2] M. H. Hartshorne, *The Faith to Doubt*, Englewood Cliffs, N. J., 1963, pp. 62–3.

persons into puppets whose strings are controlled by a divine hand. Apart from the difficult question whether a universe peopled only by "human" puppets (if that is not a contradiction in terms) would be different from one peopled entirely by wooden ones, believers have traditionally asserted that the ultimate purposes of the creator are unattainable without moral freedom.

Second, we have noted already that man's environment is a "cosmos", Kant's phenomenal sphere, a realm of law, of cause and effect, of regularity. The task of science is to penetrate this realm and comprehend it. It appears that a realm of regularity, law and prediction must logically entail the possibility of some suffering. Ninian Smart points out that "Though God is undoubtedly . . . that upon which the cosmos is totally dependent, nevertheless the cosmos has its own separate characteristics and pattern of activity."[1] If so, it follows that the misunderstanding or ignoring of the laws of nature, of gravitation or cause and effect, may entail suffering. Smart points out that a man-made machine (and a law-governed cosmos has obvious similarities to a machine), with which one continually interfered would become an area of chaos.[2] It is hard to describe what it would be like to live in a lawless and unpredictable chaos, but John Hick's attempt to envisage such an existence leads one to describe it as un-imaginably nightmarish.[3] It would appear that the demand for a cosmos in which the occurrence of natural suffering would be out of the question involves us in hopeless contradiction. It is doubtful if such a demand has any meaning at all.

Third, there is a suspicious element of "timelessness" in the sceptic's demand for a purely intellectual reconciliation of omnipotence and suffering. The demand is "timeless" in the sense that it appears to ignore the essentially historical nature of the origins of Christian belief in God. The sceptic's objection to belief based on the fact of suffering might almost lead one to suspect that Christians had dreamed up their belief in a timeless, contemplative vacuum, a belief which had then to face certain awkward facts. But Hebrew-Christian

[1] *Philosophers and Religious Truth*, London, 1964, p. 53.
[2] *Loc. cit.*
[3] *Philosophy of Religion*, pp. 45–6.

belief in God grew up in and through events of ghastly suffering. We have already mentioned the book of Job, a theodicy in which the facts of suffering are grappled with in the most realistic way. The Old Testament is a book recording the development of belief and trust in God in a people demanding the vindication of God's righteousness amidst a history of suffering, exile, cruelty, punishment and oppression. And the Passion Narrative of the New Testament Gospels contains as much cruelty, injustice, deceit, disappointment, despair and agony as any story from secular literature. The point that we are trying to make is that religious belief evolved *in spite of* suffering and evil, not in timeless and otherworldly ignorance of it. The two grew up side by side, closely inter-related. This enables us to make a point to be developed in our next chapter. It is no accident that the classical, purely speculative theodicies were composed in the so-called "Age of Reason" (approx. 1650–1780) by such thinkers as G. W. Leibniz[1] (1646–1716) and by his interpreter and popularizer, Christian Wolff (1679–1754).[2] Most religious thinkers of this period, as we shall see in our next chapter, under the influence of Descartes, despised history, rejecting it as a sphere where truth is to be found, regarding the conclusions of speculative reason as both the source and norm of truth. Hence the timelessness of their discussion of suffering which has characterized and vitiated much philosophical discussion of the issue ever since.

We turn now to the third and final type of objection that can be brought against moral arguments for theism, which concerns the satisfactoriness or otherwise of the language in which they are commonly expressed. (At this stage we can offer only a brief discussion of the issue, since in our final chapter we turn our attention fully upon the whole question of the relationship between language and theology.) We must be clear that those thinkers we have considered are not blind to

[1] *Theodicy*, 1710.

[2] Wolff's glib attempt to show on purely rational grounds that this world is "the best of all possible worlds" drew forth as a reply Voltaire's scathingly satirical novel *Candide* (1759), in which the hero, having undergone a succession of the most appalling misfortunes, refuses to allow any of them to count against his view that this world is the best of all possible ones.

their semantic inadequacies. D. M. Baillie, for example, is aware that the attempt to describe what is given in moral experience involves one in the use of inadequate symbols which give rise to perplexity. Yet moral faith demands that moral values are "somewhere perfectly realized", a demand which results in imprecise and perplexing language.[1] A. E. Taylor admits that his convictions force him to use dated seventeenth- and eighteenth-century language, that moral distinctions are "immutable and eternal".[2] Farmer, in his attempt to do justice to moral experience, is forced to use highly paradoxical language, when he describes moral values as simultaneously "real" and "not yet real".[3] Elsewhere Farmer concedes that the reality disclosed in moral awareness is not "expressible in precisely defined concepts", and he is forced to use the German *Ahnung*, a term found in the work of Otto and others.[4] Farmer also brings to our notice the ethical work of Hartmann, who in describing moral experience uses very singular language, such as that moral essences "press for their actualization", "exert an influence on human life", "take a personal interest in and engage in activity towards" their realization, "refuse to recognize what is in antagonism towards them", and so on.[5]

Farmer confesses that he is puzzled by Hartmann's "shadowy 'intermezzo of being' where values exist, or subsist, in a sort of disembodied state and yet are real enough and potent enough. . . ." W. G. Maclagan, after identifying the "order of values" which is apprehended in moral experience with "God", says this of his language: "I readily concede that to speak of an order of values is not to carry our thought to a point at which it may complacently rest. The concept is obscure and problematic in the highest degree. It challenges further enquiry which, if fruitful, might alter our language and thought almost beyond recognition . . . But in default of this enquiry, . . . it appears to me that we can neither dispense with the concept . . . nor yet relate values in any helpful way

[1] *Faith in God*, p. 195.
[2] *Does God Exist?*, pp. 102–3.
[3] *Towards Belief in God*, pp. 196 f.
[4] *Revelation and Religion*, pp. 127 f.
[5] *Towards Belief in God*, pp. 198 f.

to some other Being supposedly more fundamental. The beginning of wisdom may here lie simply in getting used to the concept of values as a concept of what *is*, though not as temporal existents are. It may no doubt take some getting used to."[1] None of these thinkers is satisfied with the language, symbols and concepts which moral experience obliges him to use, but each one is clear that he must, rather than give up his conception of moral experience, continue to use them, in the absence of better.

Nevertheless, we can only sympathize with those who feel otherwise. Ninian Smart, for example, obviously has strong reservations about moral arguments for theism, especially when they assert the "objectivity" of the moral law.[2] He notes that the word "objective" is notoriously ambiguous; it can mean either that a state of affairs so described "exists independently of human beings" or that "there are public ways of deciding the truth (etc.) about the things in question".[3] He wants to say that moral distinctions are only "objective" in this latter sense, for which he prefers the term "intersubjective", meaning that moral subjects can rationally discuss such issues. But he would feel unhappy about describing the moral law as "objective" in the former sense, and this for two reasons. First, because a moral injunction or command is not a *thing*, like an object in nature. Second, because to consider it as such would mean that we had begun a process of "thing-making", of objectification, which would involve us in regarding all kinds of truths, including mathematical ones, as objective things, a process the end of which it is hard to predict! He is clearly influenced in this by semantic considerations, believing that "it is better English . . . if we simply consider [the moral law] as a set of rules or statements"; the trouble is that "the attempt to argue that there must be a source of objective values rests on the confusion between rules and things".[4]

We ought to acknowledge the reasonableness of such objections against moral arguments for theism. Still, there

1 *The Theological Frontier of Ethics*, pp. 91–2.
2 See his *Philosophers and Religious Truth*, 4.58, 4.59 and 4.60, pp. 119 f.
3 *Op. cit.*, 4.58.
4 *Op. cit.*, 4.59.

are important things that we must continue to put forward in their support. We have already argued that moral distinctions are somehow objective partly at least because they are intersubjective; that is, because they are valid independently of the desires and wants of moral agents and because they can be rationally discussed.[1] We noted that John Hick had spoken of God as a "trans-human" source and basis of moral values, not an "objective" one. But the moral theists we have been considering would not have meant by the "objectivity" of values exactly what Ninian Smart means by it when he says that "the statement 'It is wrong to steal' is not a *thing*, like an apple-tree", or like, as he says, the moon.[2] That is, the "objectivity" of moral values is not the same *kind* of objectivity that we ascribe to objects in nature. We have already noted how Maclagan, also troubled by the "objectivity" of the moral order, makes the point that the beginning of wisdom in this matter may lie "in getting used to the concept of values as a concept of what *is*, though not as temporal existents are".[3]

That is, in some mysterious way, moral values differ ontologically from natural objects; they do not exist *in the same kind of way* that the moon and apple trees do. Maclagan makes an important point when he says that we all suffer from an "initial prejudice in favour of 'matter of fact' as the paradigm of the real", a prejudice not unconnected without reasonable objection to the idea "that qualities could somehow exist on their own and as it were 'floating in the void', in abstraction from what they qualify".[4] Nevertheless, his contention is that "moral experience in the form of our consciousness of moral demand (the experience of categorical obligation, with the values inseparable therefrom) does indeed . . . require for its interpretation reference to an order of being other than the natural, or matter-of-fact order of spatio-temporal existence".[5] He means by this that "the quality of the experience itself may

---

[1] We have described values as "underived" and "given". In so far as they are "given", it is hard to describe them as "merely intersubjective". That is, "intersubjectivity" is an unstable and unsatisfactory half-way house between "subjectivity" and "objectivity" in Smart's first sense.

[2] *Op. cit.*, 4.58.

[3] *The Theological Frontiers of Ethics*, p. 92.

[4] *Loc. cit.*

[5] *Op. cit.*, p. 93.

be such that we cannot adequately and convincingly describe it except in language of a religious character, language that has a quality . . . at least akin to that of the language in which religion speaks of God".[1] This has of course been implicit all along in our discussion of a full and adequate interpretation and description of moral experience, especially in so far as, on Lotzean lines, it has been strongly anti-naturalistic.[2]

It is hard to concede that considerations of linguistic lucidity alone must force us to abandon certain lines of argument. In everyday experience, for example, we use odd language to describe thinking processes. We say, for instance, that "I have it at the back of my mind" or that "She has scarcely an idea in her head", or something of the like. We do not mean by such language that thoughts or ideas have precise spatio-temporal location somewhere *inside* the skull, exactly as the book has location *inside* the bookcase. Clearly when we speak of certain levels of reality we are forced to use very curious language indeed, compared with the matter-of-fact language we use to describe nature. Indeed, it is very hard to say exactly what we do mean when we say that thought goes on *within* nature. Similarly, when we speak of other phenomena, for example, freely chosen courses of action, we are forced to use odd language, but language which many would be unwilling to abandon. These examples may help to cast light on language describing moral experience. There are levels of being (Hartmann), distinct from and perhaps superior to those levels which are the concern of the empirical sciences, the analysis, description and evaluation of which demand the use of language which is analogical, symbolic and metaphorical, in short, indirect and oblique.

We need not spend too long on Ninian Smart's objection that holding to the objectivity of moral values would involve us in thingmaking, in objectifying all kinds of truths, including mathematical ones. Thinkers like Farmer reject the view that mathematical truths are real in the same sense as values. There

[1] *Op. cit.*, pp. 93–4.
[2] See our sixth chapter below, where we shall argue that one of the often unstated assumptions of much modern analytic philosophy is that the norm of all meaningful discourse is the language of mathematics or of the experimental sciences.

is a significant qualitative difference between the two; moral values are active, not passive, and so stand in a different relationship to the moral agent from that of mathematical truths to the mathematician. Nor can we concede the force of the objection that it is better "if we simply consider [the moral law] as a set of rules or statements" and that moral arguments for belief rest "on the confusion between rules and things".[1] It is true that commonly we refer to and discuss moral issues in the context of rules, laws and statements, and also that our rudimentary knowledge of moral matters comes to us in concrete commands and prohibitions, such as "it is wrong to steal".[2] But this does not mean that morality is to be identified with rules and statements, or that reflection upon, criticism of and discrimination between rules does not lead to the conclusions that they are, at the best, the embodiment of "something" which transcends the rules themselves. The attempt to overcome moral disagreement shows this, because, as we have argued, the entering into rational discussion with those whose rules and statements differ from ours presupposes that amidst the conditioned, complex disagreements there is something unconditional, given, and underived, to which appeal is made.

Moreover, thinkers such as Sorley, Taylor and Farmer are agreed that it is mistaken to assume that moral values (or the moral law) are exhausted through their incorporation into laws and propositions. They agree that we only grasp and comprehend the moral law piecemeal. Our understanding of it is always only partial. Moral values transcend the comprehension and obedience of individuals and societies. They thus transcend any given set of moral rules. Considerations of linguistic lucidity are not enough to make them abandon language which, however opaque and perplexing it may seem as compared with matter-of-fact scientific languages, does appear to do justice to moral experience as they conceive it. Their language is no more opaque than that of St. Paul when he writes that "love is the fulfilling of the law";[3] that concrete rules and regulations are insufficient in themselves; that they

1 Smart, op. cit., 4.59.
2 Op. cit., 4.58.
3 Rom. 13:10.

are of value only in so far as they point beyond themselves to that ideal of love which they imperfectly, inadequately reflect and embody. To forget this, to imagine that obedience to a set of rules fulfils what is demanded, is legalism, one of the most pernicious forms of what the New Testament calls "sin".

It is true that moral experience, as it has been described and interpreted above, leads us into a highly perplexing and confusing situation, from which we rightly demand to be liberated. Ninian Smart rightly points out that the objectification of the moral law "would be imagining it as a kind of mysterious and invisible substance pervading we know not where", until "there would be a world of ideas, like those of Plato's theory, existing independently of the world of experience".[1] Beside this we may place Farmer's perplexity at Hartmann's "shadowy intermezzo of being", which his description of moral experience leads to. The whole point of moral arguments for religious belief is that they lead us towards that point of perplexity and decision where belief in God becomes possible for us as the rational, intelligible and illuminating goal of the moral pilgrimage.

[1] *Op. cit.*, 4.58.

Chapter Four

GOD AS SUBJECT

OUR thesis throughout has been that the modern *impasse* between philosophy and theology is rooted in the kind of discussion of theism we find in the writings of Hume and Kant. It is now necessary to enquire into the extent to which the negative critiques of these two damaged the fabric of distinctively Christian belief, if at all. In other words *what* precisely was damaged by their criticisms? In order to answer such questions it is necessary to understand the theological tradition of which they were so critical. In brief, Hume and Kant were critical of the theology of the so-called "Age of Reason", which lasted approximately from 1650 to 1780. This was the era of rationalism *par excellence*, when Europeans revered (if not idolized) pure, speculative reason in every sphere of life, philosophical, scientific, artistic, political, architectural and theological. In philosophy and theology particularly, rationalism involved the view that speculative, discursive reason alone is sufficient for the attainment of all necessary truth. We can single out three reasons for the almost exclusively rationalistic theology of the era 1650 to 1780.

First, the widespread European veneration of reason due to its success in the new sciences as practised by Nicolaus Copernicus (1473–1543), Galilei Galileo (1564–1642), Johann Kepler (1571–1630), Francis Bacon (1561–1626) and Isaac Newton (1642–1725). An implication of this veneration for the physical sciences was that the Age of Reason came to regard nature as the sphere the understanding of which was fundamental to the attempt to understand all reality as such. Second, seventeenth-century Europe had been convulsed by widespread bloodshed and war, of which the disastrous Thirty Years' War (1618–48) was the most appalling example. In this strife Europeans slaughtered each other over the issue of the content of divine revelation, a burning issue which the seventeenth century had inherited from the century of the

European Reformation, the sixteenth. In the circumstances, it is understandable that seventeenth-century man, wearied by intolerance, persecution and bloodshed carried on in the name of divinely guaranteed churches and revelations, should seek for and find a religion which could commend itself to all Europeans by virtue merely of its reasonableness. Hence the emergence of the tolerant "Religion of Reason" (or "Natural Religion") which tried to dispense with appeal to troublesome supernatural revelation or inspiration. The third reason for the emergence of theological rationalism is to be found in the genius of René Descartes (1596–1650), and in the philosophical and theological tradition which he founded ("Cartesianism").

Descartes is generally credited with being the "father" of modern philosophy, and some understanding of his presuppositions and viewpoint is necessary for a grasp of modern philosophy and philosophical theology. Descartes was a celebrated mathematician, and it was his conviction that both philosophy and theology should be modelled on mathematics, a programme which he himself initiated, with significant consequences for the modern philosophical discussion of religious belief. The Cartesian stress on mathematics, for instance, ascribed tremendous importance in the modern period to the ideas of "proof" and "certainty" in theology. Now a "proof", for example in geometry, is a demonstration from agreed premises to a conclusion of such a nature that disagreement with it is self-contradictory. A proof, by definition, does not *invite* agreement; rather, it *coerces* it. If one does not agree with a genuine proof one is either stupid or perverse. The reason is that in a proof the conclusion is already contained in a hidden form in the premises, and the formal proof simply makes explicit and plain what was hitherto implicit and concealed in the premises.

Two things follow. First, it is not obvious that the idea of God is implicitly contained in the premises of, say, the classical cosmological and teleological proofs of God's existence, namely in the fact of the existence of the cosmos or in certain features of it, its apparent regularity or order. It is therefore clear that these, whatever they are, are not proofs. Second, if they are not, and if they are ever so regarded, and a system of religious beliefs, practices and rites erected upon their conclusions, such a system would be dangerously precarious and unstable. In fact, this was what happened in the period 1650 to 1780, and this explains the grave crisis which occurred after the validity of the proofs had been challenged by Hume and Kant.

Another consequence of Descartes' influence was that in Cartesian philosophical theology the fundamental relationship between knower and what is known was a subject-object one.[1] In this structure, the knowing subject, a naked, abstract, thinking self, is surrounded by a world of inert but interrelated objects. Knowledge comes about either when this world of objects is penetrated and grasped by the thinking self, or when the self turns in upon itself and investigates those ideas and notions allegedly innate within its "substance". It is clear that this subject-object structure appears to be the most apt for, say, the experimental sciences, and that the introspective attitude appears to be most apt in, say, mathematics or logic. But it is not at all clear that either of these represents the most apt approach in theology or philosophy. Yet the subject-object structure dominated philosophical theologians during the Age of Reason. And a great deal of subsequent philosophy and theology has reacted away from this fundamental Cartesian presupposition.

We have already mentioned another relevant aspect of Cartesianism—the conviction that the sphere in which truth and knowledge were to be sought was pre-eminently the sphere of *nature*. We have noted the reverence paid in the period under discussion to the new and exciting natural sciences, and in an age when the insights of scientific pioneers like Kepler and Galileo were being brilliantly synthesized by Newton into a magnificent mechanical picture of the universe (a picture which was to endure until the end of the nineteenth century), it is understandable why men generally should concentrate their gaze exclusively upon nature as the exciting source of all clues to the nature of reality. Yet from the distinctively Christian point of view the consequences were disastrous. Descartes, as a mathematician and physicist, had defined God almost exclusively in terms of his function in the natural

[1] See the discussion above, pp. 113 f.

131

system, as the cause of the mechanical cosmos, and of its motion, stability and intelligibility.[1] But the "first cause" God is a shrunken caricature of the God of authentic Christian belief. Étienne Gilson has pointed out that Descartes' favourite name for God was "the Author of Nature".[2] From this type of natural theology grave consequences flowed.

The "existence" of God was established almost entirely by pointing to "functions" which must necessarily be attributed to him within nature. Physical nature, it was asserted, demanded an uncaused first cause for its existence to be intelligible; it demanded a prime mover if its motion was to be intelligible; certain features of it, brought to light by the new empirical sciences, such as orderliness, harmoniousness or regularity, demanded the existence of a cosmic designing intelligence. Hence the popularity of seventeenth- and eighteenth-century disciplines like "Physico-theology",[3] "Water-theology" and even "Insect-theology", in which attempts were made to "trace God's wisdom in Creation".[4] Hence also the popularity of the traditional "proofs" for God's existence, re-stated and defended by thinkers like Leibniz, and popularized in German (as distinct from Latin) by Wolff. This philosophico-theological amalgam was known in Kant's time as "the Leibnizian-Wolffian" philosophy, the basis of much eighteenth-century belief and practice.

From another point of view, the approach to God in terms of the functions He performed within nature had even more disastrous consequences. In this period when the purely mechanical picture of the cosmos was being constructed, filled in and elaborated, the question inevitably arose as to how God was related to the machine. In Newton's time, the regularity, stability and origins of the planetary system were still unintelligible. Newton found God in these gaps in human understanding as the originator, regulator and upholder of the mechanical cosmos. But these gaps in intelli-

---

[1] See, for example, James Collins, *God in Modern Philosophy*, III, 2, "The Cartesian God as the Foundation of Philosophical Physics", pp. 64–9.

[2] *God and Philosophy*, Yale, 1959 edition, p. 89.

[3] Kant's name for the argument from design was the "Physico-Theological Proof", *Critique of Pure Reason*, pp. 361 f.

[4] L. Charles Birch, *Nature and God*, London, 1965, pp. 20–21.

gibility were gradually and completely filled up, so it seemed at the time, by the work of Kant and of the French mathematician, physicist and astronomer, Pierre Simon Laplace (1749–1827).[1] It was he who answered Bonaparte's question as to the room left for God in the mechanical cosmos with his celebrated statement, "Sire, I do not need that hypothesis."[2] This is of course the "God of the gaps", the "stop-gap" God of that natural theology against which Bonhoeffer has raged in our time.[3] To locate God in the gaps in man's understanding of nature, we have learned, and not only from Bonhoeffer, is one of the most disastrous theological undertakings conceivable, because as science fills in gap after gap such a "God" is harried from pillar to post until in a scientific culture there is literally no place left for him.

The next significant aspect of the Cartesian tradition stems from the fact that Descartes despised and rejected history.[4] For Descartes history was a discipline merely for escapists; historical narratives are notoriously untrustworthy, so that historical study is worthless for helping us to understand our present and its problems.[5] Descartes never enquired about the

[1] In his *Exposition du Système du Monde* (1796) and *Mécanique Céleste* (1799).

[2] For this whole subject see Carl Friedrich von Weizsäcker, *The History of Nature*, London, 1951, pp. 118 f., *The World View of Physics*, London, 1952, pp. 156 f., *The Relevance of Science*, Gifford Lectures 1959–60, London, 1964, chapter 7: John Dillenberger, *Protestant Thought and Natural Science*, London, 1961, p. 122; Herbert Butterfield, *The Origins of Modern Science: 1300–1800*, London, 1949, pp. 141 f.; J. S. Habgood, *Religion and Science*, London, 1964: "Newton himself was not happy that the machine, as he understood it, would work by itself without being thrown off balance. He thought that God must continually correct the irregularities, thereby earning the scorn of those who accused God of inefficiency as a creator" (p. 36). The English classical scholar Richard Bentley (1662–1742), Master of Trinity College, Cambridge (1700–42), tried in his sermons to prove God's existence from the gaps of science in the light of Newton's physics. Newton and Bentley were contemporaries at Cambridge, (Weizsäcker, *The Relevance of Science*, p. 120).

[3] *Letter and Papers From Prison*, pp. 103–4, 120–1; Bonhoeffer was confirmed in his view by reading v. Weizsäcker's *The World View of Physics* in prison, Bonhoeffer, *op. cit.*, pp. 102–3.

[4] See Gilson, *God and Philosophy*, p. 82; The views of Descartes and the Cartesians on history are concisely summarized in R. G. Collingwood, *The Idea of History*, Oxford, 1946, pp. 59–63.

[5] Collingwood, *op. cit.*, p. 60.

origins of the Christian concept of God in the Bible or in history, a failure which evoked a notable response from his contemporary, the French mathematician and theologian Blaise Pascal (1623–62), who wrote this: "The God of Christians is not a God who is simply the author of mathematical truths, or of the order of the elements; that is the view of heathens and Epicureans . . . but the God of Abraham, the God of Isaac, the God of Jacob . . ."[1] Finding such an historical enquiry pointless he simply, but incredibly, asserted that the notion of God was universally innate in men, a position peculiarly vulnerable to attack! He not only despised history but was ignorant of it; thus Hamelin tells us that "Descartes comes after the Ancients almost as though there had been nothing else between him and them, save only the physicists."[2] He despised history as the sphere where imagination and fantasy held sway.[3] Descartes, followed by his disciples, "turned his back upon history as a source of knowledge".[4] For thinkers from Descartes to Kant, "History was considered to be man's battle against nature."[5] The views of the Cartesians regarding history were well summed up by one of Kant's greatest contemporaries, G. E. Lessing (1729–81), in his celebrated dictum: "The accidental truths of history can never become the proof of the necessary truths of reason."

Of course, the opinions of Descartes were not the sole cause of the Age of Reason's suspicion and rejection of the dimension of history. In a sense the rejection of history was but the other side of a coin already examined—the Age's almost exclusive concentration upon nature as the source of all truth. Man's gaze was so focussed upon nature as the source of all knowledge that he was almost blind to all else.[6] The

[1] *Pensées*, 153–4.
[2] O. Hamelin, *Le Système de Descartes*, 2nd edition, Paris, 1921, p. 15, quoted in Gilson, *op. cit.*, p. 78; cf. Gilson, *History of Christian Philosophy in the Middle Ages*, London, 1955, pp. 542–3.
[3] Carl Michalson, *The Rationality of Faith*, London, 1964, p. 28; cf. Collingwood, *op. cit.*, pp. 60–1.
[4] Alan Richardson, *History Sacred and Profane*, London, 1964, p. 26.
[5] Dillenberger, *op. cit.*, p. 189.
[6] Collingwood tells us that Descartes' intention, in taking up his sceptical attitude to history, was that he "meant to direct people away from it towards exact science", *op. cit.*, p. 61.

tendency, in the long run, was therefore to identify reality with nature, a tendency which bore fruit in nineteenth-century naturalism and positivism. Also, as we have already noted, Europeans had become understandably nauseated by all talk of divinely guaranteed historical revelations. Sixteenth-century religious fanaticism and seventeenth-century intolerance, persecution and bloodshed had put such a notion almost entirely into disfavour by the end of the seventeenth century. The "gentleman's agreement" of the Age of Reason in religious affairs was to find a European *modus vivendi*, a set of religious beliefs and attitudes whose norm and source was to be reason alone, and, more particularly, reason's conclusions about the origins and structure of nature.[1] But whatever the causes, the thinkers of the Age of Reason, if they did not with Descartes positively despise the dimension of history, doubted its worth and for most practical purposes neglected and ignored it.

One final aspect of the religious conceptions of the Age of Reason must be indicated. It became increasingly difficult throughout the period to assert that God was active in the *hic et nunc*. To be sure, some did, notably Newton, when he taught that the mechanical cosmos required constant supervision, interference and renewal by God. But God's *contemporary* activity was in this sense no more than activity within the order of nature, in the regulation and correction of the orbit of planets and the like. But a contemporary philosopher like Leibniz could deride such notions of the contemporary activity of God. A clockwork machine like the cosmos which went wrong and required constant attention could not have been created by a perfect deity. A cosmos created by a perfect God was one which, like a perfect clock, only required to be wound up and thereafter went perfectly without need of attention.[2] The consequences of Leibniz's views (especially as they were popularized by Wolff) were momentous. The eighteenth-century conclusion was that God was to be sought at the *beginning* of things, as first cause or designing intelli-

[1] For the seventeenth-century revolt against religious intolerance and fanaticism, see Arnold Toynbee, *An Historian's Approach to Religion*, London, 1956, Part II, "Religion in a Westernizing World", pp. 143 f.
[2] For a discussion of this, see Dillenberger, *op. cit.*, pp. 121 f.

gence. There was of course plenty of contemporary evidence of God's primeval activity in the world, analysed and impressively expounded in the "physico-theologies" of the period. But it was hardly conceivable (outside the various European pietistic traditions and communities) in the period that God should be actively present in the spheres of human history and personality, in personal relationships, in religious or moral experience, in responses to prayer, in sacramental worship. In brief, there was hardly any conception of divine "grace". But distinctively *Christian* theism had always taught that God was in some dynamic, condescending, helping relationship with His creatures. It has therefore become usual in theological circles to describe the eighteenth-century, Leibnizian-Wolffian rationalistic type of belief in a deity who created a perfect cosmos and thereafter neither interested Himself nor intervened in it, not as *theism*, but as *deism*. It has been debated if, from the point of view of *Christian* theology, the Leibnizian-Wolffian type of belief, eighteenth-century deism, is really distinguishable from practical atheism.

We are perhaps now in a better position to answer the question posed at the beginning of this chapter: What precisely was it that was undermined by the critiques of theology we find in Hume and Kant? The question is easily answered. When Hume wrote on religion he had before him two *deistic* works, Samuel Clarke's Boylean lectures, *Discourse Concerning the Being and Attributes of God* (1704), and the work of the Scottish Newtonian deist Colin Maclaurin, *An Account of Sir Isaac Newton's Philosophical Discoveries*.[1] And when Kant wrote critically of religion he had in mind the Leibnizian-Wolffian rationalistic system, in which he himself had been educated. Indeed, when Kant formulated the traditional theistic proofs in the *Critique of Pure Reason* and the *Critique of Judgment*, he gave typically Wolffian versions of them.[2] That is, by their critiques Hume and Kant undermined the thin and

[1] See Norman Kemp Smith's introduction to his edition of Hume's *Dialogues*, Oxford, 1935, pp. 34 and 97, and James Collins, *God in Modern Philosophy*, pp. 424 and 427.

[2] For this whole matter see the Introductory Essay by Theodore M. Greene to the Harper Torchbooks Edition of Kant's *Religion*, pp. ix–lxxiii. For Kant's relation to Wolffian theology, pp. xxix f.

impoverished type of philosophical theism worked out in the Age of Reason. To be precise, they demonstrated the weaknesses inherent in the Cartesian tradition of philosophical theology, obsessed by quasi-scientific "proofs", taking up a subject-object attitude to knowledge, pointing to the gaps and "mysteries" in nature as grounds for belief in the existence of the deity, turning their backs upon history, experience and revelation as sources of truth, locating God at the beginning of things, behind, above or beyond the world, or at the conclusion of a theorem. Hume and Kant undermined eighteenth-century deism.

This insight has two important consequences. The first is rather alarming. It is that a great many recent and contemporary philosophers have continued to challenge religious belief in deistic, Humean and Kantian terms. And regrettably, too many theologians have accepted the challenge, joining in the debate in these terms, consequently apparently ignoring a great many post-Kantian contributions to theology. The second is this; as we saw in our examination of the nineteenth century, since 1800 many theological trends have sharply reacted away from the understanding of religious belief typical of seventeenth- and eighteenth-century theological rationalism, the rationalism so vulnerable to Humean and Kantian criticism. These trends have done so mainly by trying to rescue genuinely Christian belief from the reductionism and distortion implicit in rationalism, and by restoring to it essential dimensions eliminated from it by deistic thinkers in the Age of Reason.

This was of course what thinkers in the Schleiermacher-Ritschl tradition were trying to do, but they represent only a few trends in a host of others. Most of the remainder of this book will be concerned with other nineteenth- and twentieth-century trends which have reacted sharply away from the positions of rationalism, and have tried to make religious belief invulnerable to critiques like those of Hume and Kant. We shall examine one such trend in this chapter and one in the next, and in our concluding chapter we shall refer to several more. The trend with which we shall be concerned in the remainder of this chapter is that type of theology initiated almost fifty years ago by the Swiss theologian Karl Barth (b. 1886).

The epoch-beginning theological revolution associated with Barth's name is rightly dated from the publication of his *Commentary on Romans* in 1919. Since then until the nineteen-sixties a flood of theological works has flowed from Barth's pen, and although his name is not uncommonly associated mainly with his attacks on natural theology, his work is nevertheless comprised of themes of great relevance for the philosopher of religion.[1] These themes really cluster around Barth's central affirmation, which is that of the eternal and indissoluble *subjectivity* of God. *God is eternal subject.* That is the central message which Barth, in a bewildering variety of forms, has not tired of lecturing, preaching and writing about for almost half a century. Barth insists that the God of Christianity acts, sends his word, takes the initiative, reveals, creates, gives, calls, elects, judges and discloses. Barth's theology develops such themes, in constant dialogue with disciplines such as the history of theology and philosophy, biblical exegesis and church history. Man's knowledge of God is possible *only* through God's action towards man in grace — beside this there is no genuine knowledge of God whatever.

The importance of Barth's central affirmation for the history of philosophical theology is easily seen. The assertion of God's subjectivity at once removes him from the place he had occupied in the Age of Reason, the era of theological rationalism beginning with Descartes and ending with Kant. For that Age, God was an *object*, an important, even the most important object in reality. The theological rationalists attempted to locate God within or above or beyond physical nature, as its creator, regulator or designer. They could hardly do otherwise, given the Cartesian structure of knowing as subject-object. If knowledge comes about by man's pene-tration of the objects with which he is surrounded, then clearly God must either be such an object or structurally linked to the system in which such objects are inter-related. But if, with Barth, the radical *subjectivity* of God be affirmed, the natural theology of the period, and the criticisms brought

[1] Our discussion of Barth must regrettably be confined to the relevance of his work for the philosophy of religion. Limitation of space forbids us to pay attention to Barth's systematic dogmatic and biblical theology, whose significance is of course immense.

against it, are undermined. How can God's existence as an *object* be shown if God is eternally and indissolubly *subject* acting towards and upon man?[1]

In the second place, the assertion of God's subjectivity is relevant for that crisis in the philosophical evaluation of theism rooted in the scepticism of Hume and Kant. Both of these engaged in a discussion about the existence or non-existence of the God of the rationalists, the God of the proofs and demonstrations, the *object*-God beyond or necessitated by physical nature. Here again, Barth's insistence upon God as *subject* tends to draw the teeth from Humean and Kantian criticisms. If God is subject, the denial that an object-God's existence is provable is irrelevant. For Barth God is not essentially and primarily the *existing* one; He is always and essentially the *coming* one; as such he cannot possibly be the *object* of man's science, intellection or quest. It is God who seeks out and finds man, never *vice-versa*! In these ways Barth's central affirmation is highly relevant to the theology of the period 1650 to 1800. Knowledge of God comes about by God's action in revelation, not within the Cartesian subject-object framework within which man investigates nature. It is futile to seek for knowledge of God within inert nature, since God, as eternal *subject*, cannot be sought at all! The God of deism, the God whose existence is thought necessary in order to explain the existence or structure of the world, must be sharply distinguished from the God who, as subject, freely and graciously comes to man and discloses Himself to him. The God sought after by philosophical theism has nothing in common with the eternal subject who acts in his own revelation towards man in Christ witnessed to by Scripture in the Church.

In the third place, Barth's central affirmation has resulted in a sharp reaction away from the German theological thought of the nineteenth century, the period which began with Schleiermacher and ended with the disciples of Ritschl in

---

[1] According to Helmut Gollwitzer, early Barthian theology conducted a polemic against the idea that we "can conceive of God . . . as one cause in a series, as one factor among other factors", "as though God and man were two things", *The Existence of God as Confessed by Faith*, London, 1965, pp. 76–7.

the years following World War I. Barth has always been a keen student of nineteenth century theologians, and has tried hard to understand their work from within.[1] Nevertheless, he has held that the trend they represented was essentially a disastrous one. He has raged against the anthropocentric standpoint they took up, and their glib assumption that there is smooth, unbroken continuity from man to God. This assumption, Barth claims, led them disastrously to deify nineteenth-century man. Their God, he claims, tended to be little more than the glorious sum total of nineteenth-century man's values, ideals, aspirations and drives, in short, a "bourgeois" God. Barth has shown lively interest in the thought of Feuerbach, which he has described as "the thorn in the flesh of modern theology".[2] Barth's position is that Feuerbach, in denying any objective existence to God apart from man, thought that he was drawing out to their logical conclusion the theologies of Schleiermacher and Hegel. Hence he holds that all anthropocentric theologies have to reckon with the real possibility of sliding down the treacherous slope mapped out clearly for the first time by Feuerbach. In the light of the dangers allegedly inherent in nineteenth-century thought, Barth's theology has been to a great extent based upon those biblical themes and trends in the history of dogma which stress God's otherness from man, His transcendence, mystery, freedom and sovereignty, which, apart from his self-disclosure, pass human knowledge. For the preface of an early volume of sermons Barth used these words of Calvin — "*Deus in sua inscrutabili altitudine non est investigandus*"[3] — a sentence which well sums up Barth's attitude to all philosophical and natural theology. Making allowance for the fact that Barth's choice of Scripture and theology to illustrate God's dissimilarity from man has been one-sided, it is clear that his God could hardly have

[1] See, for example, his *Die protestantische Theologie im 19ten Jahrhundert*, Zürich, 1952, of which eleven chapters have been translated and published in *From Rousseau to Ritschl*, London, 1959; also his essay "Evangelical Theology in the Nineteenth Century", *The Humanity of God*, London, 1961.

[2] See Barth's introductory essay to the Harper Torchbooks Edition of *The Essence of Christianity*, and his chapter on Feuerbach in *From Rousseau to Ritschl*, pp. 355-61.

[3] *Revolutionary Theology in the Making: Barth-Thurneysen Correspondence, 1914-25*, translated by James D. Smart, London, 1964, p. 17.

been derived from an analysis of man's sublime consciousness, and that he is hardly a reflection or projection of man, even bourgeois man at his best! The abrupt discontinuity between man and God has seldom, if ever, been more strongly asserted than it has been by Barth.

As we move through Barth's massive and intricate theological system, we note that again and again he moves abruptly away from typically nineteenth-century theological positions. This comes out strongly in his stern denial that Christianity is a *religion*. To describe it as such had been the fundamental error of the nineteenth-century. Schleiermacher, for instance, had pointed to the universality of that religious consciousness which had given rise to the world-historical religions, of which Christianity was, according to Schleiermacher, the supreme but not the only one. Ritschl had begun his work with a definition of religion as that by means of which man achieves transcendence over nature, and had then investigated the nature of Christianity in the light of his definition. Barth has often pointed to the long-term consequences of this theological approach in the work of the Ritschlian scholar Ernst Troeltsch (1865–1923), leader of the German History of Religions school of thought (*Religionsgeschichtlicheschule*), who thought that Christianity might conceivably be superseded as the supreme world-religion.

Barth's reaction to this trend has been the sharp denial that Christianity is a religion at all — Jesus Christ, he has insisted, is the abolition and end of all religion. Religion represents man's futile attempt to find or construct God, whereas Christ is simply God's unique approach to man from the God-ward side. The intellectual aspect of *religion* is for Barth natural or philosophical theology, man's quite futile attempt to build by reason a bridge from man to God. Barth's polemic against all forms of natural theology has been fierce in the extreme. For him natural theology has not merely been a futile nuisance — rather has it been a dreadful obstacle to God's revelation. Through it man comes to possess an idol which usurps the place of the true God and which positively hinders man from coming to know Him. Barth's denial of the possibility of natural theology casts light on another aspect of his thought; his immense respect for the theologians of the sixteenth-century Reformation, Calvin especially. This is seen in the way in which he has deplored the obsession with natural theology in the seventeenth, eighteenth and nineteenth centuries, and in which he has by-passed these three centuries in order to get back to Calvin, a theologian who also ignored man's natural "religious" faculties, emphasizing rather God's unique self-disclosure in Christ.

In a text-book on the philosophy of religion we unfortunately do not have space to dwell on the many themes which have gone to make up Barth's rich, intricate and massive dogmatic theology. We lack space, for example, to develop how he teaches that the knowledge of God occurs only in the Church, or how it is always God who chooses man and never *vice-versa*, or to develop his teaching on the significance of Scripture. This is a pity, because all of such themes are relevant to our purpose here, which is to indicate how Barth's theology has initiated a revolution against the tendencies exhibited by philosophical theology during the previous three centuries. But perhaps we have dwelt upon enough of his thought to be able to indicate the scope of that gratitude which contemporary theology owes to him. It is clear that Barth initiated a theological renaissance which is of truly world-wide importance. One of the greatest tributes paid to Barth came from the late Pope Pius XII, who described him as the greatest systematic theologian since St. Thomas Aquinas in the thirteenth century, the "Angelic Doctor" of the Roman Church. His systematic theology has greatly stimulated interest in other theological disciplines — for example, twentieth-century "biblical" theology would hardly have developed as it has without the interest in the Bible evoked by Barthian theology. Paul Tillich is surely right when he says that twentieth-century theologians have been obliged to begin their work by stating how they stand in relation to Barth.[1]

[1] *Systematic Theology*, vol. I, London, 1953, pp. 5–8; one theologian who stand in an extremely close relation to Barth is Dietrich Bonhoeffer (1905–45). A great deal has been made in English circles in the nineteen-sixties of Bonhoeffer's conception of "religionless" Christianity, or Christianity "without religion". See, for example, *Beyond Religion*, by Daniel Jenkins, London, 1962; J. A. T. Robinson's *Honest to God*, London, 1963, pp. 23,

Barth's influence on the Church has been huge. Several generations of theological students, preparing for work in the pastoral and teaching ministries of the world-wide Church, have sat at his feet and have been thoroughly trained in theological thinking by him. The Ecumenical Movement has been deeply indebted to him. Church life, even at the parochial and congregational level, has directly benefited from the ways in which his theological themes have enriched preaching during the past forty years. The Church which probably owes most to Barth's theology is the Church in Germany. In the early nineteen-thirties, the Church there was faced by a monstrous ideological challenge in the shape of National Socialist propaganda. There was a mystical, quasi-religious side to Nazism, which taught that the divine life was immanent in the different *racial* groups which comprise mankind, but uniquely evident in the so-called Nordic, Aryan or Germanic racial group. This group, it was taught, was uniquely called to lead Europe and eventually the world out of social, economic and spiritual crisis under the leadership of Hitler, by force of arms if necessary. This was the ideology behind the nonsense of the "Master Race" (*Herrenvolk*) mystique.[1]

This was a challenge which the German Church could not

35-9, 61, 75 f., 106, 122 f., 127; A. R. Vidler, "Religion and the National Church", *Soundings*, edited by Vidler, Cambridge, 1962, pp. 239-63; cf. Bonhoeffer, *Letters and Papers From Prison*, pp. 104, 107 f., 113, 114 f., 116 f., 121, 123, 124. Bonhoeffer acknowledges that in rejecting "religion" he is indebted to Barth. For Bonhoeffer, "religion" seems to have meant three things—metaphysics, inwardness, and individualism. In the context of Barthianism, "metaphysics" denotes the natural theology of the Age of Reason; "inwardness" and "individualism" are the defining marks of the nineteenth-century approaches, of which Schleiermacher's and Ritschl's are typical. Bonhoeffer's "religionless" Christianity therefore stemmed from his Barthian affinities. It follows that an estimate of this conception of "religionlessness" can only be reached in the light of the criticisms of the whole approach to theology initiated by Barth, developed in pp. 144 f. below. See also my paper, "Dietrich Bonhoeffer's Attack on Christian Existentialism" (*Renaissance and Modern Studies*, VIII, Nottingham, 1964, pp. 92–108) and my essay, "Beyond All Reason" (*Four Anchors From the Stern*, edited by Alan Richardson, London, 1963, pp. 31–46).

[1] Developed by Alfred Rosenberg in his *Der Mythus des 20ten Jahrhunderts*, Munich, 1930.

evade, and it responded under the influence of Barth's theology, sharply denying any innate or natural knowledge of God in race, history, reason or religion. Hence the emergence of the celebrated Declaration of Barmen of May, 1934, in which the German Confessional Church denied the existence of "secondary" revelations of the divine mind and purpose, beside that unique and sufficient primary revelation of God in Jesus Christ, witnessed to by Holy Scripture. That the German Confessing Church survived the ideological onslaught of Nazi propaganda is due in no small measure not only to Barth's theology but also to his personal participation in the struggle for the Church's autonomy and doctrinal purity.[1]

In spite of the immense debt of gratitude which twentieth-century theology owes to Barth, it is nevertheless true that his thought has evoked a considerable amount of controversy and criticism. Criticism has come, for example, from biblical scholars who have been troubled by Barth's use of the Bible for theological purposes. But here we can only consider difficulties which Barth's theology causes for philosophers. At the considerable risk of appearing to over-simplify and distort Barth's subtle theological system, we suggest that at two significant and related points his theology gives rise to philosophical consternation. These two points are, first, Barth's negative attitude to human reason, and, second, his apparent disregard for the thinking, aspiring and striving of men in their concreteness, historicity and individuality.

First, let us consider the business of human reason. On the popular, everyday level it is clear that if Barth is right it is very difficult to say how or in what circumstances the Christian believer could discuss his faith with his neighbour, or could in any way try to persuade his neighbour to share his religious beliefs, attitudes and concerns. Between the believer

---

[1] Critics of Barth and Barthianism are not always obviously aware that in the Germany of the nineteen-thirties the denial of "secondary revelations" and the rejection of metaphysical theology was a life-and-death matter for the Church, and not a piece of academic quibbling. For the German Church Struggle, see Rudolf Homann, *Der Mythus und das Evangelium*, Witten, 1935; A. S. Duncan-Jones, *The Struggle for Religious Freedom in Germany*, London, 1938; Karl Barth, *The German Church Conflict*, edited by A. M. Allchin, Martin E. Marty, and T. H. L. Parker, London, 1965.

and his neighbour there is a gulf fixed which is, humanly speaking, quite impassable. In the last resort, the believer has received, apparently, a revelation from God and his neighbour has not. The believer in the nature of the case is forbidden to present to his neighbour a case for his religious beliefs by bringing forward reasons which are common ground between them, because such reasons simply do not exist. Now if this is true it goes counter to the ways in which most religious people regard their beliefs. Most of them do consider that there are some grounds for believing as they do which can reasonably be discussed and examined. In fact, if they were persuaded that such grounds were illusory or worthless, the strong possibility is that they would feel obliged to abandon their beliefs. This is in fact what we have all seen happening.

Included among such grounds of course is the conviction of believers that their beliefs are inexplicable without the confirming or unifying of them by the action of God himself. And from the side of the believer's sceptical neighbour, it is clear to most of us that if he were given to understand that religious belief rests *solely* upon the conviction of the believer that he has been communicated with by God, a conviction which could neither be strengthened nor weakened, verified nor falsified by any considerations whatever apart from the allegedly God-given conviction itself, he would at once reject religious belief out of hand as an arbitrary, irrational, subjective prejudice unworthy of serious examination or assessment. This is, we must insist, the actual state of affairs, the world being as it is; and although there appear to be Christians who are not disconcerted by it, the strong probability is that most believers and their critics will feel gravely disturbed by the attempt thus to detach religious beliefs from the area of rational discussion and evaluation. Thus far, the "plain man" at any rate will find the Barthian account of religious belief rather disturbing and disconcerting.

From the more sophisticated, philosophical viewpoint, the matter is not much otherwise. Barth has sternly refused every demand of the philosopher of religion for *grounds* which might confirm or substantiate the Christian view of things. He has refused to admit that human reason or reflection could arrive at conclusions which are sympathetic towards the view of things disclosed by revelation. He has firmly set his face against the kind of view outlined in our third chapter above — that man's moral experience, taken seriously and examined thoroughly, points him in the direction of belief in God. He will have no truck with any view that suggests continuity between, on the one hand, merely human aspirations towards goodness and God, on the other. So small has his interest in this been that he has been widely accused of indifference to ethics! He has even deplored the notion that the "natural man" can discover anything at all about God by perusing the Bible. He insists that without God's grace, his act, his miracle, without that unique operation in which God removes the scales from the eyes of the spiritually blind, the Bible is for the unconverted nothing more than a block of printed paper, spiritually unintelligible and theologically uninformative!

Nor has Barth been in the least willing to acknowledge that religion and history in general are shot through with theologically informative experiences and occasions when, to use the words of Ronald Hepburn, "the world loses its ordinariness and takes on a disturbing, derivative, transfigured look; when awe deepens to numinous awe".[1] The truth of God's unique self-disclosure could not possibly be confirmed by such rapturous experiences or occasions. One has nothing to do with the other. Nor could God's revelation be linked with any merely human hopes or needs. Bland Blanshard tries to commend the religious life in these words: "The humility, the capacity for reverence, the high concern for ends neither material or selfish, the morality touched with emotion, which religion has stood for over the centuries are precious still, and deeply needed in our troubled time."[2] This may or may not be true; but for Barthians it is just irrelevant. Religious belief is grounded in God's action and in *nothing* else; man's wistful hopes and deepest intimations have nothing to do with the matter!

If this is true, clearly the philosopher is no less baffled than the "plain man". Every request of his for grounds, reasons or confirmations is turned down flat. At this point a rather unfair piece of tactics is occasionally attempted by theologians

[1] *Religion and Humanism*, London, 1964, p. 16.
[2] *Faith and the Philosophers*, edited by John Hick, London, 1964, p. 198.

of Barth's persuasion. The suggestion is made that the request for reasons is tantamount to challenging God to justify Himself. This was in effect Barth's rejoinder a few years ago to Karl Jaspers, his academic colleague in the Chair of Philosophy in the University of Basel, when Jaspers asked for grounds for accepting revelation. Accused by Barth of asking God to justify Himself, Jaspers' reply was that this was not so. He was, he claimed, merely asking for grounds upon which a certain *theological viewpoint* was to be accepted as having come from God. H. J. Paton has recently written this: "A very little modesty might suggest to the prophet that to question the truth of his message is not the same thing as to sit in judgment upon God."[1] Precisely; the man, directly confronted by God, who demands that God justify himself is indeed guilty of impiety and blasphemy. But the man who asks the preacher to indicate reasons for regarding his message as God's message is not so guilty.

Now when Barth refuses to produce any *reasons* or *grounds* for accepting "God's revelation", and when the philosopher concludes abruptly that this refusal is irrational, every sympathy must be extended to the philosopher. So-called "knowledge" of the divine appears to be so radically different from every other kind of human knowledge, without exception, that there is a real danger that the philosopher will summarily dismiss its claim to be considered as knowledge in any significant sense. For there appears to be no conceivable way in which it could be verified or falsified, regarded as plausible or implausible, probable or improbable. And, as we shall see below, many modern thinkers hold that an "assertion" which cannot be verified or falsified at all is a "pseudo-assertion"; it is not an assertion at all, it is a meaningless sound![2] Nor is it only philosophers who think in this way. Many theologians are aghast when told that belief in God has nothing whatever to do with ordinary human experience or happenings within the structure of the everyday world. Religious belief simply occurs miraculously through the agency of God quite inde-

[1] *Op. cit.*, p. 197.
[2] See our discussion of the philosophy of linguistic analysis in the sixth chapter below.

147

pendently of anything in everyday reality. It seems to occur in some dimension utterly detached from everyday human thinking, hoping and living.

This appears to stand in such sharp contradiction to the historic understanding of belief that there appears to be no alternative to rejecting it. The religious believer rightly finds it hard to credit that religious beliefs could be true within the spheres of nature, history, morality and experience which are *utterly devoid* of evidence of any kind for their truth, apart from the conviction in some minds that they are grounded in God. Nor does he suspect that his refusal is in any way impious or blasphemous. We conclude that the Barthian account of belief raises crucial questions about the rational grounds for such belief. Granted that the believer is right in regarding his beliefs as partly at least grounded upon God's revelatory action, it is clear that he must go on to enquire about wider grounds for them upon which they can be commended and by means of which they can be defended. The theology of the nineteen-fifties and nineteen-sixties has gone beyond the Barthian position, involving itself in discussion about the credibility or otherwise of a theistic world-picture, about wider grounds for religious belief which might be common ground between Christians and sceptics, believers and humanists. In doing so, theology has abandoned strict Barthian presuppositions and limitations.

We turn now to Barth's alleged disregard for man in his concreteness and historicity. This disregard has been another bone of contention between Barth and his critics, both philosophical and theological. It is easy to see what his critics mean. If he is right, if there is in human thinking, willing, aspiring and experiencing absolutely *nothing* which is a presupposition or a prerequisite for man's coming to believe, and if man's human world is utterly lacking in any evidence which would lend support to his belief, man's part in the whole scheme of things appears to have been reduced to vanishing-point. "All is of God," the Barthian theologian may say, but the logical corollary of this is, "Man is nothing"! Barth's critics rightly will not have this. Hence Barth has been accused of "dehumanization". The late John Baillie likened Barth's account of revelation to God's self-disclosure to "sticks and stones".[1] This aspect of Barth's thought has evoked considerable controversy, and that, apparently, for two reasons, one theological and the other philosophical.

The theological reason is that Barth's "natural man", utterly devoid of any awareness of God in his "natural" state, quite unable to come to any knowledge of God through his thinking, moral striving, experience of beauty and encounter with his neighbours, has appeared to many to be an unprecedented departure from the traditions both of the Bible and of historic Christianity. Both of these, it has been argued, hold that man, created in the divine image, in his intellectual, moral, aesthetic and (pace Barth!) religious experience, has the possibility of glimpsing God, from whom he originated and for whose fellowship he is intended. Hence many theologians have rejected the Barthian picture of man.

The second, philosophical reason for dissension over Barth's doctrine of man, concerns the significance ascribed to man by contemporary thought. It is a commonplace amongst historians of ideas that at least since Kant, and possibly since the Renaissance, huge interest has been shown in man, in the essentially *human*. The so-called Kantian Copernican revolution, it is argued, was in reality an *anti-Copernican* one. Whereas Copernicus' astronomy displaced man from the centre of the cosmos, Kant's philosophical revolution placed man firmly back at the centre of things as a creature of moral worth, superior to and transcendent over nature. This Kantian and post-Kantian interest in man grew in intensity throughout the nineteenth century, and in the twentieth has flowered in many ways, Freudian psychoanalysis, philosophies of personal being, and most significantly, in the philosophy known as existentialism. Thus, in a sense, Barth's theology, with its apparent disregard for man in his concrete possibilities, has gone against the stream.[2] It is evidence of his great insight that early in his career he prophesied that there would be a significant return to an *anthropocentric* theology stressing once more the *human* bases of religious belief. This has indeed come

[1] *Our Knowledge of God*, Oxford, 1939, p. 24.
[2] Barth has been great enough to realize that his theology has tended to do so in many ways; see his collections of essays, *Against the Stream*, London, 1954.

to pass in the revolt of certain theologians against Barth's undervaluation of man, resulting in theologies which have stressed *human existence*. Since such theologies have tried to work out a synthesis between Christian theology and contemporary existentialist philosophy, they have commonly been called *existentialist* theologies. We shall examine one of these, that of the Marburg theologian Rudolf Bultmann, in our next chapter.

Even if it appears that we have been critical of Barth, it is nevertheless true that philosophical theology must be deeply indebted to his work, paradoxical as this may seem. Theologians who have studied his works will not easily make certain fatal mistakes. They will not, for instance, forget the insights inherent in Barth's insistence upon God's *subjectivity*. They will not imagine, with the Age of Reason, that God is an unresponsive, functional object to be discovered within or beyond nature, or to be integrated into its structure. Against psychological projectionists like Feuerbach and Freud they will maintain the firm insistence of the Christian tradition that God is no mere image projected upon a screen by man's needs, fears, ambitions and aspirations. Under the influence of Barth, contemporary theologians will not easily fall into the nineteenth-century error of imagining that talk of man and talk of God are ultimately the same thing, that God is really man writ large. Nor will Barth's theology allow theologians to give the impression that Christian belief comes about *merely* by argument, reflection or taking thought. They have been forced to take into account that the occurrence of such belief is unintelligible without God's activity towards man, without God's revelatory action.

To say such things is to say that Barth's theological enterprise has partly at least been a loud "*Nein!*" to much of the philosophical and theological development since the sixteenth-century. Only as such does a great deal of it have meaning. If Barth's theology has been a reaction against the distortion and dilution of the Christian faith carried out in three centuries, most theologians today would agree that it has been an over-reaction. Certain historical factors in this century have combined to bring it about. Certainly, without the lunacy exhibited by Europeans in World War I it is dubious if Barth's outright condemnation of nineteenth-century thought would have received such widespread acclaim. And, without a shadow of a doubt, had it not been for the insane claim of Nazi mystics and "philosophers" to have an insight into the ultimate meaning of things, a quite crazy claim which led in the 'thirties to genocide and world war, it is dubious if the Barthian denial of all natural knowledge of God would have been accorded the status of orthodoxy it enjoyed in Europe at the end of the 'thirties.

Significantly, one of those who have admitted that it was an over-reaction has been Barth himself.[1] He has conceded that the extreme tendencies his theology took in the 'twenties and 'thirties, although justified at the time, were historically conditioned, and that they gave his theology a one-sided character. He has admitted that for him there is "humanity" in God and that this forms the basis of the God-man relationship. If so, many will wonder if this admission does not really point to there being "divinity" in man, and that therefore there is a link between man and God, and so some natural theology. Barth of course would deny this, and his followers (from whom Barth has always carefully distinguished himself) have tried to argue that this admission does not constitute any change in the substance of his theology whatever, but that it was implicit in it from the beginning! Many will rightly find this incredible, and if with Bland Blanshard they fail to grasp the odd distinction between *theanthropology* (of which Barth approves) and *anthropotheology* (of which he disapproves), they will tend to think that older types of natural theology, particularly nineteenth-century ones, which stressed similarities between the human and the divine (and thus the relevance of the divine for genuinely *human* existence) cannot be ruled out of court so summarily as they were by Barth forty years ago. To one such type of contemporary theology we now turn, the theology of human existence.

[1] See his essay "The Humanity of God" in the volume, *The Humanity of God*.

Chapter Five

GOD AND HUMAN EXISTENCE

WE turn now to consider the construction of a twentieth-century apologetic theology in the work of the Marburg New Testament scholar and systematic theologian Rudolf Bultmann (b. 1884). Bultmann's theology is not only an exceptionally interesting type of philosophical theology whose articulation has much to teach us, but represents one of the most important contemporary attempts to make theology relevant for modern man. Bultmann belongs to exactly the same generation as Barth (Barth was born in 1886), and they were both educated at the Universities of Berlin, Tübingen and Marburg. Sharing very much the same background, it is not surprising to find that they share a good deal of common ground in their fundamental attitudes and presuppositions. Although in the nineteen-sixties we are accustomed to thinking and hearing of Bultmann and Barth as being basically opposed to each other, this is only partly true, and it is important to get the common ground between the two sharply into focus. They were both educated in two Ritschlian, neo-Kantian theological schools; in that of Wilhelm Herrmann (1846–1922) in the University of Marburg, and that of Julius Kaftan (1848–1926) in the University of Berlin. Both therefore share an antipathy to metaphysical theology. Both are clear about the impotence of pure, speculative reason to penetrate to God's existence and attributes in, above or beyond the world. Bultmann has been as adamant as Barth that nature is opaque to, or at best ambiguous about, the existence or activity of the deity.[1] Bultmann has held with Barth that God is not an *object* to be sought after, analysed or described; rather God stands as *subject* over against man and addresses His word to him.

Bultmann has been even more sceptical than Barth about

[1] See Bultmann's essay, "The Question of Natural Revelation", in *Essays: Philosophical and Theological*, London, 1955.

the possibility of man finding some objective information about God in the historical records of the Bible. Since the nineteen-twenties, Bultmann has been a biblical critic of the most radical tendencies, holding, for example, that the Gospel records contain hardly a strand of reliable objective information about Jesus as he was in his "sheer factuality".[1] Moreover, Bultmann holds that the Old Testament cannot be regarded as a source-book from which we can cull information about God or build up a conception of Him; the Old Testament's talk about God is full of mystery, unintelligibility and paradox.[2] Nor has Bultmann been any more inclined than Barth to attach significance to Jesus as an ethical example or propounder of ethical wisdom. He fully shares Barth's aversion to commending Christianity in this way. With Barth he does not regard Jesus' ethical teaching as specially outstanding. The similarities between the two are obvious. No objective grounds for religious belief are to be found in speculative reason, nature, history or ethics. In what way, then, do the two differ?

The difference between them can be stated historically by saying that whereas Bultmann fully shares Barth's aversion to the natural theologies of the seventeenth and eighteenth centuries, the age from Descartes to Kant, Bultmann's attitude to the theologians of the nineteenth century has been much more positive than that of Barth. That is, he shares with thinkers like Schleiermacher and Ritschl a concern to shape the Christian faith in order to make it relevant for contemporary man, contemporary thought and contemporary problems. This concern marks Bultmann's breach with Barth. For Barth, as we have seen, the sole but indispensable condition for man coming to believe is God's miracle. God alone creates in man that faculty which enables him to grasp revelation. This, for Barth, is the one and only thing needful. There is no antecedent condition in man, intellectual, religious or moral, which could possibly assist revelation to occur. There is, as Barth has put it, no contact-point (*Anknüpfungspunkt*) in man

[1] See Bultmann's book, *Jesus*, Berlin, 1926.
[2] See Bultmann's essay, "The Significance of the Old Testament for the Christian Faith", in *The Old Testament and Christian Faith*, edited by Bernhard W. Anderson, New York, 1963, pp. 8–35.

for the Gospel, nor is one necessary. It is precisely at this point that Bultmann sharply disagrees with Barth. As a New Testament scholar Bultmann has long since come to the conclusion that much biblical language, terminology and jargon, which is of a highly technical nature, is literally meaningless for twentieth-century man. But it is more than a question of mere terminology. Bultmann is clear that the whole way of thinking, the whole way of looking at the world, the conceptions, preconceptions and assumptions of the biblical writers have all long since passed away.

Bultmann has always been acutely aware of the huge changes brought about in thinking by the passage of time, by immense philosophical, scientific and conceptual revolutions, changes which have operated to separate twentieth-century man from the thought-world of the New Testament. Hence he has looked askance at Barth's conviction that acceptance of the Christian message presupposes *only* and *merely* God's self-disclosure. Bultmann's position is that modern man does not understand, does not find meaning and relevance in biblical talk, and can thus never reach the position of either accepting or rejecting the Gospel. The theological task is therefore to close the gap between modern man's concern and the meaning of the Gospel. The theologian's job is to show that the historic Christian message is relevant and meaningful for his thinking and living. To continue to address modern man in traditional biblical terms is rather like addressing an audience of average Anglo-Saxons in fluent Japanese. Both procedures have the same result, unintelligibility. Hence the breach between Bultmann and Barth.

How then has Bultmann proposed to make Christianity relevant to, meaningful for, modern man? Obviously he has been obliged first to obtain some conception of "modern man" for whom he makes the Gospel relevant. At this point a fateful choice has faced Bultmann, a choice not always appreciated by his unsympathetic critics. Suppse that Bultmann had decided to try to make Christianity relevant for the not uncommon contemporary man who is, as we defined the terms above, both *positivistic* and *naturalistic*. Such a man, by definition, is convinced that the only knowledge which is possible is gained by the methods of the empirical sciences, and assumes that all reality is exhaustively identifiable with physical nature, the object of the empirical sciences. Clearly Bultmann has not attempted such a thankless, futile task. For it is, also by definition, impossible to make Christianity relevant for such a man, since a term like "God", for example, indicating that there is something "more than" physical nature, or that there are dimensions in reality knowable by methods other than those of the natural sciences, is a mere sound or cipher which lacks meaning. Rather Bultmann has selected a conception of man more adequate for his theological purpose, and his source for this has been the work of the German philosopher Martin Heidegger (b. 1889), a former colleague of his in the University of Marburg. In order to understand why Bultmann has tried to articulate the Christian faith by means of Heidegger's thought, we must have some grasp of its central themes.

Heidegger is, strictly speaking, an *ontologist*, a philosopher interested in the science of *being*, in the ways in which different things can be said to be, or to exist, or to come into being. It is vital to understand that Heidegger's work at many points has been decisively influenced by Christian theological conceptions.[1] Originally a Roman Catholic intended for the priesthood, Heidegger prosecuted his earliest research at the University of Freiburg-im-Breisgau into the thought of the mediaeval Catholic theologian Duns Scotus. Other Christian theologians who have influenced Heidegger's thought include St. Augustine, Luther and Kierkegaard. It is equally important to grasp that at the heart of Heidegger's thinking lies a sharp reaction against the thought of Descartes, who is, in Heidegger's view, something of the "villain" in the story of modern philosophy. A grasp of the nature of this reaction is crucial for an understanding of Heidegger.[2]

According to Heidegger, Descartes' fateful error was his

[1] See Schubert M. Ogden's essay, "The Temporality of God", in *Zeit und Geschichte: Dankesgabe an Rudolf Bultmann zum 80. Geburtstag*, hrsg. von Erich Dinkler, Tübingen, 1964.

[2] Heidegger's main work is *Sein und Zeit*, Tübingen, 1926, the 7th edition of which has been translated into English by John Macquarrie and Edward Robinson as *Being and Time*, London, 1962. Our references are to those of the margins, which refer to the 8th German edition. For Heidegger's reaction against Descartes see especially pp. 22, 24, 25, 45, 46, 66, 89–101, 203–4.

failure to distinguish between the being of humans and non-humans. Descartes defined human being as *res cogitans*, a thinking or cogitating *thing*. He thus applied to humans the categories which Aristotle had applied to things in nature, substance, quality, relation, cause and so on. By doing so, Heidegger argues, he dehumanized human being; he regarded it as a bare, abstract, intellecting object in a world of objects, denuded of individuality, personality, will, emotion and the subconscious self. Since human being was defined as a thinking *thing* or *substance*, possessing innate ideas, this implied that man was regarded as a more or less finished or completed entity, a conception which excludes the notion that man must become, develop, change. The notion that man's real self is his future, as yet unrealized self, is excluded by Descartes' definition. In short, Descartes reduced man to the status of being one object within the world of objects, physical nature, from which he was distinguished by one characteristic only, pure thought. Heidegger also argues that this Cartesian conception of man has been absolutely dominant in Western thought since the seventeenth century. One great thinker, and this is significant from the point of view of our thesis, who failed to overcome Cartesian dehumanization was Kant himself.[1]

Heidegger proposes to overcome this Cartesian dehumanization by sharply distinguishing human from non-human being. Human being differs from all non-human being because it is open to itself. Only humans know that they *are*, and only they experience the call to be different from what they are. Only they concern themselves with what it really means *to be*. Human being is quite unique; it *exists* in ways in which physical objects cannot exist. The root meaning of *exist* is "to stand out of", and so the meaning of human existence is that humans stand out of, transcend, are radically different from non-human, physical nature. To understand human existence is therefore the beginning of all knowledge — this understanding sheds light upon all reality.

Heidegger's fundamental theme is probably his distinction between *inauthentic* and *authentic* existence, and to that we now turn. According to Heidegger, man can exist inauthentically. Roughly speaking, this means that man understands himself

[1] *Being and Time*, pp. 203–4.

purely scientifically, as a natural object, substance or entity. Now almost all existentialists have reacted sharply against the dehumanization of man by purely scientific understanding. In many of them, "science stands for unauthentic existence. Science is a matter of indifference, of concern with selected objects or items, whether of nature or of history. It conceals man in his totality, in his mystery, by a concern with the multiplication of knowledge essentially indifferent to himself as an existing subject . . . Where man is an item in the historical process, history has been reduced to nature."[1] This is absolutely true of Heidegger, as we shall see if we turn to his analysis of inauthentic existence in a little detail. In this type of existence man fails completely to distinguish himself from things. This implies *anonymity*. Here Heidegger points to an everyday characteristic of inauthentic existence, the use of the noun "One". In the sphere of inauthenticity, "one says, one does, one prescribes, one dies".[2]

This mysterious, uncanny "One", who dominates man's life, is really a very sinister figure. It is a symbol of man's enslavement to the impersonal, to the determining and moulding forces of his environment. So long as man lives, speaks and behaves according to the dictates of the "One", he is sunk in inauthentic existence as one thing among others. He is indistinguishable from the mass, from the lump of human "substance"; he does not "exist". In inauthentic existence man is "naturalized"; he becomes merely a part of nature, determined by a world in which he is only an item. He lives according to impersonal laws which he does not understand. Of course, as a human, his being is flooded occasionally by *anxiety*. This anxiety is rooted in the occasional call of his authentic, real, future self. But he flees from anxiety by sinking himself even more firmly in anonymity and nature. Also, he is aware of *conscience*, the call of his future, authentic self; but this he interprets as a demand to comply more vigorously with the dictates of the impersonal "One".

The radical inauthenticity of man's life is discernible

---

[1] Dillenberger, *Protestant Thought and Natural Science*, p. 267.
[2] In *Being and Time* Heidegger's *das Man* (literally, "the one") has been translated as "the they"; see pp. 126 f. Thus, in everyday existence, "They say, they do, they prescribe, they die."

clearly in his understanding of time. Inauthentic man understands all time, including his own, in a purely scientific way.[1] In this scientific, or as Heidegger calls it "vulgar", understanding of time, the past is simply that which has already come to pass, and the future is simply that which is yet to be. Between past and future is the present conceived as an extensionless "now", a point which moves regularly and inexorably over a graduated time-scale.[2] This is countable or measurable mathematical clock-time. Now if man understands his own being in the light of such an understanding of temporality, he regards his being as swept along by the momentum of a temporal flux. Within such an understanding there is no possibility of man rising out of the flux, of his becoming something different from his past. Inauthentic man is rather like an inert branch swept along by a swollen stream. His being is firmly integrated into a process.

There is yet another way of indicating the meaning of inauthentic existence.[3] Man exists inauthentically when his being is defined merely in terms of those factors which locate him within a class, group, genus or species. The biologist naturally classifies man as *homo sapiens*. The social scientist classifies him as working-class or middle-class. But the man *solely* so defined is inauthentic man. He is shorn of uniqueness, variety, personality; he is an item within a group of identical items. Man's life is naturalized; he is born, he lives and he dies, exactly like a rabbit or a plant. As *homo sapiens* his behaviour and possibilities conform rigidly to the pattern imposed by the laws operative within his group. He cannot be said to *exist*— rather, he simply *occurs*! Such then is, in outline, Heidegger's picture of inauthentic man, the man who has been dehumanized, shrunk and paralyzed by being exhaustively understood in scientific categories, as a mere thing or substance within the interlocking processes of nature.

We turn now to a sketch of what Heidegger means by *authentic* existence. If we can keep in mind the main characteristics of inauthentic existence in the order given above, we shall more readily grasp Heidegger's meaning. Authentic man

[1] See Ogden's *The Temporality of God*.
[2] *Being and Time*, pp. 420 f.
[3] *Op. cit.*, pp. 42 f.

does not understand himself in a purely scientific way. He does not regard himself as a completed thing or a shaped substance, but rather as a being to be understood in terms of his existential possibilities, of what he might yet be, of what he is called to be. Nor can these possibilities be grasped by science. The truly existing man's set of possibilities are unique to himself. Heidegger describes this uniqueness by saying that there attaches to man "thrownness" (*Geworfenheit*).[1] By being "thrown", so to speak, into life at a certain point at a certain time with a certain genetic inheritance, a man's possibilities are limited and uniquely grouped. Each man has to come to terms with his own possibilities for himself. Authentic man does not model his life upon the demands of the impersonal and sinister "One", but upon the demand laid upon him by his possibilities. He is thus delivered from suffocating, smothering anonymity. Authentic man is thus opened up to "becoming" in a unique sense. No longer is he an item or substance of nature, fixed, hardened, shaped, completed, finalized. What he truly "is" yet lies before him.

Authentic man's awareness, like inauthentic man's, is from time to time flooded by anxiety. This anxiety is rooted in the awareness he has occasionally of his possibilities, his real, future self which beckons him, challenging him to understand his being in the light of his future and not of his past. But unlike inauthentic man, authentic man does not flee panic-stricken from anxiety to immerse himself cosily in the mass, in the average, in the uniformities and familiarities of nature. Rather does he fully accept and suffer anxiety, allowing it to drive him in the direction of authentic existence. Likewise the man on the way to authenticity hearkens to the voice of conscience. But he does not confuse this with the demand for conformity proceeding from the impersonal "One". He acknowledges that this voice proceeds mysteriously from that future self of his which is disclosed in his possibilities, that self which from time to time demands of him its own actualization. When he acknowledges this voice and its source authentic man experiences *guilt*. This is rooted in the awareness he has of his tragic alienation from his future, authentic self, an awareness which occasionally pierces the protective

[1] *Being and Time*, pp. 135 and 179.

shell within which inauthentic man usually protects himself.

The man on the way to authenticity does not understand his time in the mathematical, vulgar way. He squarely faces his past with its record of inauthenticity, his past which has determined what he is now. But he realizes that his responsibility is towards his future self disclosed in his possibilities. Whether or not authenticity is achieved depends upon how man reacts to this present responsibility. If he evades it, and allows an unbroken continuity to bridge past and future in the present, he remains sunk in inauthenticity. But if he accepts it, and by resolve or decision in the present modifies his self in the light of his possibilities, authenticity of existence becomes possible and actual. The causal nexus between past and future is broken. Thus human temporality differs radically from that which belongs to natural objects and processes, the temporality of science. It means that man must not be understood as a natural object, substance or process. He must not be defined merely as the member of a class, group or species, shorn of his uniqueness and behaving mechanically according to the laws of his group. Rather does man belong to the dimension of *history* rather than nature—to the realm of existential possibilities rather than that of rigidly operative laws. Authentic man does not *occur*—he *exists*.

In the light of the various modes of existence described by Heidegger, Bultmann approaches his data, the materials of the Christian faith, in the attempt to make that faith relevant for twentieth-century man. We must now try to give a brief sketch of that faith interpreted in the light of the philosophy of human existence. According to Bultmann, the Christian faith also regards man not as a natural, completed entity or substance, but as an uniquely personal individual, created in God's image, who cares for and encounters each person in his own way and according to his own "thrownness". For the Christian faith too, man is always "on the way"; he is never at peace, but forever restlessly seeks himself, trying to "find himself". The New Testament speaks of losing one's life or finding it. The New Testament is also clear that man's being is flooded by anxiety; he is divided against himself. Continually he tries to find his security in earthly, material things. At the same time he is not left in peace in the idolatry of the tangible and the disposable. Sunk in the world, man yet feels that the world threatens his true existence—he therefore feels unease. The Christian faith therefore portrays man's life as a battlefield; man is "at war with himself". His lack of peace also comes from conscience, whose commands transcend the conventional commands of morality, reminding man of the fundamental alienation of his empirical, here-and-now self from what he should be and what he must become. This awareness of guilt is a prerequisite of Christian conversion.

The Christian conception of time also differs radically from what Heidegger calls the "vulgar" conception.[1] For Christianity, the man constituted by his sinful past may remain immersed in his sinfulness; the causal nexus between past and future may remain unbroken. At this point there emerges clearly Bultmann's sharp break with Heideggerian conceptions. Bultmann denies that this causal connection between past and future can be fractured by any power innate in man. He rejects Heidegger's view that by the call of conscience man may resolve to break with his inauthentic, sinful past. Rather does he insist that this break can only come about by the action, the grace of God, who in Christ offers to free man from the grip of the past. God in Christ offers man the power whereby in the present moment the grip of the sinful past is broken, so that man is free for a new kind of future, in which, freed from the torment of worldly cares and concerns, he can serve God and his neighbour. God *alone* grants man those possibilities which he lost in his sinful past.

Nor does this happen only once—again and again, in the proclamation of His word of grace, forgiveness and power, God thus acts towards man. This event, the event of God's liberating action towards man, is for Bultmann the *eschatological* event—the *end*-event, the event of the *last things*, which marks the end of man's old, sinful, inauthentic existence, and gives him the possibility of a new, authentic existence, for which he was originally intended and from which he was alienated. The heart of Christianity is to be sought in that moment in which the causal nexus between

[1] The authentic Christian's "past and future become more than pure time as it is marked on a calendar or a timetable", Bultmann, *Jesus Christ and Mythology*, London, 1953, p. 75.

inauthentic past and future is broken through a decision made possible by God's grace alone. Again and again in his historical existence man is brought into situations in which he alone must decide; thus the Christian life is one of repeated encounters with the grace of God. Only through these encounters and decisions can man's possibilities be realized. Man's authentic self is always his future self. Thus man belongs to the sphere of *history* rather than *nature*; that is, he belongs to the realm of possibility rather than the realm of law.[1]

This type of Christianity is, roughly speaking, what Bultmann emerges with after his encounter with the New Testament. When he approaches the New Testament, the question which is uppermost in his mind is: What does this passage, text or saying have to say about human existence (in the sense in which it has been analysed above)? Indeed, he is convinced that this is the *only* legitimate question with which to approach the biblical text. His view is that biblical statements are to be translated, completely and exhaustively, into existential ones, so that the Bible becomes once again relevant for modern man. He is convinced that the Bible has in our time become dangerously incomprehensible and irrelevant for modern man. This is because modern man's thought-forms and language differ enormously from those of the first century when the New Testament was written.

For example, the biblical writers appear to introduce God as a cosmic force or power into nature—when they speak of God stilling a storm or healing an illness. Modern man, who is used to understanding nature in scientific categories, simply does not understand what this means. The danger, according to Bultmann, is that modern man might therefore summarily dismiss the biblical message as pre-scientific childishness, never realizing that it is of incalculable significance for his real life. Again, the Bible sometimes speaks of God in the system of concepts (*Begrifflichkeit*) of an outmoded first-century world-view which is not, cannot be, modern man's. The biblical message appears at times linked firmly to a first-century cosmology in which the universe appears as a finite three-layered system. The biblical account of the Ascension

[1] Bultmann, *History and Eschatology*, Gifford Lectures, 1955, Edinburgh, 1957.

of Christ, for example, appears to presuppose such a dated, pre-Copernican cosmology. And to describe the work of Christ in terms of the exorcism of evil supernatural spirits appears also to belong to a world-view which can no longer be that of modern man.

Again, the Bible at times appears to *objectify* God. It makes him an object open to the scrutiny and observation of all and sundry. Presumably, when in the Passion Narrative the evangelists state that the death of Jesus was accompanied by the opening of graves and the walking about of the dead, they mean that this display of divine power was experienced by all and sundry who happened to observe it, without any decision or personal commitment on their part. But modern man (both inside and outside the Church) can observe nothing of the kind in his experience, and so feels intensely puzzled by these biblical accounts. Bultmann is of course intensely sympathetic towards modern man, and so suggests that this biblical talk should be translated into discourse which is relevant for his contemporaries who wrestle with the issues of human existence.

Hence we have Bultmann's proposal to *demythologize* the New Testament. Those elements listed above which are, according to Bultmann, incomprehensible to modern man, first-century cosmology, primitive science, and objectifying talk about God, are called by Bultmann "*myth*", which, he is convinced, must be interpreted as or translated into *existential* discourse, so that the Bible can once more become relevant. The choice of the English translation "demythologize" has of course been unfortunate from Bultmann's point of view, suggesting, as it does, to Anglo-Saxon ears, "the elimination of fairy-tales" from the New Testament! The German word translated as "demythologize", *entmythologisieren*, would of course have been far better translated as "*de-objectify*", or "*existentialise*", or *de-generalize*", or something of the kind. It means really "to translate exhaustively into existential terminology", a proposal of Bultmann's at which we shall have to look closely below.

We must now try to reach some estimate of Bultmann's understanding of Christianity. Bultmann's philosophical theology is extremely interesting, because it represents one of the most significant twentieth-century attempts at a synthesis of the

Christian faith and secular thought. As such, it has evoked truly world-wide interest and controversy. It has been accompanied and followed by the international publication of a host of books, papers, article, pamphlets and essays, some in attack, some in defence, of Bultmann's proposals. His work has elicited almost every conceivable response, ranging from enthusiastic gratitude to condemnatory horror. Unfortunately, we only have space here to look at a very brief selection of controversial elements in Bultmann's synthesis. Moreover, we must limit ourselves to a discussion of how Bultmann's account of Christianity appears to the philosopher concerned with the philosophical evaluation of religion.

The attempt to describe the reactions of biblical, historical, dogmatic and pastoral theologians falls, unfortunately, outside the scope of this book. And these reactions have been fully described elsewhere. We wish to argue here that the interest and relevance of Bultmann's work, and the main philosophical difficulties it causes, mushroom around his main thesis—that all theological and biblical discourse must be translated *exhaustively*, *absolutely*, into discourse about man's existence. By making and implementing this proposal Bultmann has tried to fulfil his original intention, to make Christianity relevant to the issues which concern and perplex man. And it can hardly be doubted that he has succeeded in linking Christian belief firmly to human concerns, questionings, purposes and aspirations. In order to grasp the centrality of Bultmann's main thesis, let us pay attention to the weight of the evidence in Bultmann's writings.

"To speak of the act of God," says Bultmann, "means to speak at the same time of my existence."[1] To speak of God's act means ". . . our being addressed by God here and now, our being questioned, judged, and blessed by him".[2] To speak of God as Creator is merely to ". . . understand myself here and now existentially to be the creature of God".[3] Bultmann is convinced that "we cannot speak of an act of God without speaking simultaneously of our own existence".[4] He defines

[1] *Kerygma and Myth*, London, 1953, p. 196.
[2] *Op. cit.*, pp. 196–7.
[3] *Op. cit.*, p. 198; cf. *Jesus Christ and Mythology*, p. 69.
[4] *Kerygma and Myth*, p. 199.

"faith" as "a new understanding of existence".[1] He proposes the exhaustive translation of theological into anthropological statements when he insists that ". . . a theological proposition can only be valid when it can show itself to be a genuine component part of the Christian understanding of human existence".[2] Distinctively Christian faith is that which holds that "God acts on me, speaks to me, here and now".[3]

God can only be defined as "the power which bestows upon me life and existence".[4] Bultmann confines God to the existential sphere when he insists that he cannot speak of God's activity in general statements acceptable to anyone and everyone: "I can speak only of what He does here and now with me, of what He speaks here and now to me."[5] To speak of God as acting only makes sense for him if "we mean that we are confronted with God, addressed, asked, judged, or blessed by God"; such speech involves "the events of personal existence".[6] In other words, "only such statements about God are legitimate as express the existential relation between God and man".[7] The only legitimate interpretation of language referring to God's actions is that "God is a personal being acting on persons".[8] Can we not then speak of God as He is apart from His relationship with His creatures? No, answers Bultmann, "we cannot speak of what God is in Himself but only of what He is doing to us and with us",[9] or "only in the sense that He acts with me here and now".[10]

He gives a statement of his main theological intention when he replies to a critic: "I *am* trying to substitute anthropology for theology, for I am interpreting theological affirmations as assertions about human life."[11] He says much the same thing when he confesses that "the God of the Christian revelation

---

[1] *Op. cit.*, p. 202.
[2] *Essays: Philosophical and Theological*, p. 259.
[3] *Jesus Christ and Mythology*, p. 64.
[4] *Op. cit.*, p. 66.
[5] *Ibid.*
[6] *Op. cit.*, p. 68.
[7] *Op. cit.*, p. 69.
[8] *Op. cit.*, p. 70.
[9] *Op. cit.*, p. 73.
[10] *Op. cit.*, p. 78.
[11] *Kerygma and Myth*, p. 107.

is the answer to the vital questions, the existential questions".[1] The sheer weight of evidence for Bultmann's central proposal, to transpose the language of religion and theology into the language of human existence, and *no more*, is pretty considerable. To an examination of this proposal we must now turn.

Terrific controversy has raged over Bultmann's insistence upon this "no more". It is easy to see why. On the face of it, his critics feel consternation at Bultmann's proposals, because in spite of his protests to the contrary, they suspect that Bultmann has *reduced* theology to anthropology. Whether this is so or not, and we must raise the question below, most people will agree with John Macquarrie when he asks "whether this approach (of Bultmann's) does not detach theology from any religious basis in the activity of God, so that . . . theology itself would have ceased, and have passed over into philosophy".[2] Macquarrie feels that Bultmann's account of Christianity needs to be supplemented; "room must also be found for that transcendent element which cannot be existentially translated".[3]

But what is this transcendent element resistant to existential translation, this dimension of theology which is "more than" the merely existential? There is one term which Bultmann never tries to translate—the term "God" itself. But the philosopher will complain that Bultmann uses this term in a curiously limited way, a way which appears to reduce the scope of the conception of God. He will not deny that for Christian belief God has certainly always been He "who addresses *me*, questions *me*, blesses *me*, creates *me*, acts upon *me*, speaks to *me*, forgives *me*, and gives *me* life and existence". But he will ask if the term "God" in Christian circles has not been considerably "more than" this. He might, for example, point out that the concept "God" is one with a very long and complex history indeed, a history not identifiable with the personal histories of individual believers who acknowledge God's action towards them. The concept "God" has had a long history in the rational reflection of saints, theologians,

---

[1] *Op. cit.*, p. 108.
[2] *An Existentialist Theology*, London, 1955, p. 243.
[3] *Op. cit.*, p. 244.

philosophers and ecclesiastical councils, and has been gradually built up in and through this history.

If we do not misunderstand the terms, is not the concept "God" a *communal* and *ecclesiastical* one? Moreover, the philosopher may ask bluntly: Have not the Bible, the Creeds and the theologians spoken freely not only of what God *does* towards, in or for *me*, but also of what God *is in himself*, apart from his relationships with His creatures? For example, when theologians have spoken of God's *creative* activity, have they not meant by this "more than" my self-understanding as a creature totally dependent upon God at all times? Have they not also meant that God has somehow called into being all that is, all reality, including the physical cosmos, its contents, and the laws according to which it operates? To summarize some of these philosophical objections to Bultmann's use of the term "God", the philosopher may ask if the term is not a very much more complex one than Bultmann appears to allow, having been built up gradually over a long stretch of time, absorbing from differing contexts various constitutive elements which greatly transcend *my* experiences of or encounters with Him — elements deriving from rational reflection, theological contemplation, ecclesiastical deliberation, and the historical, communal experience of believers not only in the Christian tradition, but also in the Judaic one? It is hard to withhold sympathy from him if he complains that Bultmann appears to have eliminated many of these elements from the term when he confines the term "God" exclusively to the sphere of human existence, as he understands it. It is this elimination that shows that the complaint that Bultmann has eliminated God from his account of Christianity is not completely irrelevant. At any rate, it seems hard for Bultmann to defend himself against the accusation that in using the term "God" purely existentially, he has so reduced its scope that he has transformed its traditional meaning.

Nevertheless, in spite of Bultmann's curious use of the term "God", we must go on to enquire why he uses it as he does. Clearly, his translation of all theological language into existential (or anthropological) is not capricious or arbitrary. The reasons for it lie in the various philosophical and theological influences which are discernible in his work. Clearly, one set of such influences emanates from the nineteenth century, and from the Ritschlian school in particular, and to an examination of some of these we now turn.[1] It would be odd if Bultmann showed no signs of having been influenced by the Ritschlian tradition, since, as we noted, he was educated within two neo-Kantian, Ritschlian theological schools. Thus there is a sense in which Bultmann stands within the Ritschlian theological tradition.

For example, he is averse, as were all the Ritschlians, to metaphysical arguments for a theistic standpoint. Again and again he firmly refuses to allow that God's existence or activity is *objectively* discernible—that is, apart from faith and commitment. "God withdraws himself," writes Bultmann, "from the objective view; he can only be believed upon in defiance of all outward appearance."[2] Faith cannot be proved, says Bultmann, for "if it were susceptible to proof it would mean that we could know and establish God apart from faith, and that would be placing Him on a level with the world of tangible, objective reality".[3] He puts this another way when he writes that "God's handiwork cannot be labelled and docketed like the work of an artist or an engineer."[4] Faith "demands to be freed from any world-view produced by man's thought, whether mythological or scientific".[5] God "withholds Himself from view and observation".[6] So far as *observation* of God and his works is concerned, "the whole of nature and history is profane",[7] "the framework of nature and history is profane".[8] That is, "we can believe in God only in spite of experience".[9] Bultmann is just as adamant as were all the Ritschlians that man's "pure reason" is incapable of constructing a view of reality sympathetic to religious beliefs and attitudes, or of discerning God's existence or activity.

If Bultmann resembles Ritschl in his aversion to rational

---

[1] In the discussion which follows, cf. pp. 86 f. above, chapter two.

[2] *Kerygma and Myth*, p. 210.

[3] *Op. cit.*, p. 201.

[4] *Op. cit.*, p. 121.

[5] *Jesus Christ and Mythology*, p. 83.

[6] *Op. cit.*, p. 84.

[7] *Op. cit.*, p. 85.

[8] *Kerygma and Myth*, p. 211.

[9] *Jesus Christ and Mythology*, p. 84.

theology, the resemblance between them is no less striking in the *anthropocentric* character of both their theologies. This resemblance comes out in various ways. There is, for instance, a curious resemblance between the way in which Bultmann has been influenced by a philosopher like Heidegger and the way in which Ritschl was influenced by a philosopher like Lotze.[1] Under Lotzean influence, Ritschl had stressed the religious significance of man's uniqueness as a creature of moral worth over against the indifferent, impersonal world of nature as portrayed by nineteenth-century scientific naturalism. Under Heideggerian influence, Bultmann has emphasized the religious significance of human existence over against the sinister dehumanization of man implicit both in Cartesian thinking and in his life in scientific and techno-logical societies. In a sense, the slogan "Spirit over Nature" is just as applicable to Bultmann's theology as it was to Ritschl's. The similarity is of significance, because it indicates that Bultmann's theology might run into difficulties parallel to those which, we discovered, were encountered by Ritschl's.[2]

And this, we argue, is what has happened. For example, in the long run, in Bultmann's view man's attitude to Christian belief depends upon his attitude to himself. More precisely, it depends upon the extent to which he experiences the threat to his authentic existence implicit in scientific attitudes and in modern mass-society. Now this threat may be a very real one. Twentieth-century existentialist philosophy as a whole has protested vigorously against the contemporary insidious dehumanization of man. And naturally in this situation Christianity can be seen to possess great relevance indeed — a relevance heavily underlined by Bultmann's theology. Nevertheless, it must be conceded that if man's uniqueness, individuality, authenticity and personal worth, his radical dissimilarity to the objects and processes of nature, can be guaranteed by appeals to considerations other than Christian ones, then so much the worse for the uniqueness of Christianity. But this is almost exactly the same criticism we made earlier of Ritschl's apologetic theology.[3] In that case we argued that

[1] See above, pp. 81 f.
[2] See above, pp. 87 f.
[3] *Loc. cit.*

169

if the nature-man conflict should somehow be resolved, this would have the tendency towards making Ritschl's talk of value-judgments, and so of God, irrelevant. And this appears to be a danger against which Bultmann's theology also is vulnerable.

But even if the conflict between, on the one hand, the man pursuing authenticity of life and, on the other, contemporary dehumanization and anonymity cannot be easily resolved in the foreseeable future, another danger arises. Man may have at his disposal means of guaranteeing authentic existence other than religious ones. Here there spring to mind possibilities such as the arts, literature, music, and other aesthetic pursuits. And, paradoxically, amongst such possibilities must be included certain philosophical tendencies, including existentialism itself! Now existentialism *may* take religious forms, and in the case of thinkers like Kierkegaard, Bultmann, Marcel and Maritain, has done so, but this is by no means necessary. Heidegger himself leaves the question of God open; he has described the transition from inauthentic to authentic existence as occurring through man's decision, through his resolve, without dependence upon any power or factor approaching man from outside himself. Indeed, recalling Heidegger's dependence upon theologians like St. Augustine, Luther and Kierkegaard, his analysis of man could be described as the Christian one from which God had been eliminated!

Another existentialist philosopher, Karl Jaspers (b. 1883), also reacting against contemporary dehumanizing tendencies, holds that man's real life (which he describes as "transcendence") may be grasped without appeal to any special or unique "act of God". The power to lay hold of such real life is, for Jaspers, built into the structure of all human existence as such. Now of course Bultmann breaks with such existentialists at this point, insisting that it is only through God's gracious here-and-now activity that authentic life becomes possible. Nonetheless, the fact that existentialist philosophy, contending for human uniqueness and freedom over against contemporary dehumanization, can dispense with all talk of God and of special divine activity, draws attention sharply to the dangerous direction in which Bultmann's theology has been moving. That is, if existentialist philosophy can be a useful ally for the Christian apologist (and Bultmann has shown that it can), it may also be a secular competitor of Christianity, and one to be reckoned with at that. But this danger of *secularization* was one which Ritschl's theology also encountered.[1] In Ritschlian theology, the God who functions as a prop for man's ethical aspiration over against the pressure of nature has to face heavy *secular* competition in fulfilling his task. Similarly, if *adequate* secular methods of combating dehumanization and of reaching authentic existence were found, the possibility might arise that Bultmann's conception of God too would be regarded as redundant.

Another obvious similarity between Ritschl and Bultmann is that whereas the former insisted upon confining all theological statements to value-statements, the latter confines them to existential statements. There is clearly a similarity between the unique value God has for one's soul (Ritschl), and the unique significance God has for one's authentic existence (Bultmann).[2] The interesting question here is that just as Ritschl's theology tended to slide over into mere anthropology, and seemed vulnerable to attack by psychological naturalism,[3] does Bultmann's exhibit the same tendencies? Bultmann is clear that his theology might be considered vulnerable to similar criticisms to those directed against theologies like Ritschl's, and so takes pains to cover himself against them. Bultmann insists therefore that although the believer cannot speak of God without speaking about his own existence, "it by no means follows that God has no real existence apart from the believer or the act of believing".[4] That is, "that God cannot be seen apart from faith does not mean that He does not exist apart from it".[5] He denies that his theology means "that God's action is deprived of objective reality, that it is reduced to a purely subjective, psychological experience".[6]

[1] See above, pp. 86 f.

[2] For the similarities between the position of Bultmann and Ritschl see Paul Althaus, *The So-Called Kerygma and the Historical Jesus*, pp. 83 f., and John Macquarrie, *The Scope of Demythologizing*, London, 1960, pp. 117 f. and 123 f.

[3] See above, pp. 90 f.

[4] *Kerygma and Myth*, p. 199.

[5] *Op. cit.*, pp. 200–1.

[6] *Jesus Christ and Mythology*, p. 70.

God does not exist "only as an inner event in the soul".[1]

On the contrary, God does have a real, objective existence apart from and outside of the believer. What does Bultmann mean by this? He tries to impart his meaning by means of an analogy. He points out that our authentic existence is constituted, and our real being built up and enriched through the *encounters* we have with other persons, encounters of love, trust, devotion, and so on. Through relationships with wives, husbands, children and friends our existence is enriched and transformed, and our real being forged. So too our authentic existence is forged by means of those occasions when we *encounter* God, hearing His word addressed to us personally, a word significant for our existence, uniquely enabling us to lay hold of our real, future being. And just as a believer's wife or children, who constitute his existence, have a real existence apart from and independently of him, so too God, who constitutes his authentic being in encounters, also exists apart from and independently of the believer. And just as the love between a man and his wife cannot be objectively discerned by a spectator, and is capable of "naturalistic" explanation by a psychologist, likewise the relationship between the believer and God cannot be objectively observed, demonstrated, proved or disproved. When we encounter other human existents and God the main point is that "in each case we are no longer the same after the encounter as before it".[2] Thus Bultmann tries to guard against the psychological attacks made against nineteenth-century anthropocentric theologians.

This is an extremely interesting account of the life of the believer, and we must ask if Bultmann has defended it sufficiently against the criticism of the philosopher that for him God has no existence apart from the believer, or act of believing. It seems that the philosopher may have four points that he can raise against Bultmann. First, he can argue that Bultmann's analogy is not altogether a satisfactory one, because there are certain crucial differences between the believer's wife or child on the one hand and God on the other. Although he may concede that the inner nature of the relationship

[1] *Ibid.*
[2] *Kerygma and Myth*, p. 200.

(e.g., love, trust, devotion) cannot be demonstrated or observed in both cases, he may point out that the believer has incomparably better grounds for believing in the *factual* existence of his wife or child than in the factual existence of God. In the former case he has the evidence of sense-experience (e.g. sight, touch, hearing) which Bultmann would strongly forbid him in the latter. He might therefore conclude that Bultmann's analogy between our relationships with human existents and our relationships with God is not altogether satisfactory.

Second, he could argue that a man's existence may be as readily changed by holding a false belief as by a true one. If a man believes himself to have moral freedom, this may make a considerable psychological difference to his conduct and character. If he believes that his sins are forgiven by God, this may assist him to accept himself and deliver him from crippling self-loathing, making a large difference indeed to his existence. A *transforming* "encounter" (or experience) *by itself* does not guarantee that what is "encountered" exists factually outside, apart from and independently of him.

Third, the philosopher may object that even if Bultmann's analogy were sound, it implies that for Bultmann God is just another factor (even the most significant factor), which assists the achievement of authentic existence. And he may protest that this is more proof that Bultmann has a *reduced* conception of God, having confined him to the sphere of human existence. Nor does such a protest come only from the philosopher; a distinguished theologian has recently protested that for Bultmann "God can . . . only become perceptible in his function of serving man's interest in authenticity".[1] Bultmann reduces the Christian faith "to those statements which have to do with the interest of man".[2] The gist of this criticism is that Bultmann has not simply re-interpreted but also somewhat transformed Christian language about God.

Fourth, the philosopher may confess a certain unease about an ambiguity in Bultmann's concept of encounter. Although Bultmann loudly insists upon God's independent existence "apart from" the believer's "encounter" with him, he

[1] Helmut Gollwitzer, *The Existence of God As Confessed by Faith*, p. 33.
[2] *Ibid.*

sternly forbids any investigation of or talk of this "apart from". Hence the philosopher's bewilderment — "God" is not just a description given to a (hidden) transforming experience, but what he is "more than" this he is forbidden by Bultmann to investigate or talk about! Hence the ambiguity in Bultmann is that despite his sincere protests about God's objective existence, his language "could also be taken to mean that God's being is identical with the event of this encounter . . . , that 'God' is a title for this event and this experience, and that to make any confession of a real being of God outside this event is already to fall into an objectifying metaphysic".[1]

What do such criticisms add up to? In general, they remind us of the great amount of common ground shared by Bultmann and Barth, of which we spoke earlier. Both have overstressed the theological impotence of reflective reason; both have insisted that nature, history and moral experience are utterly devoid of any evidence whatever which would lend support to religious belief. The philosophical and theological critic is therefore surely justified in asking that Bultmann's account of Christian faith be supplemented by wider grounds by means of which it can be defended and commended.

Finally, there is another influence operating in Bultmann's theology, an understanding of which helps to clarify his conception of God — the effect of Lutheranism in general, and Luther's interpretation of the Pauline doctrine of justification by faith in particular. Luther had taught that to be justified by God involves the radical abandonment of all attempts to find security through merely human works and achievements. Justification depends upon perfect faith and absolute trust *in God alone*. Now Bultmann obviously has widened (as have many German theologians under Luther's influence) the scope of such "works" or "achievements". They include for him not merely "works of the Law" (attempts at moral self-improvement through outward obedience to a moral code), and dependence upon the efficacy of an outward religious rite (such as the rite of circumcision), against which St. Paul had argued so fiercely in his Epistles, but also works of *knowledge* or *speculation*, by means of which a man might claim to apprehend something of God, apart from justifying faith

[1] *Op. cit.*, p. 34.

itself. Thus Bultmann holds that "we can believe in God only *in spite of* experience, just as we can accept justification only *in spite of* conscience".[1] "There is," writes Bultmann, "no difference between security based on good works and security based on *objectifying knowledge*."[2]

Heinz Zahrnt is right when he says that Bultmann "fights for the preservation of the *sola fide* of the Reformation".[3] John Macquarrie tells us that Karl Barth has concluded of Bultmann that he "is simply a Lutheran, with Herrmann, Ritschl, Melancthon and Luther himself behind him",[4] and "that Bultmann tends to make the Pauline writings a 'canon within the canon', as followers of Luther have often done".[5] Clearly one's estimate of this Lutheran influence upon Bultmann will depend largely upon one's estimate of Lutheran theology in general. But speaking from the side of the philosopher, it is clear that Luther's utter rejection of all rational attempts to gain knowledge of God is very problematic indeed. He will almost certainly agree with A. E. Taylor that although vital theology and religion cannot get along without God's revelation and self-disclosure, the average man "cannot be expected to receive anything as such a communication from God until he is at least satisfied that it is reasonable to believe that there is Some One to make the communication".[6]

Nor will the philosopher find support here from his philosophical colleagues alone; the Lutheran rejection of *all* natural knowledge of God is unacceptable to many theologians, especially those concerned with the theology of the Old Testament. Many of these would argue that within the Old Testament writings we can perceive the firm outlines of the Hebrew-Christian concept of God taking shape, a concept which forms the backcloth against which the work and teaching of Jesus has its meaning, and one which for long has been central to the dialogue between theologians and philosophers. Old Testament theologians have exhibited considerable unease about Bultmann's negative attitude to the

[1] *Jesus Christ and Mythology*, p. 84, italics mine.
[2] *Ibid.*, italics mine.
[3] *The Historical Jesus*, London, 1963, pp. 88–9.
[4] *The Scope of Demythologizing*, p. 123.
[5] *Op. cit.*, p. 170.
[6] *Does God Exist?*, p. 7.

Old Testament. Particularly, they have been disturbed about some statements of his such as "to the Christian faith the Old Testament is no longer revelation", and "to us the history of Israel is not history of revelation".[1] Thus biblical theologians have cast doubt upon his extremely sceptical attitude to knowledge of God apart from that knowledge implicit in here-and-now, God-elicited faith.

We have been critical of Bultmann's theological proposals and have pointed out the perplexities involved in his conception of religious belief. Nonetheless, in Bultmann's as in Barth's case, we must acknowledge the immense debt of gratitude contemporary philosophical theology owes to him. It is to Bultmann's great credit that he has made out such a positive case for man's essentially "religious" nature. That is, that man's essential nature is pervaded and shot through with inalienable and profound questionings, anxieties, thrusts and drives, which propel him towards that vital point where a decision about religious belief becomes agonizingly urgent. In doing so, Bultmann, influenced by modern existentialist analyses of man, has fatally undermined the acceptability of the Cartesian caricature of man as a finished, polished piece of thinking substance, whose sole object is to penetrate the structure of physical nature as an inert and impersonal collection of objects over against him. In the fulfilment of this task, Bultmann has worked out an interpretation of religious belief which modern philosophical theology cannot ignore except at its peril.

Yet, having examined Bultmann's theology and having grasped gratefully its significance for our thinking, we must go on to enquire about the possibility of wider grounds for a religious outlook upon things than he would allow. That is, to ask if twentieth-century man can find an over-all conception of reality within which religious beliefs, attitudes and practices make sense. To such an enquiry we now turn.

[1] From Bultmann's paper, "The Significance of the Old Testament for the Christian Faith", *The Old Testament and the Christian Faith*, p. 31; the entire volume is very relevant for Bultmann's theological position. Bultmann's paper is interesting if read in conjunction with his essay, "The Significance of Jewish Old Testament Tradition for the Christian West", *Essays: Philosophical and Theological*, pp. 262–72.

Chapter Six

LANGUAGE, GOD AND METAPHYSICS

IN the last two chapters we have looked at thinkers in the Continental tradition. But in this chapter we consider the theological discussions of philosophers who have worked within and influenced the Anglo-Saxon tradition. Without being unduly dogmatic, we may say that since the First World War Anglo-Saxon philosophers, particularly in England, and more particularly within the universities of Cambridge and Oxford, have tried to limit philosophy fairly strictly to the *analysis* of words, concepts, sentences, statements and propositions. They have been interested in the ways in which language works and should work. They have been interested in the *logic* of language. Such philosophical work has therefore been labelled the philosophy of linguistic analysis, analytic philosophy, philosophical analysis, or something of the kind. The words *analytic* and *analysis* here are used in strict contradistinction to *synthetic* and *synthesis*. That is, analytic philosophers have generally held that philosophical synthesis, the construction of a unified, overall, encyclopaedic view of reality, is to be regarded as an impossible and therefore a futile task. This rejection of synthetic philosophy implies of course the abandonment of the age-old view that philosophy's subject-matter concerns some ultimate, metaphysical, or supersensible sphere. Rather, the subject-matter of philosophy concerns the everyday, commonsense world of man's experience in space and time, and the language he uses to describe it.

Another significant aspect of analytic philosophy is its almost obsessive concern with concepts like *meaning, meaningful* and *non-meaningful* (or *nonsensical*). Analytic philosophers have occupied themselves with distinguishing strictly between meaningful and meaningless propositions, a distinction fraught with significance for their attitude to religious or theological language. Without being unduly dogmatic again, we can say that there has been a tendency to single out two broad classes of meaningful utterance. The first class are those that can be labelled as *definitions*. In a definition-sentence the predicate term merely *defines* the subject term; or, since the predicate *analyses* the subject, the sentence may be called *analytic*. We can put this in several other ways. Since in such a sentence the predicate simply repeats in a different form what is already implicit in the subject, the sentence in question can be called a *tautology*. Or an analytic or tautologous proposition, a definition, may be defined as one the denial of which is self-contradictory.

It is not hard to think of examples of such analytic propositions. They occur fairly frequently, for example, in mathematics and logic. Given that $x = 2$, the statement $6 = 3x$ is analytic and tautologous. In everyday discourse too, much of our language is analytic. Thus, "all spinsters are unmarried women" is an analytic proposition, since the phrase "unmarried women" *analyses* or *defines* the term "spinsters". Clearly also much theological language is analytic. The proposition "God is immortal" is analytic, because implicit in the notion of "God" is the idea of "not being subject to death". The proposition "God is mortal" is a *nonsensical* one, since it fails to define correctly the concept "God". That is, it fails to use linguistic symbols correctly. It might likewise be argued that all propositions denying God's essential attributes, such as "omnipotence", "omnipresence", "omniscience", and so on, are nonsensical for the same reason. Such considerations bring us to what is, from our point of view, the most significant aspect of analytic statements. The fact that such propositions as "all spinsters are unmarried women" and "God is immortal" are *analytically* meaningful, does not mean that either "spinsters" or "God" actually exist. The concession that these propositions are meaningful only means that they use words and symbols in a correct, that is, generally-agreed way. But they do not establish facts, either that there are actually unmarried women in the world, or that the world is God-created or God-governed. Since they are not factual, and do not give us information or knowledge about what exists in reality, such merely analytic propositions are generally described as *non-cognitive*.

The second type of statement admitted to be meaningful by philosophical analysts is a *synthetic* one (i.e. a factual one, claiming to give us knowledge about reality), which is capable of being broken down into further statements, or of being translated into another statement, which refer to or describe tests or experiences which would tend either to *verify* or *falsify* the statement. In such a statement the predicate term does not analyse or define the subject term, but makes an assertion about the subject of the statement which can, in principle at least, be checked or tested in some way. It thus claims to be *cognitive*. Its meaningfulness depends upon the possibility (even if it is only a remote or future one), of its being shown to be true or false in a factual sense. Thus the proposition that "one volume of water yields 1,696 volumes of vapour at atmospheric pressure" only has meaning if tests can be conducted to show its truth or falsity. If the possibility of such tests were quite out of the question, the proposition would have to be abandoned as meaningless. Even the proposition "the other side of the moon is made of chocolate" is meaningful, for in the second half of the twentieth century it is not implausible to argue that tests to verify or falsify it, such as feeling, tasting, seeing and chemical analysis, are within the realms of possibility. Synthetic statements can be meaningful but false. But a statement which claims to give knowledge about reality and which yet is utterly incapable of being translated into a statement describing a test (or tests) which would show it to be either true or false is meaningless and nonsensical, and unworthy of serious consideration. The consideration of competing but quite untestable assertion-statements is a complete waste of time and effort.

We now enquire about how theological or religious language fares within the context of such a linguistic analysis. As we have noted, much theological language is analytic, and as such there are meaningful and meaningless ways of using it. But obviously the most important theological statements claim to be synthetic, cognitive assertions. They claim to be inter-pretations or descriptions of, or to give information about reality, and no amount of talk about Christianity being "a way of life" should be allowed to obscure this. To be sure, Christianity is a way of life, involving our subjective attitudes, decisions and perspectives, but it is a great deal more than this. It also claims to describe the ultimate nature of things and to give information about reality otherwise unobtainable. Thus, when Christians use propositions such as "God exists" or "Man is immortal soul", when they recite the Creeds or sing hymns in church, they are partly at any rate making cognitive assertions. What is the philosophical analyst's estimate of the claim of such theological statements to be cognitive? The analyst has not infrequently estimated the cognitive value of such statements by putting to them one of the forms of the so-called *verification-principle*, "the meaning of a statement is the method of its verification".

He has wanted to know if the theological statements in question can be translated into a statement (or set of statements) which refer to tests or experiences enabling us either to verify or falsify them. The meaning of a theological statement, in common with the meaning of other statements claiming to be cognitive, is the statement of *the possibilities of its verification*. Hence it has often been concluded that theological statements, for example, statements about God, the supernatural or the supersensible, are not analysable into statements about states of affairs, tests, observations or measurements which would verify or falsify the statements themselves. Analysts have not uncommonly pointed to the presence within the same world of theists and atheists, each group insisting upon the truth of its interpretation of reality, but neither possessing any means whatever of verifying its own standpoint, or of falsifying its opponents'. The conclusion about religious belief in analytic circles has therefore very often been that of radical agnosticism—*agnosticism*, we must note, and not *atheism*. An atheistic, that is, God-less interpretation of reality is just as nonsensical as a theistic one, for it claims to *know* the godlessness of reality just as a theistic one claims to have *knowledge* of the divine origin of and providence over things. For most philosophical analysts the claim that there are tests or experiences which would show the non-existence of God is just as questionable as the claim that there are tests to show the opposite.

Before taking a closer look at such an analysis of theological language, there is one question worth asking: What are the possible theological responses that can be made to it? There are (at least) three significant ones which we must note. First, if the above analysis of theological language as non-cognitive were accepted, this acceptance can lead to the complete abandonment of all attempts to find a philosophical basis for and justification of religious belief, together with the abandonment of all religious practices, attitudes and endeavours. Instead, there is accepted some attitude to the world which dispenses completely with all transcendent, supernatural reference, such as the attitude of *scientific humanism*. The agnostic humanist abandons religious attitudes and exercises because he considers (rightly, many feel) that they only make sense within the context of a philosophical outlook which holds that the universe has a theistic origin, oversight and goal. Scientific humanism is the accepted "religion" of very many in our time, simply because they feel that today, partly due to philosophical criticism, the rational grounds for a theistic viewpoint are either non-existent, or so few or thin as to be negligible.[1]

Second, it can be held that even though the "verificational analysis" (to use Frederick Ferré's term[2]) of theological language conclusively demonstrates that such language is non-cognitive (that is, that it does not yield any verifiable knowledge about the world), this does not necessarily mean that religion is thereby stripped of value, or that all religious practices and attitudes ought to be given up. Religion may have another task to perform beside that of trying to give a factual description of the ultimate nature of the universe, a task which is indispensable for man's personal, ethical and social life. Now this is clearly a very old conception of religion's function, which was common, for example, in ancient Greece and Rome.[3] Although, as we shall see below, it has become extremely widespread in the nineteen-fifties

[1] For the historical beginnings of scientific humanism in England see Rudolf Metz, *A Hundred Years of British Philosophy*, London, 1938, Part I, chapter IV.

[2] See his *Language, Logic and God*, London, 1962, chapter 2, "The Logic of Verificational Analysis", pp. 8 f.

[3] J. B. Bury, *A History of Freedom of Thought*, 2nd edition, Oxford, 1952, p. 19.

and nineteen-sixties, it is enlightening to glance at a few of the earlier versions of this view.

It was, for instance, a fairly common view of religion in the seventeenth and eighteenth centuries in England. One notable Archbishop of Canterbury, John Tillotson (1630–94), defended the Christian religion mainly, if not wholly, because it regulated civic and social life by promising rewards to the virtuous and punishments to the wicked. This tended also to be David Hume's conception of organized religion, especially so far as the lower, more uninstructed and unreflective classes were concerned. Feuerbach, whose views we examined above,[1] also held that religion was incalculably valuable so long as its statements were interpreted as applying to man rather than to God—for Feuerbach, religion had an important humanistic task to perform. Feuerbach's *The Essence of Christianity* was translated into English (in 1854), and his views popularized in England, by the novelist George Eliot (1819–80). And according to the English poet and critic Matthew Arnold (1822–88), religion's central themes are morality and conduct, which are inspired with emotional fervour by it. Arnold's *Literature and Dogma* (1873), expounding this view, was immensely influential.[2]

One of the greatest figures in the history of British philosophy, John Stuart Mill (1806–73), held that the so-called ultimate truths of religion are incapable either of proof or disproof. Nevertheless, religion had for him a certain moral utility of great benefit to human society. Especially Mill admired the moral education of children commonly undertaken in religious societies, the way in which religious beliefs engender in society public opinion which praises virtue, blames vice and fears shame. So far as the Christian religion is concerned, Mill was grateful for its assertions that the greatest are those who serve, that the weak and humble should be reverenced, and that we should do as we would be done by. Nevertheless, Mill, in trying to strip Christianity of its "rituals" and "trappings", was left with "Christianity

---

[1] See above, pp. 74 f.
[2] Cf. the account of religion given by R. B. Braithwaite, pp. 184 f. below.

without Christianity", with "something that is not much more than morality itself, but that casts a mystique of a sort around the body of moral principles".[1]

The twentieth-century Spanish-American poet and philosopher George Santayana (1863–1952), although philosophically a materialist, yet developed an impressive defence of religion, not on the grounds that its beliefs about fact were literally true (he held that they were not), but because religion provides man with lenses, so to speak, through which the world appears as a place where life demands, if it is to be lived fully and richly, love, devotion, loyalty, commitment and the other moral virtues associated with religion. The distinguished British biologist Julian Huxley, in his *Religion Without Revelation*,[2] argued that traditional religious beliefs about supernatural beings and divine revelations are in the twentieth century intellectually intolerable; so far as *describing* the real world is concerned, scientific techniques have replaced theological ones. Nonetheless, religion possesses unique value. It holds that human life is sacred, and that truth, beauty and goodness are ultimates, to be desired for their own sake. By giving up its pretensions about possessing ultimate supernatural knowledge, religion would become more accessible to more people, and would be able to contribute enormously to the progress and happiness of the human race.

It is likely that the nineteen-fifties and nineteen-sixties will be specially remembered by historians of theology because of the world-wide publication of books and articles rejecting religion as a set of doctrines giving information about the ultimate nature of things, on the ground that they are incapable of being verified or falsified, and interpreting it rather as something that engenders, reinforces or preserves certain indispensable moral attitudes or human insights. Amongst the most significant of these publications are R. B. Braithwaite's *An Empiricist's Account of the Nature of Religious Belief*,[3] J. H.

[1] From Max Lerner's introduction to *The Essential Works of John Stuart Mill*, (including his "The Utility of Religion"), New York, 1961, p. xxvii.

[2] The Thinker's Library, no. 83, London, 1941 (first published in 1927).

[3] The 9th A. S. Eddington Memorial Lecture, Cambridge, 1955; it has been reprinted in full in the collection of readings, *The Existence of God*, edited by John Hick, New York and London, 1964, pp. 229–52.

Randall's *The Role of Knowledge in Western Religion*,[1] Peter Munz's *Problems of Religious Knowledge*,[2] T. R. Miles' *Religion and the Scientific Outlook*,[3] and Paul van Buren's *The Secular Meaning of the Gospel*.[4] We have space here to glance at only two of these, perhaps the most significant of them, Braithwaite's and Van Buren's points of view.

We turn first to Braithwaite's argument. He asserts that statements whose claim to truth can be tested in some way can be divided into three classes — statements of matters of fact, scientific hypotheses and mathematical statements.[5] The first of these are verifiable (or falsifiable) by direct observation; but since it can hardly be maintained that divinity is directly observable, the significant propositions of theology do not fit into this first class.[6] And since there are no experienceable grounds for preferring a theological explanation of the world to scientific explanations supported by factual evidence, theological propositions do not fall into the second class either.[7] And since the propositions of mathematics and logic are non-cognitive, that is, since they make "no assertion about there being any things in the world",[8] theological propositions can hardly be classed with them. Although Braithwaite believes that theological statements cannot be fitted into any class of statements whose truth can be tested by generally recognized methods, he does not therefore classify them as meaningless. If, with many modern philosophers,[9] we substitute for the verification principle (the meaning of any statement is given by the method of its verification) the use-principle (the meaning of any statement is given

[1] Boston, 1958; see the discussion of Randall's position in Hick, *Philosophy of Religion*, pp. 86–8.

[2] London, 1959; see the discussion in E. L. Mascall, *The Secularization of Christianity*, London, 1965, pp. 20–1.

[3] London, 1959; see the discussion in Mascall, *op. cit.*, pp. 16–19.

[4] London, 1963; see the long discussion in Mascall, *op. cit.*, chapter II, pp. 40–105. With these five books it is interesting to read also J. N. Findlay's paper, "Can God's Existence Be Disproved?", *New Essays in Philosophical Theology* (paper-back edition), London, 1963, pp. 47–56.

[5] *An Empiricist's View of the Nature of Religious Belief*, p. 4.

[6] *Op. cit.*, pp. 4–5.

[7] *Op. cit.*, pp. 5–8.

[8] *Op. cit.*, p. 8.

[9] See pp. 198 f. below.

by the way in which it is used), Braithwaite's opinion is that *religious assertions are used for moral purposes*.

Since he believes, further, that moral propositions are used by moral agents in order to indicate their intention to follow certain moral policies, he concludes that religious assertions are used in an identical way.[1] Thus the Christian's "assertion that God is love (*agape*)" is really a declaration of "his intention to follow an agapeistic way of life".[2] One discovers what is meant by an agapeistic way of life within the context of Christianity by means of the concrete examples one finds in Christian teaching—for example, in the behaviour of the good Samaritan.[3] At this point we may want to ask—Why must we drag religion into morality? If we cannot be religious believers in a cognitive way, why cannot we simply adopt moral policies and act in accordance with them? Braithwaite's answer to this is that morality doctored with religion is superior to morality neat. The reason is that religion is concerned not only with changes in exterior behaviour-policies, but also with interior changes, changes of the heart and the feelings, with giving a new "frame of mind".[4] The Christian religion does this for moral agents because the "stories" of Christianity, when entertained in thought (without necessarily being believed as true), reinforce the agent's intention to follow the way of life enshrined in the stories; because "it is an empirical psychological fact that many people find it easier to resolve upon and to carry through a course of action which is contrary to their natural inclinations if this policy is associated in their minds with certain stories".[5]

This insight is of course a very old one, and Braithwaite rightly associates it with the views of Matthew Arnold.[6] It is interesting to compare here some words of a famous Oxford don written almost sixty years ago: "Theism of the Christian type is the creed which secures the maximum emotional hold of human Morality upon the mind. Action motived by

[1] *Op. cit.*, pp. 11–16.

[2] *Op. cit.*, p. 18.

[3] *Op. cit.*, p. 20.

[4] *Op. cit.*, pp. 21–2.

[5] *Op. cit.*, p. 27. Compare with this what we said of Kant's theory, that there is a *felt need* to believe in God, p. 48 above.

[6] *Op. cit.*, pp. 24–5.

185

no other desire than the desire to fulfil the Moral Law for its own sake, accompanied by no emotion but what is produced by the direct consciousness of duty, is undoubtedly not impossible. But such a desire is not commonly the sole or (unless reinforced by other feelings or emotions) the habitually dominant motive of action even in the best men.''[1] Beside this we may set these words of Braithwaite: ''There is one story common to all the moral theistic religions which has proved of great psychological value in enabling religious men to persevere in carrying out their religious behaviour policies — the story that in so doing they are doing the will of God.''[2]

Braithwaite's thesis has been subjected to detailed criticism since 1955 which it would be pointless to repeat here.[3] Nevertheless, there are some obvious points that we should note before leaving Braithwaite's argument. First, it is obvious that his account of Christianity is crudely ''reductionist''; in limiting the function of Christianity to that of providing stories which reinforce moral living, he has not merely reinterpreted it but has thoroughly tranformed it. Second, Braithwaite has apparently ignored that Christian attitudes, expectations, decisions, policies and actions are inextricably bound up with various beliefs *about* reality, *about* the origin, nature, and destiny of the world; he has ignored that the religious man believes ''that his religion gives him some insight into the kind of world in which he has to follow his way of life''.[4] He appears not to have taken account of the ''great extent to which it is men's beliefs about God which impel them to an agapeistic way of life''.[5]

Third, it is instructive to enquire about the *difference* (if any) between Braithwaite's position and that of sensitive and morally serious humanists. One such, R. W. Hepburn, has pointed out that one simply cannot sacrifice ''the language of 'transcendence', the thought of God as a personal being,

[1] Hastings Rashdall, *The Theory of Good and Evil*, Oxford, 1907, vol. II, p. 259.

[2] *An Empiricist's View of the Nature of Religious Belief*, pp. 30–1.

[3] See, for example, E. L. Mascall, *Words and Images*, London, 1957, chapter IV; R. W. Hepburn, *Christianity and Paradox*, London, 1958, pp. 192 f.; Frederick Ferré, *Language, Logic and God*, pp. 124–8.

[4] John Macquarrie, *Twentieth-Century Religious Thought*, p. 316.

[5] J. Hick, *Philosophy of Religion*, p. 92.

wholly other to man, dwelling apart in majesty", without leaving Christianity behind.[1] Hepburn disagrees that Braithwaite's account of Christianity is compatible with traditional Christianity,[2] and to read Hepburn leaves us in little doubt that he, regarding himself as a humanist outside the Church, holds views about the moral value of Christian stories and parables which come fairly close to those of Braithwaite.[3]

Fourth, and this point is perhaps the most important of all, we must not overlook the *structure* of Braithwaite's argument. It does little good to denigrate the account he gives of religious belief if we do not take into account his reasons for reaching it. Basic of course to Braithwaite's views on religion are his views on the *unverifiability* of theological statements, and consequently on the necessarily *non-cognitive* character of religious assertions. If we shared his views that religious statements are untestable and that consequently it is impossible to regard them as conveying knowledge of reality, it is hard to see how we could escape either agnostic humanism or the view that religion's only value is the psychological reinforcement it provides for moral living. For this reason we must soon turn to an examination of this whole business of the verification and testing of religious propositions.

We must next take a brief glance at the starting-point of Paul van Buren's *The Secular Meaning of the Gospel*.[4] In this case, considerations of space must limit our discussion to part of the basic *structure* of Van Buren's argument, especially again the extent to which his account of Christianity has been predetermined by his acceptance of a certain critique of the truth-claims of Christian language. Van Buren's case springs to a large extent out of his conviction that "few men are able today to ascribe 'reality' to (the supernatural) as they would to the things, people, or relationships which matter to them".[5]

[1] *Christianity and Paradox*, pp. 193–4.
[2] *Op. cit.*, p. 194.
[3] See e.g., p. 195.
[4] See the excellent review of Van Buren's book by Langdon B. Gilkey, "A New Linguistic Madness", *New Theology*, No. 2, edited by Martin E. Marty and Dean G. Peerman, New York, 1965, pp. 39–49; the review first appeared in *The Journal of Religion*, University of Chicago Press, July, 1964.
[5] *The Secular Meaning of the Gospel*, p. 4.

One of the reasons for this is that "our English-speaking culture has an empirical tradition and that the world today is increasingly being formed by technology and the whole industrial process".[1] The man whose life is set in the context of such a culture "thinks empirically and pragmatically".[2] Van Buren is sufficiently influenced by analytic philosophers to demand "verification"; but he puts forward a "modified" (some British philosophers would describe it as "weak") version of the verification-principle — "what sort of things would count for an assertion and what sort of things would count against it".[3]

Speaking for empiricists, he says: "We do not know 'what' God is, and we cannot understand how the word 'God' is being used".[4] The existentialist theologian's " 'non-objective' use of the word 'God' allows of no verification and is therefore meaningless".[5] He accepts enthusiastically Braithwaite's demolition of the truth-claims of traditional theological language on the ground that they are unverifiable and therefore non-cognitive.[6] He rejects the cognitive approach to theological language because "it tends to mark off a certain area of experience as 'religious', and it argues for a religious way of knowing, in contrast to other (secular?) ways of knowing".[7] For Van Buren, "the language of faith has meaning when it is taken to refer to the Christian way of life; it is not a set of cosmological assertions".[8]

He focusses attention upon a question which sharpens for him the real contemporary issue in theology: "Jesus or God, Christology or Theology?", and indicates his own preference for the former terms in these two pairs, because *the* contemporary theological problem "is that the *word* 'God' is

[1] *Op. cit.*, p. 17.
[2] *Ibid.*
[3] *Op. cit.*, p. 15.
[4] *Op. cit.*, p. 84.
[5] *Op. cit.*, p. 83. See our discussion above of Bultmann's conception of "God", where we raised the question as to the way in which God exists "apart from", "outside" the believer, pp. 171 f.
[6] *Op. cit.*, pp. 92–6.
[7] *Op. cit.*, pp. 98–9.
[8] *Op. cit.*, p. 101. Cf. Braithwaite's thesis.

dead''.[1] In this way Van Buren indicates the nature of his own theological programme as Christianity without theism, some kind of belief in Jesus of Nazareth without belief in God, since in our contemporary world the latter type of belief has become meaningless. This "Christianity without God" is described by Van Buren thus: "The Gospel claims that in the history of Jesus of Nazareth something universal, eternal, absolute, something it calls 'God' was manifested."[2] That is, "he who says, 'Jesus is Lord', says that Jesus' freedom has been contagious and has become the criterion for his life, public and private".[3] The logic of taking the confession in this way implies "that Christian faith involves a way of life".[4] If the Christian is asked whether there is some absolute being "behind" or "beyond" all created things, "he will be wise to remain silent".[5] He admits that in his restatement of Christianity "the word 'God' has been avoided because it equivocates and misleads".[6]

We have included this brief glance at Van Buren's thesis (as we included our analysis of Braithwaite's) almost wholly in order to show the way in which the glib acceptance by a theologian of the view that religious discourse is non-cognitive disastrously affects his subsequent attempt to give an adequate account of the Christian faith. But we must not leave it without making several comments. The first is that most of the points we made about Braithwaite's are relevant to Van Buren's, so that there is no need to repeat them here. The second is that it is interesting to enquire if Van Buren's restatement of Christian faith impresses modern "empirical" and "secular" men.

The basic thesis of Van Buren's book was in fact fully debated on the B.B.C.'s Third Programme by two theologians and two agnostic, empiricist philosophers, Alasdair MacIntyre and Bernard Williams.[7] The reactions of the philosophers were interesting—they looked askance at Van Buren's proposals,

[1] *Op. cit.*, p. 103.
[2] *Op. cit.*, pp. 139–40.
[3] *Op. cit.*, p. 142.
[4] *Op. cit.*, p. 140.
[5] *Op. cit.*, p. 144.
[6] *Op. cit.*, p. 145.
[7] On 2nd September, 1964.

because they had difficulty in distinguishing his basic presuppositions from other atheistic ones! They made it clear that the significance of Jesus (if any) was to be looked for in the claims made (by himself and the Church) linking him to a supreme transcendent Being. If this were denied, the alternative appears to be some kind of "Christian atheism", but atheism, after all, is atheism, however it is qualified. But could not Van Buren's thesis, that Jesus, standing alone without God, is able to command men's admiration, allegiance, loyalty and devotion, evoke respect? The philosophers made it clear that in their view Jesus, *by Himself*, is simply not able to bear the weight of the significance and devotion heaped upon him by the Bible and the Church.

If Van Buren's thesis were correct, they made it clear that Jesus would have to compete *solely on human terms* with all other religious leaders and holy and wise men. It is feasible that some might be intoxicated by the liberating story of Jesus, but this could not be guaranteed—modern man could take his pick, and might well prefer to Jesus the Buddha or Socrates as giving him the most significant perspective upon life, or indeed he might prefer a liberating perspective derived from a combination of all of them, or a combination derived from other holy men, including none of them![1] But, might it not be argued, does not the *ethical* teaching of Jesus (and its effect upon men) guarantee him a significance denied to other religious leaders? Again the philosophers were frank — Jesus' ethical teachings *alone* might win for him a *minor* place in the history of morals, and perhaps a rather more than minor place in the history of the conflict of morality with legalism, but it was emphasized, the philosopher might not be prepared to award higher marks than that! The trouble with estimating Jesus' significance solely on the basis of his ethical teaching is, first, that his ethical sayings are often in

[1] Compare what has been written by Gilkey: "Surely contemporary modern man . . . would find the self-surrendering, altruistic 'perspective' and 'freedom' of this ancient martyr (i.e. Jesus) as strange, as unintelligible, and as offensive as are the old 'myths' in which is story is ordinarily phrased" *op. cit.*, p. 44). Speaking about Van Buren's book, Gilkey says that "one cannot help but ask why all this interest in Jesus and his story; is he not . . . merely one other interesting and inspiring example of the possibilities of human freedom?" (p. 45).

the form of aphorisms exceedingly difficult to interpret, and, second, that the changed circumstances of 2000 years later make his ethical teaching difficult to apply. Such reactions as these from contemporary philosophical empiricists should make us, to put it mildly, wary of the apologetic value of Van Buren's restatement of Christianity, designed to command the respect and discipleship of modern man.[1] The third point that must not be lost sight of is that the fulcrum upon which Van Buren's thesis turns is his acceptance of the "non-cognitive" character of the discourse of Christian theism due to its alleged "non-verifiability", an acceptance which we must examine.

We now turn to the third possible theological response to the analytic critique of religious discourse. This involves us in the examination and criticism of the (not always apparent) presuppositions and implications of much philosophical analysis, and in an enquiry into how far such a philosophical method is adequate for an evaluation of *genuine* religious belief and discourse. The sketch we gave above[2] of the analytic critique of theological propositions gives a deceptively simple appearance to philosophical analysis, as though it were a generally agreed method amongst Anglo-Saxon philosophers, or had had a simple, smooth, uneventful history.[3] This is by no means the case, as a reading of, for example, Mr. J. O. Urmson's book, *Philosophical Analysis: Its Development Between the Two World Wars*,[4] makes plain. In fact, analytic philosophy has had a curiously complex history within which philosophers have held varying estimates of the value of religious discourse. Generally speaking, we may say that in the initial stages of its history analytic philosophy (in the form of *logical positivism*), was extremely sceptical of the truth-claims of religious utterance, but that in the later phase of its history it (as

[1] See the interesting discussion of "Christian atheism" in E. L. Mascall, *The Secularisation of Christianity*, p. 104, n. 2.

[2] See pp. 177–81 above.

[3] Father Copleston warns us of the danger of supposing that in Britain "the dominant current of thought is the only current". Many British philosophical scholars of great repute have stood apart from and have been critical of the trends of analytic philosophy; for this see Frederick Copleston, S. J., *Contemporary Philosophy*, London, 1956, pp. 18–21.

[4] Oxford, 1956.

functional analysis or *logical empiricism*) was much less dogmatic about the meaninglessness of theological propositions. We now turn to a closer examination of these two phases.

Logical positivism is the name given to the standpoint of a number of philosophers (especially logicians and philosophers of science), who formed the so-called Vienna Circle in the years after World War I, a group whose head was Moritz Schlick (1882–1936), Professor of the Philosophy of the Inductive Sciences in the University of Vienna. The group's views were eventually popularized in English by Professor A. J. Ayer in his *Language, Truth and Logic*, first published in 1936.[1] Logical *positivism*, as its name implies,[2] contended that since all knowledge is derived from sense-experience, the only genuine way of acquiring and extending our knowledge is that employed by the natural sciences. Its adherents argued that this conception of knowledge is our key for understanding all the language we use to describe the world. Language which really does this can be broken down into more elementary propositions, each one related to a piece of sense-experience. The task of the philosopher is therefore to examine propositions and other pieces of language claiming to describe the world (that is, cognitive ones), with a view to finding out if they can be broken down into observation-statements or experience-statements. If they could, they were classified as meaningful; if not, as meaningless.

Of course, logical positivists allowed that the necessary propositions of mathematics and logic were meaningful, but, since they did not claim to give us knowledge of the world, they were non-cognitive. It is plain that if meaningful propositions are restricted to either mathematical statements or propositions testable by sense experience, at least *three* classes of statement are at once ruled out of court as meaningless—ethical, metaphysical and theological ones. In fact the positivists alleged that ethical statements merely reflect the subjective, arbitrary emotional attitudes of those who use them (they were described as "emotive" and non-cognitive), and that both metaphysical and theological statements, since they cannot be checked by appeal to sense-experiences,

[1] 2nd revised edition, London, 1946.
[2] See above, pp. 78 f.

192

measurements or observations, are nonsensical. Frequently they were described as "pseudo-propositions". Traditional theological and metaphysical problems were "pseudo-problems", that is, quite incapable of solution.

Although it is not unknown for religious belief still to be criticized as though the tenets of logical positivism were self-evidently true, these were in fact being severely criticized in the nineteen-thirties, not only by theologians and moralists, but also by devotees within the movement itself. It is clear that, at least so far as theological statements are concerned, everything must turn on the so-called verifiability-principle (the meaning of a statement is the method of its verification). We now note some of the most telling criticisms brought against it. Before World War II one question was much discussed. What exactly is the *logical status* of the verifiability-principle itself? The extreme positivists of the nineteen-twenties had classified *all* meaningful propositions (without exception) as either definitions (tautologies, analytic statements), or empirically testable statements. Into which of these two classes did the principle fit?

If it fitted into neither, it would apparently be meaningless. Now the positivists had already loudly insisted that philosophy was essentially a non-cognitive science; its scope was the logical clarification of concepts and statements. It was therefore impossible to fit the principle into the second class, that of empirically verifiable propositions. Anyway, to regard it as such would have entailed examining every conceivable theological, metaphysical and ethical statement, with a view to discovering if there were a method of testing it—an impossibly huge task, even if a method for carrying it out could be suggested. If so, the only remaining class it could be inserted into was the first one—the class of definitions, of analytic statements. But will it fit into this class any more easily?

The verification-principle cannot be defended as a definition, that is, as a proposition whose meaningfulness depends simply upon its correct use of symbols and concepts. The proposition "all meaningful cognitive statements are those testable by sense-experience" is not at all a definition *in the same sense as* "all spinsters are unmarried women". In the latter case everyone familiar with English usage agrees that the word "spinster" means "an unmarried woman". To use the word in some other sense is simply to break a universally agreed rule. But in the former case this is not so. Many who are linguistically competent, including theologians, moralists and metaphysicians, are by no means agreed that the word "meaningful" means "empirically verifiable"! This is the very bone of contention, the precise meaning of "meaningful". Thus the positivist was accused, not without justification, of having arbitrarily altered everyday language to suit his philosophical persuasion. For example, generation upon generation had made statements like "cruelty goes against the nature of things", or "cruelty goes against the grain of the universe". In making such statements, these generations were agreed that they were making sense, that their meaning was clear. But according to logical positivists such statements were nonsensical; they were prize examples of meaningless statements. But in saying so the positivists were tampering with linguistic usage. They were trying to force their own sense of "meaningful" upon those who disagreed with them.

How then was the verifiability-principle to be classified? What was its precise logical status? One cannot help feeling sympathy for the hostile critics of the principle, who bluntly declared that it was itself a prize example of what the positivists loathed most—*metaphysics*! That is, that it expressed an attitude to the nature and scope of *knowledge* which was not itself capable of being tested by observations and other sense-experiences. That is, at the heart of logical positivism lay a metaphysical attitude to knowledge. But there was a corollary to this suggestion; it was that the positivist's dogmatic use of the verifiability-principle had a (concealed) metaphysical view of *reality*. It is easy to see the grounds upon which the suggestion rests. These are that if one has a metaphysical attitude to the scope and nature of *knowledge*, it is impossible to escape from a parallel metaphysical attitude to the scope and nature of what is there to be known, to *reality*. It was hard for extreme logical positivists to deny that the language they considered normative reflected their assumptions concerning the nature of reality. Thus William Alston has pointed out that the verifiability-principle is apt enough for the language we use to describe observable physical objects, adjectives connoting directly observable properties, and verbs concerned with directly observable activities.[1]

As such, the verifiability-principle appears to operate at a comparatively simple, crude, even childish level of experience, with a much reduced and impoverished conception of reality. Alston argues further that words that would be ruled out as meaningless by the principle would include, for example, "society", "conscientious", "intelligent", "education", "brilliant" and "neurosis".[2] It is just not true that what these words indicate is directly observable or measurable. "Observation" is of course not irrelevant in applying these terms, but there is a great deal more to it than that. Alston is convinced that we must talk of semantic levels, or strata of language, and that "no one has ever made a plausible case for the possibility of defining all meaningful words in the language of the lowest level",[3] which is just what logical positivism tried to do. The lowest level of reality reflected by the norm of logical positivism is of course the level of sense-experience, the level of physical nature, of what is studied by the natural sciences. The early positivists talked of "propositions picturing facts", and of course such language reveals their preference for this low-level, rather unsophisticated level of experience.

Speaking historically, the verification-principle is implied by a metaphysical view called "logical atomism", a view brilliantly set forth by Ludwig Wittgenstein (1889–1951) in his *Tractatus Logico-Philosophicus*,[4] but one from which Wittgenstein later departed because of its metaphysical basis. In order

[1] William P. Alston, *Philosophy of Language*, Englewood Cliffs, N. J., 1964, p. 67.

[2] *Ibid.*

[3] *Op. cit.*, p. 68. Compare with this what has been written by J. O. Urmson: " 'This is red', 'This is near that', and 'This hit that', were thought of as being as near to paradigms of linguistic usage as ordinary language could achieve, and not merely as basic empirical statements. Any satisfactory use of language was thought to be a replica or complication of this use. This preconception was the more insidious and dangerous in that it was taken for granted as a commonplace requiring no argument, and, if thought of at all, was regarded as a self-evident truth rather than as a speculation", *Philosophical Analysis: Its Development Between the Two World Wars*, p. 197.

[4] London, 1922.

to attain to consistency, logical positivism was driven to desperate straits which today can only be regarded as ludicrous. The early positivists disliked so-called "general statements", ones that could not be broken down into statements referring to sense-experiences or observations. When they encountered statements describing the actions of groups, nations, communities and societies, these, to be considered meaningful, had to be broken down into statements referring to individuals, in most cases, of course, a futile task. Further, even if statements referring to individuals were achievable, there was to be no talk of anything else, to quote A. J. Ayer, but descriptions "in terms of their empirical manifestations — that is, in terms of the behaviour of their bodies, and ultimately in terms of sense-contents".[1] Ayer goes on to reject "the assumption that 'behind' these sense-contents there are entities which are not even in principle accessible to my observation".[2] But clearly, despite this, the plain man will go on regarding statements about states, nations and societies as meaningful (as he always has done), rather than accept such a crude, low-level account of interpersonal relationships and of how one person acquires knowledge of another. Logical positivism gets involved in such embarrassing difficulties because of its basic (but often concealed) arbitrary assumption that all there is to be known is the world of physical, observable and measurable nature, the world approached and known by the senses alone.

There is still the other sense in which logical positivism seemed involved in what it had set out to destroy, metaphysics. It assumed that since the model of all meaningful discourse was the language of the natural sciences, the only method of gaining and increasing knowledge was the method employed by these sciences. This of course is positivism, a thoroughly metaphysical attitude, since it cannot itself be verified in those scientific ways recommended by the positivists. It is, however, a tempting attitude; John Habgood tells us that "science achieves its successes by restricting its questions to those to which straight answers can be given. This is one of the main reasons for its attractiveness. It provides

[1] *Language, Truth and Logic*, 2nd edition, p. 130.
[2] *Ibid.*

definite information in a limited field. The only trouble is that its questions are not always the most interesting and relevant ones for our lives; and when scientists try to ask those particular questions they become just as confused as anybody else".[1]

The choice of its title alone points to the metaphysical assumptions in logical *positivism*. The leader of the Vienna Circle, Moritz Schlick, was appointed to the University chair in Vienna that had been occupied from 1895 to 1901 by Ernst Mach (1838–1916), the famous scientific positivist.[2] Schlick attempted, on semantic (rather than metaphysical) grounds, to implement Mach's programme of making all knowledge worthy of the name conform to the kind of knowledge we get from the natural sciences. If we grasp this aim, we can grasp the true significance of the verifiability-principle. It has become apparent that the logical positivist was really arguing in such a manner as this. "I put forward the verifiability-principle — the meaning of a (cognitive) statement is the method of its verification. That is, by *cognitive* I mean *verifiable by experience*. I am convinced that the only statements really imparting knowledge about the world are scientific ones, actually or in principle testable by experiences, observations and measurements. *So far at any rate as I am concerned*, scientific statements are infinitely preferable (from the point of view of cognition), to all other kinds, for example, metaphysical or theological ones. I am persuading you to share my preference. In putting forward the verifiability-principle I am really indulging in a special piece of pleading on behalf of the supreme intellectual respectability of the natural sciences, to the detriment of all other attempts to acquire knowledge of the world."[3]

In short, the positivist equates all knowledge with scientific knowledge, all meaningful cognitive statements with scientific ones. But this equation is, as we have seen, a metaphysical one, untestable by experiment and observation, the methods

[1] *Religion and Science*, p. 10.

[2] For nineteenth-century scientific positivism, see pp. 77 f. above.

[3] In constructing this argument, I am indebted to C. L. Stevenson's paper, "Persuasive Definitions", *Mind*, XLVII, July, 1938, pp. 331–50. According to Stevenson, the verifiability-principle is a "persuasive definition" of meaningfulness.

adulated by the positivists themselves. That is, the verifiability-principle was not a definition of everyday meaningfulness, but a polemical party-slogan devised to attack certain classes of utterance (including theological ones) as nonsensical, in the name of the empirical sciences. As Alston has put it neatly: "Positivists would never have made such a fuss over the (verifiability) criterion in the first place if it were not for the fact that the use of sentences that violate it is so widespread."[1]

It might be objected at this point that we have been tilting at a windmill, because, due to the difficulties we have described, dogmatic logical positivism had become untenable by the outbreak of World War II. Nevertheless, a sound grasp of logical positivism is necessary in order to understand contemporary philosophy and theology. For one thing, such an understanding shows the considerable difficulties involved in dogmatically asserting the unverifiability and so the non-cognitive character of certain classes of statement, notably the theological one. Further, logical positivism represents a valuable analysis both of scientific method and scientific language. Although as a coherent movement or school of thought it is no longer with us, its demand for verifiability in the case of cognitive statements lives on in the second, post-war phase of the history of analytic philosophy, to which we now turn our attention.

It is hard to give this later phase a generally agreed title, due to unhappy inconsistencies between historians of recent thought. Some call it logical empiricism, despite the fact that others give this title also to logical positivism, thus making the two interchangeable. Others term it functional analysis (Frederick Ferré), and others, rather vaguely, linguistic philosophy (Ernest Gellner). Perhaps we may, at the risk of some confusion, simply call it logical empiricism, which fits it pretty well. It is not too difficult to indicate at least the general characteristics of this way of philosophizing; we may point to two methodological slogans, "Don't ask for the meaning, ask for the use", and, "Every statement has its own logic."[2] Both of these show the much less dogmatic approach of logical empiricism; it allows that statements may have a

[1] *Philosophy of Language*, p. 78.
[2] J. O. Urmson, *Philosophical Analysis*, pp. 179 f.

198

valid *use*, even if they are neither definitions nor empirically verifiable cognitive ones. In the later phase of analytic philosophy we find much being made of "the multiplicity of the tools of language", of language being "multi-layered", of "semantic strata", of linguistic "dimensions of meaning", of "language-levels" and so on.[1] Post-war analytic philosophers have written much of the multiplicity of language-games, each with its own "logic" or rules. Amongst such language-games Wittgenstein included such activities as giving orders, guessing riddles, translating languages, asking, thanking, speculating and so on.[2]

In view of the greater flexibility and lack of dogmatism in this new approach, we must ask this: Does it regard the truth-claims of religious discourse in a kindlier light than did the older logical positivism? The answer appears to be this: Since the "use" of statements is stressed rather than their "meaning", the tendency has been to allow that theological discourse has a "use" without conceding that it has cognitive meaning, that it describes or gives information about the real world. To return to Braithwaite's 1955 thesis about religious belief, we have seen that while conceding that religious discourse has a use in reinforcing moral patterns of living, he refuses to concede that it is cognitive. This position has been fairly typical of post-war philosophical analysts. J. O. Urmson, describing in 1956 the approach of contemporary analysts, points out that we must examine individual statements in order to discover their use. If in so doing we find that any statement "is unverifiable, then its job *is clearly not to describe the world about us*, but perhaps it is used for some quite different purpose".[3] John Macquarrie warns us that analysts of the modern school, however friendly they may appear to be towards religion, "are unwilling to readmit the traditional metaphysical concepts of God and the soul", and that they try to find a meaning for religion "without the embarrassment of the old-fashioned metaphysical trappings".[4]

[1] See, for example, L. Wittgenstein, *Philosophical Investigations*, Oxford, 1953, p. 12ᵉ.

[2] Wittgenstein, *op. cit.*, pp. 11ᵉ–12ᵉ.

[3] *Philosophical Analysis*, p. 179, italics mine.

[4] *Twentieth-Century Religious Thought*, p. 310.

Ernest Gellner, writing of the contemporary crisis in the humanities (with special reference to contemporary philosophy) says this: "The educated public in developed countries turns to the scientific specialist when it wants information about some facet of the world."[1] He continues: "The deprivation of the humanist intellectual of his full cognitive status has happened fairly recently."[2] Because of "the towering superiority of science as a source of knowledge about the universe" the humanist intellectual "can no longer claim . . . that he is, primarily and above all and more than anyone else, a *knower*".[3] Gellner asks, and his question is immensely significant for contemporary theology: "How are the concepts in terms of which we see ourselves and live our lives to be related to those we take seriously as genuine knowledge of the world", the latter being acquired by science.[4] He can sum up *the* problem facing the humanities in this way: "The language of the humanities is incomparably closer to what we *are*, to the life we live, than is the language of science; but on the other hand it is not obvious that the humanities contain, in any serious sense, genuine knowledge."[5] And while Gellner deplores the approach to language in terms of narrow positivistic verification, he nevertheless points out that "systematic verification happens to be a crucial part of certain forms of life, of industrial-scientific societies".[6]

What can the theologian learn from this discussion of his subject by linguistic analysts? A great deal which is absolutely crucial. Whether it is carried on by doctrinaire positivists in the nineteen-twenties, or by less rigid contemporary practitioners, he must learn, above and before all else, that *science and religion are very different things indeed*. Ernest Gellner rightly points out that "positivism starts from the chasm between that which is science and that which is not".[7]

[1] *Crisis in the Humanities*, edited by J. H. Plumb, Pelican Books, 1964, p. 72.
[2] *Ibid.*
[3] *Op. cit.*, p. 78.
[4] *Op. cit.*, pp. 78–9.
[5] *Op. cit.*, p. 79.
[6] *Op. cit.*, p. 80.
[7] *Op. cit.*, p. 74.

Urmson draws attention to C. L. Stevenson's important interpretation of the verification-principle (in "Persuasive Definitions") as "a demand to distinguish more radically between metaphysics and science, combined with a preference for science".[1] The verification-principle, says Urmson, "draws attention to the fundamental difference between science and metaphysics".[2] Ferré rightly points out that verificational analysis makes it abundantly clear that "the religious person, when he talks about 'God', is not merely speaking in a disguised way about the world".[3] And he rightly issues a warning that "theists who suppose that their speech is somehow like scientific language will do well to learn, once and for all, this lesson".[4] John Macquarrie makes very much the same point when he tells us that "what the positivists do succeed in showing pretty decisively is that assertions about God are quite different from assertions about any particular facts . . . The question, 'Is there a God?', is not to be settled in the same way as the question, 'Are there subatomic particles?' "[5]

At this point it might be objected that to learn that theology differs radically from science is precious little. This objection is unreasonable. It is so partly because, since we live in a world dominated by scientific thinking, there may well be a tendency to regard religious beliefs (if they are to be intellectually respectable) as meta-scientific theories. It is also unreasonable because to know what religious beliefs *are not* is to be set partly on the right road to knowing what they *are*. And if philosophical analysis helps us to do this, it renders a great service indeed. Frederick Ferré may be right when he says that few theists are in danger of confusing religious with scientific discourse,[6] and so may Macquarrie when he says that the positivists' sharp distinction between assertions about God and empirically factual ones is no discovery, "but something that would be clear to anyone who had even a sketchy acquaintance with the history of religious thought".[7]

[1] *Philosophical Analysis*, p. 171.
[2] *Op. cit.*, p. 172.
[3] *Language, Logic and God*, p. 43.
[4] *Ibid.*
[5] *Twentieth-Century Religious Thought*, p. 315.
[6] *Language, Logic and God*, p. 43.
[7] *Twentieth-Century Religious Thought*, p. 315.

But it is hard to establish these opinions, and it is significant that both writers feel it necessary to state them. And it is far from certain that all sceptical philosophers realize that Christian theists do not regard and defend their beliefs as meta-scientific theories, just as it is uncertain whether these philosophers themselves do not regard religious beliefs in this light. This must be stressed, because the discussion of religion by linguistic philosophers makes it clear that the most unpromising method open to theologians is to urge religious explanations so as to make it appear that they can compete with (or that they are superior to) scientific theories or explanations. Philosophical analysis has made it clear, especially by its studies of the language of physics in the nineteen-twenties, that meaning and verification are inseparably related in the language of science, and that the impossibility of such empirical, observational verification within the context of religion must distinguish it sharply from the realm of science, and distinguish also its discourse from scientific language.

This is important, because within the Anglo-Saxon philosophical tradition, as we have seen, there has been a strong tendency, by no means dead, to regard religious beliefs as something like meta-scientific theories. We have already explored this tendency. We have looked at the older natural theology of the seventeenth and eighteenth centuries, in which a functional deity had been introduced as an *explanation* of the sheer existence of (the cosmological argument), or the structure of (the teleological argument), the physical universe. It is enlightening to recall the line taken against these arguments by Hume. In the case of the first, Hume asserted that the argument for a causal God must fail, because a causal connection between God and the world cannot be *observed* in the same way that we *observe* the causes of other artefacts. Causal connections only hold between observable states of affairs. In other words, those of the twentieth century, there is no empirical way of *verifying* or *falsifying* the propositions of the cosmological argument. It should therefore not surprise us that twentieth-century positivists and empiricists should look back with admiration to the empiricism of Hume, and to his rejection of the possibility of natural theology.

In the case of the second, Hume put against it the hypothesis of Epicurean materialism. In doing so, he was really trying to demonstrate the absurdity of supposing that either of these hypotheses could be *verified* or *falsified* by observations in our experience. Thus, in the *Dialogues*, when Philo revives the Epicurean hypothesis, he does so with this introduction: "Without any great effort of thought, I believe that I could, in an instant, propose other systems of cosmogony, which would have some faint appearance of truth: *though it is a thousand, a million to one, if either yours or any one of mine be the true system.*"[1] And Hume's agnosticism about the possibility of *verification* and *falsification* comes out clearly when Philo, after comparing the Epicurean hypothesis with the design hypothesis, sums up the discussion thus: "A total suspense of judgment is here our only reasonable resource."[2] It is therefore not surprising that when contemporary empiricists discuss "the existence of God", they should depend heavily upon the criticisms first formulated by Hume against deistic natural theology.[3]

Nor is it uncommon to read in contemporary philosophical discussions of religious belief of the difficulty or impossibility of such belief on the ground that it cannot function as an *explanation* of the natural order. One of the grounds upon which R. B. Braithwaite rejects the cognitive meaningfulness of religious statements is that they do not function as scientific hypotheses or theories.[4] R. M. Hare, while discussing the falsifiability of religious statements, quotes from the Psalms: "The earth is weak and all the inhabiters thereof: I bear up the pillars of it." He then points out that it is a mistake "to regard this kind of talk as some sort of *explanation*, as scientists are accustomed to use the word. As such it would obviously be ludicrous. We no longer believe in God as an Atlas—

[1] *Dialogues*, edited by N. Kempt Smith, p. 224, italics mine.

[2] *Op. cit.*, p. 230. In discussing Hume's refusal to call himself an atheist, Richard Wollheim makes an interesting suggestion. Hume felt, as do modern empiricists, that atheism was intellectually arrogant, laying "claim to a form of knowledge that essentially lay outside man's capacities". Hume's philosophical standpoint "was prepared to question all knowledge, even of a negative kind", *Hume on Religion*, p. 29.

[3] See, for example, J. J. C. Smart's paper, "The Existence of God", in *New Essays in Philosophical Theology*, pp. 28–46.

[4] *An Empiricist's View of the Nature of Religious Belief*, pp. 5–8.

nous n'avons pas besoin de cette hypothèse.''[1] Van Buren's agnosticism comes out strongly in these words: ''Certainly the
Christian possesses no special sources *for the scientific description
of the universe.* Before such questions as whether there is some
absolute being . . . which is 'behind' or 'beyond' all we know
and are, some final 'ground and end of all created things', he
will be wise to remain silent.''[2]

These quotations appear not to lend much support to the
optimism expressed by Ferré and Macquarrie that there is
little risk of theological statements being confused with those
of the empirical sciences. We repeat therefore: *the assertions
of science and those of religion are very different indeed.* How then
can we characterize religion and its discourse? What is the
''logic'' of theological language, if it is distinct from that of
science? How can we (to adapt a useful phrase of Gilbert
Ryle's), ''plot the logical geography'' of theological concepts
and statements? Before we can attempt to answer such questions, we must note the danger which attends using a group
of crucial common terms uncritically or unreflectively — terms
such as ''world'', ''factual'', ''real'' and ''cognitive''. Within
the context of much analytic philosophy and much philosophy
of science, such words have come to have sharply anti-
theological meanings. A failure to notice this would be
disastrous, and would make our attempt to plot the logical
geography of theological discourse futile.

For example, when many philosophers use the term
''world'', they mean by it (although this may not be explicit),
the ''world of nature'', the world known by the senses,
whose structure is investigated by the empirical sciences.[3]
Thus when Urmson talks of language ''describing the *world*
around us'', and when Gellner talks of concepts ''we take
seriously as genuine knowledge of the *world*'', they are clearly

[1] *New Essays in Philosophical Theology*, p. 101; Hare is here quoting Laplace's
words to Napoleon, see p. 133 above.

[2] *The Secular Meaning of the Gospel*, p. 144, italics mine.

[3] Speaking of Oxford philosophers in the nineteen-twenties, R. G.
Collingwood tells us that when they discussed theory of knowledge, ''they
regarded the word 'knowledge' in that phrase as more or less equivalent
to knowledge of the world of nature or physical world'', *An Autobiography*,
Oxford, 1939, p. 84.

using the term in this loaded sense.[1] And so is Wittgenstein when he writes: "God does not reveal himself in the world."[2] Empiricists have simply taken over the term "world" and have tacitly assumed that theirs is its only meaning. But there are other meanings of the world, and theologians can use it, must use it, in a different but quite meaningful sense. "Man's world" does not at all mean, as we shall see, only man's physical environment.

Much the same is true of the terms "fact" and "factual". By these many positivists and empiricists mean that which is physical; that which is observable and measurable in a scientific sense. Ferré accuses positivistic philosophers of having failed to analyse the various meanings of the term "fact"; as they have used it, it has been "invested with powerful emotional content". Their use of it is classifiable as one of Stevenson's "persuasive definitions". Their use of the term has suppressed the insight that there can be mathematical and moral "facts".[3] If we understand this, we can see that theologians may also regard their language as being "factual", though not in this narrow, loaded, positivistic sense. Empiricists have also almost completely dominated the term "real" in much the same way. Almost universally they mean by it, belonging to the real world, the world of nature, the world known through the senses and explored by the sciences. Clearly again this is an arbitrary usage, a persuasive definition.

John Hick has raised the question of the meaning of the words "real" and "fact" within the context of theology, of language about God.[4] He makes the profound suggestion that at the root of such terms is the idea of "making a difference". And for Hick one of contemporary theology's most pressing tasks is to analyse the *difference* which would distinguish one's experience in a theistic environment as compared with an atheistic one. We find something of the same thing in Hume. In Part XI of the *Dialogues*, Hume puts this question into the mouth of Philo: "Is the world considered in general, and as it appears to us in this life, *different* [italics mine] from what a

[1] See above pp. 199–200.
[2] *Tractatus Logico-Philosophicus*, 6.432.
[3] *Language, Logic and God*, pp. 42–3.
[4] See *Philosophy of Religion*, pp. 105–6.

man or such a limited being would, *beforehand*, expect from a very powerful, wise and benevolent Deity?"[1] The theologian is called upon to answer Hume's question, but without sharing Hume's limited, empiricist meaning of the term "world".[2]

Rather similarly, positivists have tended to give the terms "cognitive" and "non-cognitive" meanings of their own. In his paper, "Persuasive Definitions", C. L. Stevenson tells us that according to positivists, " 'cognitive' is used to mean 'empirically verifiable or else analytic', and with exclusive laudatory import". He continues: "If metaphysicians answer, 'Our statements, even though neither empirically verifiable nor analytic, are still respectable', they are scarcely to be led away from their position by mere exhortation."[3] Thus, theologians must claim that religious beliefs and language are *cognitive*, that they give us genuine knowledge of the *real world*, although they will not use them in the hiddenly persuasive way in which positivists use them. If we keep these semantic distinctions in mind, we can understand that the theologian may say: Theological language is *cognitive*, giving us genuine knowledge of man's *world*, speaking of what is *real* and *factual*. We must now investigate what the theologian means when he says this.

This brings us close to the core of our discussion, and of our attempt to plot the logical geography of theological discourse. Since, as we have seen, religious beliefs and convictions differ radically from scientific theories and hypotheses, what is the exact nature of the difference? Briefly, it is that in religious and scientific cognition *knower* and *what is known* differ radically. The attempt to describe these differences will involve us in recapitulating briefly some lines of thought developed in chapters two, three, four and five above. There is a good reason for this. One of our central themes has been that since the older natural theology (the quasi-scientific

[1] Edited by N. Kemp Smith, p. 251. In discussing the existence of God, M. H. Hartshorne makes this statement: "To put it another way, his existence makes no empirical *difference* anywhere in the world", *The Faith to Doubt*, p. 45, italics mine. "His presence . . . makes no empirical *difference* anywhere", p. 50, italics mine.

[2] See below, pp. 214 f.

[3] *Mind*, July, 1938, p. 340.

attempt to make inferences from nature to God) was undermined by Humean and Kantian criticism in the last quarter of
the eighteenth century, theological trends have developed so
as to meet and disarm this kind of scepticism. These trends
have altered either the conception of the knower or the
sphere of what is known. They have done so by giving a
religious description and interpretation of human nature on
the one hand, and, on the other, by analysing and describing
that dimension within which man attains religious knowledge.
We now glance at both sides of this religious theory of knowledge; since most of these trends were examined in detail
above, most of what follows will consist of a drawing together
of various threads of thought and lines of argument. This may
help us to see them all in perspective and perceive their composite relevance for the attempt to outline a viable religious
theory of knowledge.

Let us begin with the side of the *knowing subject*. Many of
the philosophical and theological trends we have examined
have reacted very sharply away from the conception of man
as pure thought, as a being exhaustively definable in terms of
knowing, thinking, cogitating. Yet this is the conception of
man presupposed by the empirical sciences. Elements other
than man's capacity to think and understand are, strictly
speaking, irrelevant to these. Yet it can be argued that such
an understanding of man represents a thin and shrunken
caricature of the rich reality of humanity. And if we take
those descriptions of man outlined in chapters two, three and
five above, we see that these conceptions of man give a picture
which differs radically from the bare, abstract, knower presupposed by the sciences. Indeed, most of the thinkers we
surveyed there would argue that the exhaustive understanding
of man in terms of his attempt to know the external physical
world involves a destructive dehumanization.

Briefly, what has gone before has portrayed man in a three-
fold way — first, as a *religious* being (chapter two), second, as a
moral being (chapter three), and third, as an *existential* being
(chapter five). We must glance at each of these in turn. First,
man as an essentially *religious* being: much is made here of
man's consciousness (sense, taste, awareness) of the infinite
and the unconditional, of the interpenetration of human

consciousness by thoughts of God. Man is described as aware of God's inescapable presence, a primal awareness which lies at a deeper level than mere discursive reason. This approach, making much of man's essentially religious experience, appeals to his inner consciousness of God, a consciousness which precedes and is presupposed by all philosophical reflection upon and criticism of religion. Theologians of this experiential tradition have looked for signs of the divine image in man's feelings, awareness, aspirations and drives; it has looked above all else to the structure of man's inner consciousness, a phenomenon of which one can only make sense when the reality of God is admitted.[1]

Second, man as an essentially *moral* being: here much is made of man's experience of the ultimate, the absolute, the unconditional, the underived and the given. It points to the universal inevitability of morality for all, insisting that man is essentially and inalienably a moral being, making distinctions which are neither arbitrary, mutable nor temporary. It points to man's experience of having unconditional demands made upon him, of being confronted with moral imperatives, and insists that to destroy the unconditional nature of moral imperatives is to destroy man's essential nature. Further, it insists that man's moral experience sharply distinguishes him from every other being, entity and occurrence in reality, and that man's moral experience is a phenomenon of which one can only make final sense when one confesses a theistic standpoint.

Third, man as an essentially *existential* being: this approach claims that man is a being who, being "open-to-himself", is the clue to all being as such; in Heideggerian terminology, that man is a lantern which sheds light on being as a whole. More particularly, man is a being who exists uniquely in a present in which future possibilities are realizable. That is, man is a being who must be understood in terms of existential possibilities which derive from his real, future self through conscience. Man is thus a being whose awareness is flooded by demands *to be*, to become, to grasp his authentic self

[1] Probably the most notable attempt to do this has been Rudolf Otto's book, *Das Heilige*, first published in 1917; English translation by J. W. Harvey, *The Idea of the Holy*, Oxford, 1923, Pelican Books, 1959.

which lies before him, and which bring him into the situation of *Angst* (care). Thus in existentialist theologies, the "logical geography" of talk about God and grace is the existential sphere, the sphere of human existence. Talk of God and grace is the talk of man when conscious of the inauthenticity of his past and of the possibility and actuality of the transition to an authentic future in the present. Within this type of theology, man's essential nature is such that he is propelled towards that point where a decision about religious beliefs, responses and attitudes becomes urgent.[1]

Several comments may be made about these anthropologies (doctrines of man). The first is this: man is portrayed in them as radically other than the mere knower of the sciences, the detached observer and investigator of physical nature. These anthropologies insist that the acquisition of religious (as distinct from scientific) knowledge depends upon the fulfilment of certain *subjective* conditions.[2] These are that man takes with utter seriousness and follows up his insights as a religious being, that he uncompromisingly engages in and tries to make sense of moral activity, and that he comes to grips with himself as a being called to attain an existence which transcends the natural world. The second comment is that these analyses of man as a religious, moral and existential being are truly *cognitive*, and this in two senses. They are cognitive because man is a part of reality, indeed, the most significant part, and therefore when man knows himself he truly knows reality. Man's being, accessible to each of us in our humanity, is *the* clue to all reality as such. But they are cognitive also because they point man towards the ultimate *explanatory* ground of his existence and nature, God himself.[3]

So much for the side of the knowing subject. Let us now consider the character of *what is known*. Just as many trends since the Enlightenment have reacted away from the conception of man defined exhaustively as the detached observer of

[1] This kind of theological approach has been outlined in John Macquarrie, "How is Theology Possible?", in *New Theology No. 1*, edited by Martin E. Marty and Dean G. Peerman, New York, 1964.

[2] In this connection, it is interesting to reflect upon the dictum of the founder of modern existentialism, Kierkegaard: "Truth is subjectivity."

[3] See G. F. Woods, *Theological Explanation*, London, 1958, Part III: "Ultimate Explanation."

nature, so have many reacted away from any conception of what is to be known defined exhaustively as impersonal and inert physical nature. In doing so, they have stressed the dynamic, living, responsive, even personal character of what stands over against man, as that which moves towards man and enters into relationship with him. Briefly, these trends have pictured man's world under three dimensions — first, as a world of *moral values* (chapter three), second, as a world in which reality *reveals* and *discloses* itself to him (chapter four), and third, as a dimension of *history*. Let us glance at each of these in turn.

First, man's world as a realm of *moral values*: thinkers in the tradition of moral theism have all been strongly "anti-naturalistic". They have insisted that reality transcends physical nature. In particular, they have insisted that thinkers must take account of moral "facts" and moral "data" in their over-all picture of things. They have reminded us that if we talk of a "physical order" or a "biological order", we have even more right to speak of a "moral order". They have insisted that the distinction between right and wrong is as much part and parcel of the structure of the universe as biological or meteorological processes. They have made it hard for us to forget that reality is multi-layered and that amongst the ultimate constitutive and creative factors in it moral values must have a significant place. They have pointed, in the language of Otto, to a moral reality over-shadowing and penetrating the immediately given world.[1]

More particularly, they have described how moral values stand in a peculiar relationship to man: they impinge upon man's consciousness, exercising claims upon him; they thrust themselves in upon man's life, drawing him towards themselves; they indulge in activity towards him, demanding their own realization and actualization in space and time. In doing so, they bear witness to the continual pressure of God upon man and point towards God's concrete self-disclosure in history.

Second, we have the theological movement which emphasizes God's reality not as an inert, unresponsive object sought

[1] In this connection it is interesting to ponder L. W. Grensted's definition of "reality": "that is real for me which I cannot by any volitional act cause not to be", *Psychology of Religion*, Oxford, 1952, p. 149.

after in man's intellectual and religious activity, but as a subject who takes the initiative towards man and *discloses* himself to him. This approach stresses God's activity towards man and not *vice versa*; God comes, God reveals, God acts, God chooses. Within this tradition, genuine religious knowledge is unique in that it is wholly created in or evoked from the knowing subject by what is known. It is total *response* rather than self-initiated *activity*. The God known within this tradition is not merely man writ large, not merely the quintessence or reflection of man's highest ideals and deepest aspirations, but the God who transcends and differs from his creatures, who is discontinuous with them, distinct from, beyond and sovereign over them.

Third, man's world as the dimension of *history*: clearly, amongst the greatest philosophical and theological revolutions of our time will be reckoned the revival of the interest of thinkers in the sphere of history as a source of truth and understanding. It is generally reckoned that the springs of this historical revolution are to be found in a period as recent as the last third of the nineteenth century, and that it is associated with the work of thinkers like Wilhelm Dilthey (1833–1911)[1] in Germany, Benedetto Croce (1866–1953) in Italy, and Robin George Collingwood (1889–1943)[2] in England. This revolution could of course hardly have occurred without the neo-Kantian revival of interest in man (as distinct from nature), associated with the work of a thinker like Lotze. Ultimately, of course, the Dilthey-Collingwood revolution has been a revolt against the anti-historicality of the Cartesians.

Very briefly, to characterize the thought of Dilthey and Collingwood, a sharp distinction is made between man and nature, and thus also between the historical and the natural sciences, their subject-matter and methods. History is essentially the story of man, his inner life and experience. For

[1] See H. A. Hodges, *Wilhelm Dilthey, an Introduction*, London, 1944, and *The Philosophy of Wilhelm Dilthey*, London, 1952.

[2] See *An Autobiography* and *The Idea of History*. The theological relevance of the latter is clear if read in conjunction with Collingwood's *The Idea of Nature*, Oxford, 1945. Cf. the use made of Collingwood's interpretation of history in Bultmann's *History and Eschatology*.

Dilthey, historical interpretation is possible because of the human *substratum* which underlies all history and gives it unity, a substratum which enables us to re-live (*nacherleben*) in the present the experience of past humans. For Collingwood, history is the story of thought and reflection, of mind; historical interpretation involves the sympathetic, imaginative re-thinking of those thoughts and decisions which lie "inside" historical actions. In history interpersonal encounter takes place. In historical work we encounter man himself, the essentially and perennially human. Thus in investigating history the interpreter is informed, enriched, enlarged, corrected and judged. History is distinct from nature because it is impossible to reduce historical events to "processes" which operate according to historical "laws". The approach which assimilates history to nature ignores the fact that all past actions have a constitutive human element which evades scientific investigation and generalization. "The laws of nature have always been the same, and what is against nature now was against nature two thousand years ago; but the historical as distinct from the natural conditions of man's life differ so much at different times that no argument from analogy will hold."[1] Collingwood warns us that "all kinds of historical fallacies are still current, due to confusion between historical process and natural process: not only the cruder fallacies of mistaking historical facts of culture and tradition for functions of biological facts like race and pedigree, but subtler fallacies affecting methods of research and the organization of historical inquiry . . ."[2]

This historical revolution has had of course tremendous repercussions amongst biblical and systematic theologians. Biblical theologians have focussed their attention upon the intimate connection between religious convictions and the concrete interpretations of historical events within the Hebrew-Christian tradition. Stress has been laid upon God's action through historical events, upon those acts to which Old and New Testaments alike bear witness. This has been seen in the so-called "biblical theology" of the third, fourth and

[1] Collingwood, *The Idea of History*, p. 239.
[2] *Op. cit.*, p. 228. For the theological consequences of confusing nature and history see Carl Michalson's *The Rationality of Faith*.

fifth decades of the twentieth century. But the impact of this historical revolution has been even greater upon systematic theology. If theological statements concern history rather than nature, and if history is essentially the history of human experience and reflection, the consequences for theological understanding are immense.

What, for example, do theological terms like "God" and "grace" mean in the light of this historical enquiry? They can only be understood if we know that they have a history and what this history is. The term "God", for example, is not the name of a *natural* thing, entity or process whose existence or non-existence, whose operation or non-operation, can be demonstrated by "on-the-spot", here-and-now tests, like the existence of a new chemical element or planet. Nor is "grace" a quasi-substance or quasi-natural energy whose operation or non-operation can be checked here and now in response to the positivistic demand for "evidence". These terms can only be understood within the context of a long, complex and continuing process of commitment, obedience and reflection, in which experience of all kinds, moral, religious, affective and intellectual, has been sifted, evaluated and interpreted. The term "God", far from being an explanation of the physical cosmos, is rather like an eyepiece through which we are introduced to a brilliantly rich panorama, stretching back from the present into an indefinitely long human past. "Affirmations like 'God is love' are essentially historical in character; they are based upon long, intelligent and illuminated reflection upon events which have actually passed before the eyes of men."[1]

To summarize, the "logical geography" of theological discourse is the sphere of the human, in which man, as an essentially religious, moral and existential creature, is sharply aware of a realm of moral values, is grasped and illumined by a reality which stands over against him, and is convinced that what can be real for him must be grasped through a radically historical approach to the dimension of human existence. The thought of the religious believer who tries to make sense of his belief must move amongst the poles of the religious consciousness,

[1] From a B.B.C. Third Programme lecture, *When is a Word an Event?*, by Alan Richardson, reprinted in *The Listener*. June 3rd, 1965.

moral experience, human existence, the sphere of revelation and that of history. This attempt to plot the logical geography of religious discourse casts light on earlier discussion of crucial terms like "world", "fact", "real" and "cognitive", terms which, we argued, had been taken over and filled with meaning by positivists. There is every reason why the theologian may use terms like these also, restoring to them meanings of which they have been sadly exhausted. The theologian should make it clear that there is a "world" of religious, moral and existential experience, that moral demands, existential decisions and historical events are "factual", that the dimensions of value, revelation and history are "real", and that the religious, moral, existential and historical approaches to things are "cognitive", yielding knowledge of "reality".

The attempt casts light also on another earlier discussion — the discussion about the fundamental meanings of terms like "fact" and "real". We discovered that at the root of such terms lay the notion of "making a difference".[1] What difference, it may be asked, would there be in a theistic world as compared with an atheistic one? What difference does God's alleged existence make within human experience (John Hick)? These questions may be linked with the contemporary agnostic's important charge that the religious believer never seems to allow that any conceivable state of affairs or happening "in the world" could *falsify* his assertions about religious reality.[2] The agnostic complains that the believer would apparently retain his belief no matter what "the world" were like. He appears to be, claims the agnostic, completely insensitive to the falsifying power inherent in certain distressing aspects of "the world", which the agnostic never tires of pointing to. The agnostic therefore complains in exasperation that religious belief is compatible with "any kind of world" whatever. He maintains that religious belief is an odd kind of belief which does not involve its holder in pointing to any *differences* in "the real world" which religious realities (e.g. God) are alleged to make.

[1] See above, p. 205.
[2] The *locus classicus* of such a charge is of course Antony Flew's paper, "Theology and Falsification", in *New Essays in Philosophical Theology*, pp. 96–9.

Now of course the religious believer realizes that there is a *prima facie* case for regarding a world devoid of cancer, early deaths and earthquakes as more compatible with traditional theistic belief than our present one. And theologians, as Basil Mitchell has pointed out, have not been insensitive to Flew's difficulties, as their wrestling with the problem of evil testifies.[1] Nevertheless, an answer must be given to Flew's challenge. In the context of our present discussion, the answer suggested is something like this: the "world" in which religious beliefs would be *untenable* would be one in which huge stretches of our experience would differ from our present experience. It would be a "world" in which man had no religious awareness and experience whatever, in which moral values did not operate as they do, in which the essential structure of human existence did not involve man in decisions for and against a religious attitude to reality; in which man was completely unaware of any reality, independent of himself, taking the initiative towards him, evoking from his trust and commitment; in which the history of man was quite devoid of the revelational and redemptive activity of God. Throughout this discussion the term "world" has been placed between quotation-marks for a special reason—within such discussions, as often as not, the term "world" is surreptitiously used by agnostics (as it used by Flew) for the "world" of nature, man's natural environment, which does indeed often appear indifferent to human concerns and values, the "world" in which "natural" catastrophes and accidents cause acute difficulties for religious belief.[2] But this "world", at times impersonally indifferent to man, as we have tried to show, is by no means man's only world, nor is it by any means so uniformly ugly and hostile as reading agnostic literature would lead us to suppose.

We argue then that these dimensions of reality that we have analysed, often ignored or discounted by positivists, may give a richly composite context in which religious belief may be regarded meaningfully and sympathetically. It is clear that recent theological programmes which have reformulated

[1] *New Essays in Philosophical Theology*, p. 103.
[2] The difficulty put forward by Flew for religious belief is an inoperable throat-cancer.

theological materials on the bases of religious experience, moral experience, the idea of revelation, existentialist thought and the philosophy of history, have exhibited great promise. They raise several questions which are at once important and difficult. Do they point towards some new *metaphysics*? Do they enable us to believe once more in *supernature*, in the *supernatural*? These are hard questions, and we must beware of the linguistic traps into which they can lead us. To deal first with metaphysics, we must stress here the word *new*. The majority of theologians are today rightly distrustful of the older pre-Humean and pre-Kantian kind, and are conscious of the acute difficulties in which they involve us. *Metaphysics* means literally *after-physics* (it received this name because the mediaeval editors of Aristotle placed his *Metaphysics* after his *Physics*).

We mention this because there lingers in many minds the notion that *after* nature has been almost exhaustively explored and explained by *physical* means, there may remain some remnant, incomprehensible by the methods of the natural sciences, which is the reserve of the metaphysician and theologian. It requires but a little reflection to realize that this is almost the worst conceivable way in which to do theology! It would mean that theologians would be dependent upon the morsels (if any) which fall from the tables of the natural scientists. What if the scientists claimed to be able to provide exhaustive explanations of their subject-matter?[1] Besides, as we saw in examining logical positivism, religious beliefs and scientific theories are very different things indeed, and it is disastrous to confuse them. It is disastrous to suppose

[1] Compare these significant remarks made by von Weizsäcker: "Later modern times have often used the concept of life in a semi-religious sense. One spoke of life where he did not dare speak of God. A concept of life for which a place has to be made by interrupting the physical coherences, seems to me a stopgap twice over. This concept substitutes itself for a god who, in turn, can be recognized only in the gaps in those laws that he himself created. *I myself would say that we do not fail in true reverence for life if we acknowledge complete physical coherence in the material processes of life*", The History of Nature, p. 119, italics mine. Cf. J. S. Habgood, "The Uneasy Truce Between Science and Theology", Soundings, pp. 24–5: ". . . It is clear that theology ought never to be a competitor with science in the empirical realm. Theological systems are not cosmological hypotheses set up in opposition to scientific cosmology."

that religious assertions can even begin to compete with verifiable scientific hypotheses as meta-scientific explanations.

Thus, these approaches do not imply any new *metaphysics*
in this sense of *after-physics*. Nevertheless it is true that they
do imply that reality as a whole must be approached by methods
other than those of the sciences since reality transcends nature.
This comes out clearly if we reflect upon the meaning of
terms such as "supernature" and "supernatural". The
unreflective are too apt to assume that these terms point to a
layer or dimension "above", "on top of", or "beyond"
nature. We do right to be suspicious of such crude spatial
interpretations. The prefix "super-" also means "more than",
"in excess of". If so, in the light of our discussion, there is in
reality "more than" physical nature, for example, the dimensions of morality, human existence, history and so on. But we
do not mean that theology should be the serving-maid of
science, waiting patiently for science to explore and explain
nature, in the expectation that the "more than" with which
science cannot cope will provide sufficient raw material for
theology. Rather, the method of theology must be to select
her own independent starting-points, whether that of history,
of inner experience, of moral experience, of human existence,
of revelation, and work outwards from there. Within this
methodological framework, physical nature might be considered as the "metahistorical" or "superhistorical", "the
meta-existential" or the "super-existential", the "meta-
moral" or the "supermoral". Only with these reservations in
mind may theologians use terms like "metaphysics" and
"supernature".

In the light of our discussion of the relations between faith
and philosophy in the past two centuries, what tentative
conclusions can we reach about philosophical theology,
present and future? What are the growing-points in the debate
between theologians and philosophers? Which areas of discussion will require particular attention in the future? What
are viable ways forward and what are not? In order to suggest
answers to these questions, we point to three rather broad
themes which might repay attention.

The first theme is that of *nature*. It is a theme which has
cropped up on page after page of this book, one that is un-

avoidable in contemporary philosophical and theological discussion. Theologians, we suggest, must continue to give attention to it. Questions like these still urgently require exploration: What *is* nature? Can theology hand nature over intact to the empirical sciences, while she concerns herself, say, with man? What is man's place in nature? How is he related to it? We have only space to outline very briefly the lines along which such questions might be answered. It is hard to describe nature as a thing, an object, an entity, a system of things. Rather nature is, if we may put it in this way, a *methodological presupposition*. That is, it is an abstraction from the whole of reality, an abstraction based upon measurement, manipulation, observation, regularity, prediction and law. And we do have to face the fact that working with this abstraction has yielded impressively accurate information which has immensely benefited mankind.

Nevertheless, it is dangerous not to recognize that nature is an abstraction from a greater whole. Other attitudes to the reality which includes nature are clearly possible, for example, religious and aesthetic ones. Scientists have no monopoly over that reality from which scientific method abstracts "nature". To imagine that they do is to transform a methodological abstraction into a hideous reduction of reality. But this transformation can happen, and has happened, most obviously in the human sphere. In a scientific and technological society it is understandable that men should ask: Is man basically only a bit of nature, and what we sometimes call his "spirit", his deepest intimations, his sublime awareness, his inner, existential life, his metaphysical searchings, intricate but (in principle at least) perfectly explicable qualities or attributes of his *natural* life? Or, alternatively, is man basically a sublime, spiritual, moral and historical creature, who is yet linked mysteriously (and sometimes tragically) to what we call "nature", and, in part at least, dependent upon it? It is, we submit, to questions like these, concerning alternative views of the nature of man, which theologians and philosophers will have to devote attention, if the dialogue between believers and unbelievers in a scientific society is to continue in a significant way.

The second theme is not unconnected with the first—it is

theology which takes *man* as its starting-point. We have learned from our discussion that since the beginning of the nineteenth century many systematic theologians have tended to begin their work with an analysis of man. We have already pointed out that Kant's so-called Copernican revolution was in effect an anti-Copernican one, since it replaced man at the centre of human concern and so of the cosmos. Post-Kantian theologies, linked closely to the spheres of moral and religious experience, of human existence and history, have heavily underlined the *anthropocentric* character of much modern theology. The kind of questions to which theologians will have to give attention are these: What estimate are we to make of this historical trend? Has it been on the whole a fortunate or unfortunate one? The kind of answer we would urge to these is that it would appear to be impossible to reverse this historical trend, and that the development itself is by no means an altogether unfortunate one. Anyway, we can no longer, even if we wished to, do natural theology as it was done, say, in the thirteenth, seventeenth and eighteenth centuries. Systematic theologians will have to devote more and more energy to the exploration of the foundations of theology to be found in man, in the *human*, in the widest possible sense. Our discussion has made it clear that an anthropological approach to theology is fraught of course with difficulties and dangers. These are clearly to be encountered, we suggested, from psychological and other forms of naturalism. But the existence of dangers and difficulties should not be allowed to deter us from seeing that there is a job to be done, and from doing it.

In this connection, it is instructive to ponder some words of H. E. Root:

"The great problem of the Church (and therefore of its theologians) is to establish or re-establish some kind of vital contact with that enormous majority of human beings for whom the Christian faith is not so much unlikely as irrelevant and uninteresting. The greatest intellectual challenge to faith is simply that secularized intelligence which is now the rule rather than the exception, whether it expresses itself in science or philosophy or politics or the arts. It is by no means clear that anything like Christian faith in the form we know it will ever again be able to come alive for people of our own time or of such future time as we can imagine. It is just as uncertain that Christian ideas and ways of thought, as we know them, will be able to engage an intelligence now so far separated from them."[1]

Relating this problem to our problem of working out a contemporary natural theology, Mr. Root has this to say:

"Before natural theology can begin to function in our day it must have a sense of the inwardness of the lives we lead. Where do we look now for faithful, stimulating, profound accounts of what it is to be alive in the twentieth century . . . We look to the poet or novelist or dramatist or film producer. In creative works of art we see ourselves anew, come to understand ourselves better and come into touch with just those sources of imagination which should nourish efforts in natural theology."[2]

Our third theme concerns "provincialism" and "cosmopolitanism" in contemporary and future theology and philosophy. The main theme of this book has been two-fold: first, the challenge to natural theology which stemmed from Enlightenment thinkers, Hume and Kant particularly. Second, the attempt by theologians to overcome this scepticism and to reinstate religious belief on a reasonable footing. A careful examination of this two-fold structure is illuminating. On the one hand, the empiricist, positivist, and agnostic attitudes generated by a thinker like Hume were continued and developed within the English philosophical tradition by nineteenth- and twentieth-century philosophers like John Stuart Mill, Herbert Spencer, G. E. Moore, Bertrand Russell, Ludwig Wittgenstein, A. J. Ayer and Karl Popper. In fact, as we hinted above, it is arguable that the critique of religious belief by logical positivists and logical empiricists does not really add much to the views of Kant and Hume, but is essentially a re-statement of them on logical and semantic grounds.[3] Anglo-Saxon empiricism and positivism have of

[1] *Soundings*, pp. 6–7.

[2] *Op. cit.*, p. 18.

[3] "In our own time the analytical philosophers, the logical empiricists, have further underlined Kant's critical work", H. E. Root, *op. cit.*, p. 16.

course idolized the fruitfulness of science and venerated the precision and clarity of its language and concepts.

But, on the other hand, the challenge to belief issued by the Enlightenment was taken up, and theological opposition to it developed very largely by Continental (mainly German) thinkers. Since Kant, Protestant systematic and philosophical theology has been dominated (but by no means monopolized) by thinkers like Schleiermacher, Kierkegaard, Ritschl (and his school), Barth, Brunner, Otto, Buber, Bultmann, Bonhoeffer and Tillich. And some of these have utilized the insights of philosophers like Lotze, Dilthey, Jaspers and Heidegger. Each of these philosophers and theologians has in various ways been critical of pre-Enlightenment and Enlightenment conceptions of theology and philosophy, which is why we have given consideration to some of them in this book. Much Continental philosophy and theology has differed from its English counter-part in another significant respect.[1] Far from idolizing the scientific approach to reality, many of these thinkers have been strongly, even violently, anti-positivistic and anti-naturalistic, drawing attention sharply to the dehumanization of man and the hideous reduction of reality inherent in positivism, naturalism and the uncritical adulation of scientific ideologies.

Strongly anti-positivistic and anti-naturalistic tendencies throng the pages of writers like Kierkegaard, Lotze, Dilthey, Ritschl, Tillich, Jaspers, Heidegger and, above all, Martin Buber. This has given much Continental theology a tough vitality and a sturdy independence. Is there much hope that these two traditions will come together and some kind of cross-fertilization result? To be frank, from the point of view of philosophy, there does not appear to be too much to hope for. Mr. G. J. Warnock has recently written:

"Except in Scandinavia, continental Europe has recently paid scant heed to philosophy in English. (This has really been the case, in fact, for some hundreds of years.) Continental philosophers, on the other hand, are in English perhaps

[1] Scotland must not be included within the typical "Anglo-Saxon" theological tradition. Scottish theology has been influenced by Continental theology and philosophy, especially during the sixteenth, seventeenth, nineteenth and twentieth centuries.

less strenuously vituperated than in the Positivist heyday. It must be confessed, however, that they are not much read, except by some serious toilers in the vineyard of ethics. Philosophy is still far from achieving its Common Market."[1] But from the point of view of theology, the outlook appears to be brighter. In the nineteen-sixties there has been considerable evidence that some English theologians are beginning to be interested in and to utilize the methods and insights of Continental thinkers, such as Bonhoeffer, Bultmann and Tillich. It is not too much to say that the future vitality and vigour of English theology will depend partly, but not of course wholly, upon a growing rejection of intellectual provincialism, combined with a fostering of intellectual cosmopolitanism, which will be prepared to absorb insights not only from Continental Europe, but also from America, Africa and the East.

[1] "Modern European Philosophy: Some Major Connections", *Common Factor*, vol. 1, no. 2, October, 1964, p. 30.

INDEX

224